MW01491629

THE ARCHAEOLOGY OF CONTEMPORARY AMERICA

The American Experience in Archaeological Perspective

UNIVERSITY PRESS OF FLORIDA

Florida A&M University, Tallahassee
Florida Atlantic University, Boca Raton
Florida Gulf Coast University, Ft. Myers
Florida International University, Miami
Florida State University, Tallahassee
New College of Florida, Sarasota
University of Central Florida, Orlando
University of Florida, Gainesville
University of North Florida, Jacksonville
University of South Florida, Tampa
University of West Florida, Pensacola

The Archaeology of Contemporary America

William R. Caraher

Foreword by Michael Nassaney and Krysta Ryzewski

UNIVERSITY PRESS OF FLORIDA

Gainesville/Tallahassee/Tampa/Boca Raton
Pensacola/Orlando/Miami/Jacksonville/Ft. Myers/Sarasota

29 28 27 26 25 24   6 5 4 3 2 1

Library of Congress Cataloging-in-Publication Data
Names: Caraher, William R. (William Rodney), 1972– author. | Nassaney,
  Michael S., writer of introduction. | Ryzewski, Krysta, writer of
  introduction.
Title: The archaeology of contemporary America / William R. Caraher ;
  foreword by Michael Nassaney and Krysta R. Ryzewski.
Description: Gainesville : University Press of Florida, [2024] | Series:
  The American experience in archaeological perspective | Includes
  bibliographical references and index.
Identifiers: LCCN 2023042345 (print) | LCCN 2023042346 (ebook) | ISBN
  9780813069968 (hardback) | ISBN 9780813070728 (pdf) | ISBN 9780813073064
  (ebook)
Subjects: LCSH: Social archaeology—United States. | Material
  culture—United States. | Urban archaeology—United States. | Household
  archaeology—United States. | Excavations (Archaeology)—United States.
  | BISAC: SOCIAL SCIENCE / Archaeology | SOCIAL SCIENCE / Anthropology /
  Cultural & Social
Classification: LCC CC72.4 .C364 2024 (print) | LCC CC72.4 (ebook) | DDC
  973—dc23/eng/20231115
LC record available at https://lccn.loc.gov/2023042345
LC ebook record available at https://lccn.loc.gov/2023042346

The University Press of Florida is the scholarly publishing agency for the State University System
of Florida, comprising Florida A&M University, Florida Atlantic University, Florida Gulf Coast
University, Florida International University, Florida State University, New College of Florida, University of Central Florida, University of Florida, University of North Florida, University of South
Florida, and University of West Florida.

University Press of Florida
2046 NE Waldo Road
Suite 2100
Gainesville, FL 32609
http://upress.ufl.edu

For Susie

CONTENTS

FIGURES

FOREWORD

The concept of an "archaeology of the contemporary" might disorient those who have long thought of archaeology as a field that studies ancient relics for the sake of understanding what life was like long ago. This familiar genre of archaeology that focuses on the material remains of old ruins often from distant lands operates with a temporal gaze that looks backward. In doing so, conventional archaeologists have neatly structured the study of the past according to absolute and relative chronologies within geographic regions. Still today, many archaeologists tie their professional expertise to particular temporal and spatial boundaries. They might proclaim, "I'm a Bronze Age Mediterranean archaeologist," "My work focuses on the Western European Neolithic," or "I'm an eighteenth-century New England specialist—I don't work on nineteenth-century sites." An archaeology of the contemporary disrupts these tidy temporal categories and circumscribed areas of study; it encourages practitioners to consider how the traces of these pasts co-exist in the present. It requires different ways of thinking about the archaeological record and the questions we ask to probe it. Indeed, it is the only timeframe in the field of archaeology whose range is always shifting—or perhaps knows no bounds. While the temporal boundaries of the field are in constant flux, most contemporary archaeology focuses on cultural contexts within living memory.

Instead of seeking to reconstruct the past at certain points in time, an archaeology of the contemporary is decidedly situated in the present. It is socially and politically engaged and has a forward-looking orientation. Its contemporary focus redirects the perspective of archaeology, casting it as a practice that considers the disordered traces of the past in the present and the overlap or co-existence of multiple temporalities in one space. Increased recognition of the recursive relationship between past and present has led to greater archaeological attention on the recent past.

An archaeology of the contemporary simply has a different scope and impact than its antiquarian cousin. It encourages interventions that place archaeological knowledge in conversation with contemporary issues in ways that heighten archaeology's relevance to broader conversations about social, environmental, economic, and other conditions as lived in the present and as possibilities for the future. Contemporary archaeology is equally at home studying the materiality and immateriality of videogames, urban life, massive landfills, subaltern populations, everyday spaces, graffiti, sidewalk chalk, and obsolete buildings, to name just a few examples.

Given its relatively unconventional and "unbounded" practical scope, some might consider the archaeology of the contemporary to be an emergent or novel subfield in the discipline. That assessment also depends on one's temporal frame of reference. The archaeology of the contemporary has slowly crept closer to mainstream academic anthropology, archaeology, and heritage discourse over the past forty years. Its emergence in Europe (notably in the UK and Scandinavia) and in North America traveled along different intellectual trajectories, each of which shaped the scholarly outcomes of the first generations of contemporary archaeologists. In Europe, scholars who focused on the archaeology of the contemporary tended to be associated with stand-alone archaeology departments or heritage programs, and their traditions of engagement—led by such scholars as Victor Buchli, Paul Graves-Brown, Dan Hicks, Gavin Lucas, and Angela Piccini among others—contributed studies about contemporary art and archaeology, material culture, ephemera, ruination, and conflict to the subfield. In the United States, early contributors to the subfield—Richard Gould, Michael Schiffer, Bill Rathje, and Mary Beaudry, for example—emerged from departments of anthropology and were trained in traditions of processualism, ethnoarchaeology, excavation-based archaeology, and North American historical archaeology. The creation of the Contemporary Historical Archaeology in Theory (CHAT) group in Bristol, England, in 2003 brought these two disparate traditions together on an annual basis. Some two decades later, contemporary archaeology is internationally recognized as a robust subfield, and it is well represented by the *Journal of Contemporary Archaeology*, as well as by several prominent monographs, edited volumes, exhibits, and multidisciplinary research projects. To date, though, none of these major publications have been focused primarily on North American scholarship.

It is high time for a monograph that reviews the emergence of the archaeology of the contemporary in the United States and establishes a base for future contemporary scholarship in North America. In *The Archaeology of Contemporary America*, William Caraher fills this gap by introducing the subfield of contemporary archaeology in North America to the discipline. He draws on a significant body of literature in archaeology and related fields along with his own original fieldwork to demonstrate how materiality can express aspects of the American experience that often go undocumented and unspoken. This book is an important starting point for situating and inspiring future scholarship in North American archaeology.

As Caraher is quick to acknowledge, it is challenging, if not impossible, to offer a concrete, stable definition of contemporary archaeology because the subfield defies the temporal and spatial bounds of conventional archaeological specializations and is subject to change. Instead, Caraher employs a more relational definition of the archaeology of the contemporary that focuses on experiences within a world enveloped (for the most part) by supermodernity (i.e., a concept that refers to life in the contemporary modern period, which is characterized by excessive quantities of information and things, as well as an accelerated pace of time). It is, in his words, an "archaeology of events, objects, relationships and situations that overlap in time," generally coinciding with the past fifty years (beginning around 1970).

One distinct challenge in writing about contemporary events and processes with reference to a geographic space (here, the United States) is that supermodernity operates on a global scale. Caraher recognizes that the "American experience cannot exist outside of its global context," but he nonetheless creates a space in this volume that foregrounds scholarship to illuminate the American experience. The case studies Caraher introduces are often local expressions of global processes that require him to contend with the tension between global networks of capital, goods, and people, and local situations.

Caraher introduces a wide range of case studies to illustrate events and processes in the contemporary United States that connect with emotions and circumstances of joy, shame, conflict, frivolity, waste, and itinerancy. Deposits of 1980s Atari video games excavated from the Alamogordo Dump in New Mexico are artifacts of childhood and nostalgia as much as they are indicators of changing technology and critiques of Americans' rampant consumerism. Temporary workers' housing in the Bakken oil patch of North Dakota invites consideration of the relationships among commercial environmental resource extraction, labor, temporary buildings, masculinity, and living spaces. References to the temporary city constructed for the Burning Man festival in Nevada employ an archaeology of the contemporary as a tool for documenting ephemera and social organization. Discussions about archaeological interventions in post-Katrina New Orleans position an archaeology of the contemporary as a diachronic approach to questions of resiliency, disaster recovery, and preparedness for future climate-induced weather events.

Readers will find that contemporary archaeological case studies evoke strong feelings that can be depressing, dehumanizing, and traumatic, as well as creative, optimistic, and entertaining. They are never neutral, though, which speaks to the poignancy of an archaeology of the contemporary; it is a tool to provoke, engage, and encourage action. In addition to their evocations, most of the case studies Caraher references share in common the ways in which they apply archaeological methods, theories, and findings to address real-time, present-day issues affecting, and in some cases defining, American society. Caraher demonstrates how an archaeology of the contemporary can operate both in and of the present, and how the practice uses traces of the past to inform present-day conditions and envision future circumstances.

The archaeology of the contemporary past may mark the last frontier in archaeological inquiry as it exposes and assesses important trends in American life within the context of broad global processes inherent to late capitalism and the Anthropocene. No matter how disorienting or uncertain one might be about embracing the archaeology of the contemporary as a lasting, mainstream component of our discipline, there is no question that it boldly goes where no archaeology has gone before, giving us the tools to interrogate the contemporary predicament we experience as individuals, Americans, and global citizens in the present and future.

Krysta Ryzewski, Series Coeditor
Michael S. Nassaney, Founding Series Editor

ACKNOWLEDGMENTS

This book has two origin stories. The most proximate is Michael Nassaney's happy invitation to submit a proposal to the University Press of Florida's The American Experience in Archaeological Perspective series for a book on the archaeology of the American experience. His support and that of incoming series editor Krysta Ryzewski, as well as Mary Puckett at the Press, has been outstanding and deeply appreciated.

The other story starts with the Eastern Korinthia Archaeological Survey in Greece, where my colleagues and mentors cultivated my interest in the modern period. Tim Gregory, Lita Tzortzopoulou-Gregory, Tom Tartaron, Daniel Pullen, P. Nick Kardulias, Dimitri Nakassis, and Richard Rothaus helped and encouraged me to document nearly abandoned modern settlements in the southeastern Corinthia. David Pettegrew was an eager collaborator on this project. He and I returned to the site of Lakka Skoutara many times for almost two decades to document its changes and ongoing use. I continued this work with colleagues on the Western Argolid Regional Project where Dimitri Nakassis, Sarah James, Scott Gallimore, Guy Sanders, and Ioanna Antoniadou welcomed my interest in the modern period, and team leaders Rachel Fernandez, Alyssa Friedman, Melanie Godsey, Machal Gradoz, Stephanie Steinke, and Joseph Frankl helped devise methods for documenting abandoned and near-abandoned modern sites within the methods developed for Mediterranean intensive pedestrian survey. My understanding of the archaeology of modern and early modern benefited immensely from sustained collaboration with Grace Erny and Dimitri Nakassis on the publication of the site of Chelmis and its landscape.

Some colleagues with whom I worked in Greece became close collaborators on my projects in the United States. Richard Rothaus and Kostis Kourelis spent many hours traversing the Bakken, discussing settlement, industrial archaeology, domestic space, and resource booms on the North Dakota Man Camp Project. This project was codirected by Bret Weber and

Richard Rothaus, who shared their understanding of historical archaeology, housing, the history of the American West, and oral history methods during fieldwork and as friends and colleagues. They also collaborated on the Alamogordo Atari Excavations, which were directed by another alumnus of the Greek scene, Andrew Reinhard, whose relentless interest in the archaeology in and of videogames remains an inspiration. The conversations with Richard, Bret, and Kostis contributed immensely to this book. They also read chapters and provided moral support when my energy and spirits flagged.

While writing this book, I've had the pleasure of serving on the standing committee of the Contemporary and Historical Archaeology in Theory (CHAT) group. This opportunity came about through the encouragement of Rachael Kiddey and Hilary Orange, who welcomed me to the CHAT ranks and pushed me to get involved. I deeply appreciate their scholarship, kindness, and approach to the discipline (and life).

My colleagues at the University of North Dakota have been generous and supportive while I toiled on this project. In the Department of History and American Indian Studies, Cynthia Prescott, Caroline Campbell, Eric Burin, Nikki Berg Burin, Ty Reese, Hans Broedel, and Jim Mochoruk listened to my ideas and gave me a congenial space to work them out. Former and current colleagues in the Department of English—Sheila Liming, David Haeselin, Adam Kitzes, Crystal Alberts, and Sharon Carson—not only allowed me to teach a graduate seminar on things in their department but also pushed me to reconsider disciplinary and epistemological borders. Mark Jendrysik from the Department of Political Science and Public Administration served as this book's adviser on all things utopian. Michael Wittgraf and Todd Hebert reminded me of the value of music, art, and practice. Micah Bloom of Minot State University has generously allowed me to use two images from his Codex project in this book. A University of North Dakota Arts and Humanities Scholarship Initiative Grant in 2018 helped fund this project by providing me with a course release.

While writing this book, I've also had the good fortune to serve on the Grand Forks Historic Preservation Commission with a cadre of dedicated colleagues who care deeply about the historical and contemporary past of their community. Gordon Iseminger, Paul Conlon, Sandy Slater, Doug Munski, Brian Carlson, and our chair Chuck Flemmer reminded me at our monthly meetings that our past is a community concern for and in the present.

My parents, Fred and Nancy Caraher, and my brothers, Joe and Fritz, kept me grounded over the years and supported my work in too many ways to count.

Finally, this book would not possible without the encouragement, humor, dogs (Argie the Bargepole and Milo), and love provided by Susan Caraher. I dedicate this book to her as a small gesture of my appreciation for her patience with me, enthusiasm for my schemes, and consistent tolerance for this project.

Introduction

In April of 2014, I stood with a team of archaeologists at the side of a landfill at the edge of the town of Alamogordo, New Mexico. A film crew had invited us to participate in an excavation, and we were surrounded by contractors, consultants, minor celebrities, and a crowd of enthusiastic onlookers as a massive bucket loader tore into the stratigraphy of an abandoned landfill and extracted loads of household discard from the 1980s. The goal of this excavation was to confirm the urban legend that videogame maker Atari, struggling to remain solvent, had dumped truckloads of game cartridges into the Alamogordo landfill in 1983. The excavation attracted international attention and was the climax of a documentary film that framed the dig for the Atari games as the excavation of an era in both videogame development and American consumer culture (Reinhard 2015).

Some 350 miles (~560 km) to the west of Alamogordo lies the Sonoran Desert. Each year, hundreds of undocumented migrants attempt to cross this arid and unforgiving terrain to enter the United States. Many die. Jason De León's Undocumented Migration Project documented and analyzed the material culture and forensic evidence for migrant border crossing. He interweaves archaeological evidence with ethnographic accounts of the immigrants who made the harrowing journey to cross this lethal landscape. This work humanized the cost of national borders and immigration policies that rely, in part, on the Sonoran Desert as a deterrent. By documenting traces of immigration across this landscape, De León's work outlines how U.S. policy served to push the experience of our inhumane immigration policy to the margins of American consciousness. The resulting book, the *Land of Open Graves* (2015), is a powerful critique of U.S. border policy and demonstrates how material culture reveals a tragic aspect of the American experience meant to be invisible.

As the excavator brought to the surface dirty and damaged Atari game cartridges, it was painful to contemplate the relationship between the human costs of the global economy and artifacts of my childhood in this abrupt juxtaposition of my private past and our contemporary present (Wheeler 2014). Shannon Lee Dawdy's study of contemporary New Orleans considers the experience of time's circuitous route through the city's past. Her book *Patina* (2016) explored how residents of post-Katrina New Orleans both experienced and understood the multiple temporalities visible in the historical fabric of their city, in their heirlooms, and in their community's vibrant rituals. In Dawdy's hands, the visibility of patina offers a material counterargument to our faith in modern, linear progress that always values the new over the old. In its place, she introduces the reader to the complicated and recursive history of New Orleans, which embodies an experience that seems to escape the hegemonic reach of contemporary consumer culture. The value that New Orleans residents put on patina parallels in some way the value that collectors put on the stench associated with the dirty and broken Atari cartridges excavated from a New Mexico landfill.

Some 1,500 miles (~2,415 km) to the north of New Orleans, in the Bakken oil patch of North Dakota, drillers, pipeline "cats," "fishers," geologists, and even a few curious archaeologists gather for a Southern-style meal in the dining hall of a temporary "man camp" (Caraher and Weber 2017). These modular structures appeared almost overnight to house the influx of people to the region during the twenty-first-century Bakken oil boom. Some of the units across the region installed to house temporary labor had sheltered families in Louisiana who had lost their homes to Katrina. Transported from the patinated disaster site of post-Katrina of Orleans to the boom-time contingency of North Dakota's Bakken, the reuse of these trailers reflects a quintessentially modern landscape shaped by the flow of people, capital, and fossil fuels. Extractive industries, especially in the American West, continue a long tradition of exploiting the region to support the seemingly insatiable desire for consumer goods at home and abroad. The role of fossil fuels in both the shaping of the American landscape and in accelerating anthropogenic climate change further connects displacement caused by catastrophic weather events with the experience of oil workers in remote landscapes.

Despite their different contexts, the archaeology of patina in New Orleans and the contemporary Bakken oil boom represent opportunities to interrogate the experiences of both American capitalism and global climate change. The archaeology of undocumented migration in the Sonoran Desert offers a distinctly American window to the tragic experience of transnational migration perpetrated by ponderous persistence of the modern nation-state. The Atari excavation, for all its sensationalism and frivolity, reflects the key role that technology—particularly videogames—played in both our collective nostalgia for childhood and the global economic connections required to materialize these memories. Archaeological approaches to the contemporary world serve not only to document the ephemerality of the present but also to reveal the hidden and the overlooked alongside the visible, material features that define the contemporary American experience. As Richard Gould observed in one of the earliest arguments for an archaeology of the contemporary world: "modern material culture studies have shown us that we are not always what we seem, even to ourselves" (Gould 1981: 65).

Defining the Field

Readers of books in this series (and, indeed, the reviewers of early drafts of this manuscript) often expect a tidy, or at least clear, definition of archaeology of the contemporary world. The archaeology of the contemporary world, however, is a comparatively young field, especially in an American context, and because it continues to develop, any definition is provisional. Thus, while it might be appealing to hope for a single-sentence definition, the emergent character of the field makes it particularly resistant to the kind of chronological, geographic, and material definitions common to other forms of archaeological specialization. This introduction will thus develop a more relational definition situated within recent discussions of time in archaeology, archaeological methodology, and the shifting terrain of the archaeology of experience. The introduction then pivots to discuss in a more formal and traditional way the place of the American form of archaeology of the contemporary within the larger context of the field's history. The introduction's final section provides a brief outline of the book.

Readers will quickly come to realize that, similar to many emergent fields, the definition of an archaeology of the contemporary American experience is fuzzy, and this complicates our ability to produce a canonical origin story for the field. Thus the definition of the field offered here, and my explanation of the origins of the discipline, will likely not satisfy all readers. In fact, an earlier version of this manuscript evoked divergent responses from reviewers and editors alike. As the introduction and the following pages will argue, my view of this field seeks to preserve the broad, if fuzzy, boundaries of the contemporary discourse, while also recognizing my own positionality as an archaeologist within the field and its definition.

In most cases, archaeologists define their field of study based on chronological periods. This accounts for the field's long-standing interest in periodization in general in that it has shaped the profession in significant ways. Over the last twenty years, however, archaeologists have joined scholars across the humanities and social sciences to critique and challenge our professional chronologies and attitudes toward time and temporality more broadly (for a useful summary see Tamm and Olivier 2019 and Lucas 2021). This expansive and often deeply theoretical discourse offers a complex backdrop to any definition of archaeology in and of the contemporary world. Indeed, the very notion of the contemporary requires particular attention. As Gavin Lucas notes, the concept of the contemporary implies that two events discernable in the archaeological record occurred at the same time (Lucas 2015). This does not mean, however, that they occurred simultaneously, but rather that the possible chronological span for their occurrence overlapped for some duration. When describing the archaeology of the contemporary world, then, we are describing the archaeology of events, objects, relationships, and situations that overlap in time with the publication of this book and, slightly more broadly, my lifetime. The challenge of this approach is that objects can have very long lifespans, and events can be part of complex diachronic and continuous processes, as any number of recent archaeological publications have emphasized. Even "sealed contexts" often include artifacts that while contemporary at their moment of deposition represent a range of time spans (see Olivier 2015 for the classic treatment of this issue). In other words, we are contemporary with the Parthenon, the Great Zimbabwe, and the White House as well as the latest iPhone, a 1970s shopping mall, and material from the 1980s in a New Mexico landfill. Of course, no scholar studying the archaeology of the contemporary world would include lengthy discussion of the architectural development of the Parthenon in their work, although they might include a discussion of our reception of the Parthenon or its relationship to the landscape of Athens in the present time (e.g., Hamilakis and Ifantidis 2015). At the same time, an approach that emphasizes contemporaneity must recognize that a plurality of temporalities make up the contemporary. Shannon Dawdy famously called this coincidence of multiple temporalities a clockpunk archaeology, after the science fiction genre set in a world featuring the juxtaposition of objects, fashions, and technologies from multiple time periods (Dawdy 2010).

This recognition coincides with the growing awareness that the modern present is a distinctive experience. Laurent Olivier, drawing on the work of

French cultural historian François Hartog (2016), describes our experience of the contemporary as "presentism" and defines the present as an era characterized by a radical break both from the past and the future (Tamm and Olivier 2019). Olivier argued that the contemporary present is bracketed between a past that no longer seems relevant for our current situation and a future that is either completely foreclosed by the impending catastrophe of anthropogenic climate change (or the irrepressible forces of capitalism or a nuclear holocaust) or exceeds our ability to comprehend (for a useful discussion of the future see Bryant and Knight 2019). Thus, archaeologists now study "what the present does to the world" and have abandoned earlier efforts to reconstruct the past as the past. In the place of efforts to create a past as and for the past, archaeologists now seek to define and reconstruct a past that already exists in the service of the present (Olivier 2019: 30).

This rather theoretical intervention has contributed to Olivier's interest in how the technological developments of the modern age shape our experience, including our understanding of our pasts. Archaeologists working in the present recognize how the global scope and the massive destructive capacities of modern technology have transformed the world in ways and at a scale inconceivable even a century ago. Massive mines (Witmore 2021; LeCain 2009), the detritus of global conflicts such as the Cold War (Hanson 2015; McWilliams 2013), climate change–induced catastrophes (Dawdy 2006), forced migration (Hamilakis 2016), and the challenges associated with discarding unimaginably toxic detritus (Joyce 2020) characterize an era of supermodernity that transforms the particularity of human existence into a ruinous landscape of non-places indistinguishable from one another (Augé 1995; González-Ruibal 2008). The archaeology of the present in this context emphasizes the dehumanizing and destructive capacities of technology and economic regimes in the service of mass consumption. This awareness of the present as a global regime shaped by the massive material forces of twentieth- and twenty-first-century technology has also transformed our own understanding of time. Such expansive views of the present or the contemporary poses certain challenges to archaeology. As Olivier himself notes, not only does the dehumanizing and global experience of the twenty-first century exceed description at the small scale associated with traditional archaeology, but the spatially expansive character of the supermodern present also risks obfuscating the differences among those who are experiencing the present. On the other hand, as LouAnn Wurst has noted, such emphasis on the fractured nature of the present threatens to impair our capacity for the collective action necessary to resist the forces that have created supermodern displacements and produce new futures (Wurst 2015, 2019).

The tension between the collective experience of supermodernity and the diverse ways in which individuals and communities understand and experience their present likewise informs this book. Different groups bring different definitions of the present to how we understand the contemporary world. Our ability as archaeologists to engage with different experiences of time consistently complicates our work. While the concept of contemporaneity allows for multiple overlapping views of the present, archaeology has tended to cling to an absolute framework that defines our approach to disciplinary temporality. For the purposes of this book, the last fifty years offer a useful, absolute chronology for the present. The 1970s mark a period when neoliberal economic policies came to the fore both in the United States and in Europe. These policies contributed to supermodernity by producing vast new networks of globalized, private capital that challenge and exceed the economic, social, and political power of states (Harvey 2005). There are more prosaic reasons to identify the last fifty years as a convenient duration for this book. Among American archaeologists, the span of the last fifty years represents a period that falls outside conventional dates for historical significance according to federal guidelines (Yoder 2014). This also happens to coincide with my life experience, as a white, male, academic archaeologist born in 1972. To reinforce this self-referential framework of the contemporary, I have included brief first-person preludes to each chapter that serve as reminders of chronological coincidence of my perspectives and experiences with the objects, situations, landscapes, and contexts that this work studies.

This book acknowledges the complicity of academic institutions and archaeology in constructing a view of time that culminated in the modern present and marginalized alternate forms of temporal experience. Johann Fabian referred to this tendency to subordinate other forms of temporal existence to the dominant academic, modern measure of time as allochronism and part of the difficult legacy of anthropology, archaeology, and colonialism (Fabian 1983; Lucas 2021: 110). While this book's dependence on my own sense of the present will invariably shape its perspective, I will also work to recognize that my experience of the contemporary nevertheless embodies multiple views of the present. In practice, this means viewing my present as sometimes more narrow and sometimes broader than the fifty-year measure I propose in this introduction. For diaspora, Indigenous, Black, Queer, and immigrant communities, the concept of the present might be narrowly circumscribed by the experience of migration or might extend for generations through the collective memory of an irreducible landscape or the nefarious working of intergeneration trauma. For example, Jennifer Morgan has argued that in the study of the early American republic, conventional patterns of periodization poorly represent the lives of enslaved Black women, whose experiences in the early republic were fundamentally similar to their experiences before the revolution (J. Morgan 2016). Limited views of the present likewise do little for descendants of the Tulsa and Rosewood massacres (González-Tennant 2018; see chapter 7) or the Japanese concentration camps (Skiles and Clark 2009; Camp 2010; Burton and Farrell 2001; Farrell and Burton 2019), who continue to endure the consequences of lost generational wealth and contemporary trauma from "historical" events. Locating these experiences in "the past" serves to marginalize their ongoing contemporary impact on these communities. Conversely, Native American groups who protested the route of the Dakota Access Pipeline (DAPL) through the unceded treaty lands of the Standing Rock Reservation understood their protests as part of an uninterrupted tradition of Indigenous resistance. Thus Nick Estes's recent book on the DAPL protests is titled *Our History Is the Future* (2019) and demonstrates an expansive view of the present that embodies the past and future of Indigenous experiences and rights. Dawdy's work in post-Katrina New Orleans shows how the devastation of the 2005 hurricane amplified the city's diverse attitudes to the past and present (Dawdy 2016). New Orleans' Black residents often felt ambivalent about the city's ongoing efforts to preserve traditions and places associated with the city's past, whereas many white residents placed great value on the artifacts and buildings that connected them to the city's history and their pre-Katrina lives. In this way, the experiences of white residents were similar to many of the older residents in my community of Grand Forks, North Dakota, which endured a destructive flood in 1997 and depended heavily on a state-supported historical preservation commission in its aftermath as a way to manage the preservation of historic buildings that survive the inundation. As Olivier has noted, our inclination to cling fiercely to fragments of the past often manifests in our anxieties about the present (Olivier 2019).

If the contemporary includes multiple temporalities, it also consists of multiple spatial extents. As Gavin Lucas has noted, the larger the area covered by a periodization scheme, the more abstract and reductive these schemes tend to become (Lucas 2021: 66). This tendency finds its ultimate expression in the concept of supermodernity, which is a chronological framework—"modern" is part of the term—that also explicitly operates on a global scale. The supermodern manifests in the wide distribution of non-places such as airports, shopping malls, and open pit mines that exist outside of any local traditions of design or use. Thus, the supermodern operates outside of chronological indicators anchored in geographically determined practices, architecture, or styles. Workforce housing in North Dakota's Bakken oil patch consisted of designs and arrangements that found their most ready parallels with guest worker housing at construction sites at the Persian Gulf, housing constructed by immigrants on the U.S.-Mexico border, and lodging for oil workers on the North Slope of Alaska (see chapter 8). Global supply chains both require and ensure a seamless flow of capital that sustains the movement of workers, goods, and material (see chapter 3). These connections likewise trace the global dissemination of the American suburb, factory, and military base in the post–World War II decades and ensured that in many contexts supermodernity took on a distinctly American cast (see chapter 6). In other words, any view of the contemporary defined by supermodernity will require a global perspective to understand how and why we experience the contemporary world as we do and how we define the elements of an experience that are distinctly "American."

That said, this book will seek to prioritize the experience of the supermodern in contexts defined within the United States' borders. For example, the experience of migrants struggling to endure a brutal crossing of the Sonoran Desert speaks both to the intensely local experience of the desert landscape on the U.S.-Mexico border and to global policies associated with "late sovereignty" that alternate between increasingly permissive policies regarding the movement of money and goods and increasingly restrictive policies on the movement of humans (Walker 2003; see chapter 5). In New Orleans, global climate change intensified the devastating impact of Hurricane Katrina, but the destruction occurred in a city with its own distinctive temporal identity defined by a deep awareness of its history amplified by long-standing rituals such as Mardi Gras parades (Dawdy 2016; Wilkie 2014; see chapter 3). Massive multinational corporations finance much of the extraction of oil in the Bakken oil patch of North Dakota and provide accommodations for many of their workers. At the same time, however, workers who came to the oil patch but were not affiliated with these massive companies lived more casually in RVs, which they adapted to accommodate long-term use and the cold North Dakota winters (Caraher et al. 2017; see chapter 8). In this way, it becomes possible to locate examples of the global supermodern that shape our experiences in North America and the United States, while also exploring how the experiences of the contemporary preserve geographically and culturally distinctive responses. This balance will allow the book to reflect the priorities established by the field of historical archaeology, with its emphasis on the modern world and definitions developed in a white European American context, as well as elsewhere in the humanities and social sciences where national specialties remain prominent.

Methods

The tensions among the global scope of the supermodern, the local focus of most archaeological investigations, and the tendency for archaeologists to be specialists in a single period brings us to the matter of method. There are relationships among the notion of contemporaneity, methods that archaeology deploys to document our world, and an experience that we might recognize as "American." In this context, a brief consideration of methodology can contribute to our definition of an archaeology of the contemporary American experience. Cristián Simonetti (2018) has recently observed that archaeology uses an "ego reference point" for its reckoning of time. By this, he means that time is relative to the present experienced by the archaeologist both in the abstract and in the physical practice of the archaeological method. Excavation, for example, reveals "deep time" by literally removing earlier layers of earth to reveal "deeper" pasts below. Archaeologists assume that the surface is contemporary with the archaeologist themselves, although we also recognize that contemporary deposits might occur below the literal surface, throughout the plow zone, and buried below very recent depositional events. Typically, however, archaeologists refer to contemporary objects in strata excavated from below the surface as "contamination" because they upset the conventional relationship between the archaeologist and the subterranean past. Likewise, earlier artifacts present in an excavated context or assemblage are deemed "residual" largely because they are not useful for dating purposes or predate the depositional event that formed the assemblage. Simonetti contrasted this "ego reference point" approach familiar to most excavators to the perspectives of survey and landscape archaeologists whose attention tends to focus on the contemporary surface. The contemporaneity of the archaeologists and the surface, however, does not suggest that all objects that appear within a surface assemblage have the same temporality. Even a casual field walker knows it is possible to find objects from deep prehistory on the surface immediately next to an object dropped moments before. Archaeological methods that privilege work on the scale of the landscape have already recognized how this approach pushed the discipline to consider the co-existence of multiple temporalities (Harrison 2011). Thus, for Simonetti, the methods employed by an archaeologist often dictate the archaeologist's attitude toward time.

My description of Simonetti's work oversimplifies his complex arguments at the intersection of time, experience, and archaeological methods, but it serves as a useful point of departure for considering the relationship between the concept of the contemporary and the methods that have emerged to document the recent past. It is unsurprising, for example, that excavation has played a relatively minor role in the archaeology of the contemporary world. As this book will show in chapters 1 and 2, it remains possible to excavate the contemporary when, for example, digging in a landfill in search of Atari games or to understand wider consumption patterns as performed by William Rathje and his team after years of surveying garbage. The intense community interest surrounding the careful excavation of the remains of individuals interred in a mass grave in Tulsa's Oaklawn Cemetery who died in the Tulsa race massacre of 1921 (Messer 2021; Odewale and Slocum 2020; Franklin et al. 2020: 758–759; see chapter 7) serves as a reminder that temporal distance from the present alone is not an adequate measure of contemporaneity. In fact, excavations can continue to speak to contemporary descendant communities in significant ways, whether through the excavation of material associated with Indian residential schools or race massacres (chapter 6) or the discarded objects from Japanese internment camps. These excavations can likewise contribute to the healing of trauma, enrich a community's sense of place, and create new and expanded sense of contemporaneity. Awareness of the power of archaeology on contemporary communities has contributed to the development of the fields of public- and community-centered archaeology in the last few decades (e.g., Matthews 2020a). This book will not address directly many of these important and increasingly specialized discussions, but I hope their impact will be visible in discerning how archaeology contributes to our experience of the present more broadly.

To return to issues of methodology, the archaeology of the contemporary world has tended to embrace methods that underscore the contemporaneity of the archaeologist and the surface of the ground. As the second part of this introduction will show, this accounts for the field's affinity for phenomenological methods in archaeology. Most famously developed by Christopher Tilley and his colleagues, phenomenological approaches stressed that the archaeologist's experience in the present could inform how they understand past experiences in the landscape (Tilley 1994; Shanks and Tilley 1987). Among archaeologists, these approaches recognized the contemporaneity between the archaeologist and their situation as a way to allow the past to remain present in both its lived experience and temporal complexity.

This awareness of contemporaneity between the archaeologist and their present has likewise informed approaches involving active site archaeology such as Carolyn White's work at the Burning Man festival in Nevada (White 2020; see chapter 7), my own research amid active workforce housing in the Bakken (chapter 8), and at sites undergoing continuous transformation in response to the ongoing COVID pandemic (Angelo et al. 2021; Magnani et al. 2022). In these situations, it is obviously both inappropriate and often impossible to excavate. In response, archaeologists of the contemporary adapted a wide range of modern technologies, from mobile phone cameras to satellite imaging as well as time-based media such as video and audio to document active contexts. The use of methods associated with ethnography and oral history have likewise come to the fore in archaeology of the contemporary world, leveraging approaches developed in anthropology to document the "ethnographic present" (Trigger 1981; Simonetti 2018: 135–138) that is contemporary to archaeological work (for more on the convergence of archaeology and anthropology see Garrow and Yarrow 2010). As we will see later in this book, Jason De León's ethnographic interviews with undocumented migrants coincided with his use of intensive survey methods to document individuals entering the United States across the Sonoran Desert (De León 2015); Miriam Rothenberg similarly combined interviews and systematic documentation to understand the remains of volcano-damaged homes in Monserrat (Rothenberg 2021); and Davina Two Bears combined ethnographic practice, archaeology, and archival work in her effort to document the Leupp residential school on the Navajo Reservation (Two Bears 2019). The close relationship between archaeology and anthropology in the U.S. academic tradition supported the development of especially rigorous ethnographic practices that often prioritize approval by institutional review boards, anonymity, and clear policies for records preservation. This contrasts with some of the more informal or loosely defined ethnographic techniques that have sometimes characterized archaeology of the contemporary elsewhere in the world (e.g., Harrison and Schofield 2011).

Archaeologists of the contemporary world have likewise followed the lead of anthropologists in their use of photography and video to create a foundation to critique the contemporary situation. Once again, Jason De León's landmark work *Land of Open Graves* offers a model by featuring photographs by Michael Wells (De León 2015). My own project in North Dakota's Bakken collaborated with photographers Kyle Cassidy, Ryan Stander, John Holmgren, and Andrew Cullen (Caraher and Weber 2017). Shannon Dawdy's most recent project, *American Afterlives: Reinventing Death in the Twenty-First Century,* is a collaboration with filmmaker Daniel Zox (Dawdy and Zox 2021). In many ways, these approaches reflect the growing prominence of activist-artists such as Ai Weiwei and Christoph Buchel who have controversially used artifacts associated with migrants to make both political and aesthetic statements. Like these artists, archaeologists vary the intent and basis for their artistic interventions according to the projects. In chapter 3, we will show how the use of photography contributes to our understanding of the complex webs of agency in the aftermath of the devastating Minot floods of 2011 (Bloom 2017). This work and others like it reflect a growing willingness among archaeologists of the contemporary world to embrace not only new media but also new collaborations and aesthetics in documenting their own world.

A recent trio of projects dedicated to documenting and analyzing the archaeology of the COVID pandemic reflects the methodological diversity present in how archaeologists have approached a very contemporary situation in different ways. Despite the rather preliminary status of these works, they nevertheless demonstrate the plurality of approaches embraced by archaeologists of the contemporary world as they seek to navigate the often complicated intersection of local and supermodern landscapes. A project codirected by Matthew Magnani, Anatolijs Venovcevs, and Natalia Magnani in the town of Tromsø, for example, documented discarded objects associated with the pandemic using geotagged cellphone photographs (Magnani et al. 2022). This revealed that local attitudes toward COVID, particularly the need to wear latex gloves, did not align precisely with the policy statement from the Norwegian government. A collaborative project published by Dante Angelo, Kelly M. Britt, Margaret Lou Brown, and Stacey L. Camp developed a photographic archive documenting the impact of the virus across multiple sites in the United States and Chile and recently published a photo essay based on this work (2021). This kind of multisite project revealed anxiety for the future, the stress of the global collapse of home, school, and work divisions, and different approaches to enforce new forms of conformity. A photo of a supermarket in Chile (Angelo et al. 2021: figure 12) will likely strike an American viewer as deeply familiar with its oversized logo and brightly colored floor markers. But the presence of soldiers enforcing social distancing will likely appear quite foreign. Finally, a project led by John Schofield harvested data captured from social media feeds as a way to sample discard patterns of COVID-related objects from around the world (Schofield et al. 2021). Schofield combined this data from material recovered from such unlikely places as the stomach of a seal turtle off the Australian coast to reveal how single-use polypropylene masks will find their way into the environment far from the location of their intended use. While it is unlikely that the recovery of material from other organic lifeforms could represent a viable or scalable archaeological method for documenting the impact of public health policy, it does make clear that the persistence of modern material in the broader ecosystem will reinforce the supermodern scope of the contemporary experience.

The American Experience

Thus far we have considered how the archaeology of the contemporary world must contend with the multiple temporalities that make up the contemporary. We have also recognized that the late twentieth and early twenty-first centuries introduced new concepts of space, particularly the concept of global, supermodern non-places that complicate and complement traditional views of the local. The multitude of temporalities that constitute the contemporary and startling new notions of spatiality require that archaeologists in and of the twenty-first century embrace a wide range of methods. On the one hand, conventional excavation and survey practices can and do reveal multiple temporal and spatial extents in relation to the archaeologist, and these methods continue to play a familiar role in archaeology of the contemporary. On the other hand, archaeologists of the contemporary world have consistently recognized the challenge of global crises and active, developing sites through multisite approaches, digital and time-based documentation practices, ethnographic methods, and art. It is useful to note that the diverse methods associated with archaeology of the contemporary are not exclusive to this field and many of these practices have played a role in archaeology in general, but archaeology of the contemporary world has shown a greater eagerness to embrace new and sometimes even experimental approaches to capture the complexities of the modern moment.

In this book, this distinct understanding of time, space, and methods will inform how we understand the archaeology of the contemporary American experience. In fact, the diversity of times, spatial scales, and methods is essential for exploring and defining a concept as complex as the American experience. As an example, we can all understand how at a very simple level the American experience represents the experiences of Americans. As Stacey Camp has shown in her book *The Archaeology of American Citizenship* (2013), however, the idea of being American must extend beyond what it means to be a legal citizen to encompass the experience of all individuals living within the United States and neighboring areas. Thus, the concept of an American experience necessarily embodies a wide range of legal status as well as a wide range of encounters. Archaeologists have long understood the role of race, class, gender, age, and various regional identities in contributing to how individuals experience America. The concept of "America" or the "U.S." in this context extends well beyond the interaction among individuals and communities and the various apparatus of the United States government (or the governments of other American states). It is undeniable, however, that the state has played a key role in defining the American experience through various positive, negative, and ambivalent encounters with institutions such as the military (Hanson 2015), education (Skowronek and Lewis 2010), prisons (Casella 2005), internment camps (Burton and Farrell 2001), and internal and national borders (McAtackney and Maguire 2020). Of course, state institutions represent but one aspect of how groups and individuals experience America, and archaeologists studying the twentieth-century American experience have looked to consumer practices and goods, especially with the rise of mass-produced material culture, as a medium through which collective and individual identity manifests (Mullins 2011; see chapter 3). From cars to Barbie dolls, Americans have regularly used consumer goods both to consolidate social standing and to transmit the values across generations and within communities. Archaeologists have also looked for evidence in labor practices in the same period for fundamental experiences that define the diverse encounters that constitute American life (Shackel 2009; Roller 2018). For these scholars, the factory, the mining camp, the company town, the urban slum, and the protest site represent the crucibles in which American experience and identity are formed. Others still have looked to the wide range of public rituals manifest in sports to religious architecture, coming-of-age practices, festivals, and forms of commemoration as important loci for the American experience. In short, the diverse spaces and aspects of the American experience within the borders of the United States create an equally diverse range of encounters.

At the same time, archaeologists of the contemporary world recognize that the American experience is not confined to the limits of the nation-state but manifests itself in geopolitical and economic outposts, flows through global supply chains, and follows the growing output of digital media. The most literal example of the American experience beyond the borders of the United States is the military installations and corporate outposts that housed workers and soldiers in American-style suburbs (chapter 6). Recent work by Barbara Voss, Laura Ng, and Kostis Kourelis, for example, has emphasized the transnational character of immigrant worlds. Their work has expanded the model for an American experience developed in Stacey Camp's work on the archaeology of American citizenship to demonstrate that the American experience was not limited to national boundaries and manifests in how immigrants expressed their identity in their countries of origin (Voss and Allen 2008, Ng 2021; Kourelis 2020). Other examples of the global reach of the American experience are less tangible. For example, every Apple phone laden with applications, every streamed music video or game, and every major motion picture represents an expression of the American experience whether encountered in Singapore, Santiago, Athens, or Perth. The material traces of this globalized America, in turn, impact lives in the United States and abroad in unexpected ways. In fact, as I am writing this introduction, disruptions to the global supply chains brought about by the COVID pandemic have caused shortages in American supermarkets and made consumers worry about getting the latest gadgets and gifts during the holiday season. Such disruptions highlight America's dependence on offshore sites for extractive industries, manufacturing, and, increasingly, the disposal of waste. The lives of miners for cobalt and tantalum in Congo (chapter 4), factory workers in dormitories in China (chapter 8), and processors of e-waste in Asia and Africa (chapter 2) are similarly shaped by American experience as suburban consumers in the United States and workers in the Bakken oil patch of western North Dakota. Finally, if the production and consumption of the American experience happens on the supermodern scale, it is hardly surprising that the crises transforming the American experience are global as well. From the series of twenty-first-century megastorms fueled by global climate change to the pain and disruptions caused by the COVID pandemic, the American experience cannot exist outside of its global context.

At this point, it might be useful to return to the matter of defining the archaeology of the contemporary American experience (and thereby acknowledge the urging of reviewers and editors alike). For the purposes of this series, I will define the archaeology of the contemporary American experience as the study of material, situations, and encounters that occurred within the last fifty years in North America or more narrowly in the United States. When this definition proves inadequate to encapsulate the range of times, spaces, and circumstances, I will expand it chronologically and geographically. Archaeologists are adept at recognizing when their chronological assumptions are inadequate for understanding the history of a site. It is not unusual to encounter earlier material associated with a feature or a stratigraphic level dating to a later time. As a result, our discipline has developed a remarkable ability to recognize the multiple temporalities present in an assemblage and to discern whether this is meaningful for understanding its history. I will do all I can to apply this same aptitude to this book.

A Short History of the Field

The approach in this book to the temporal character, spatial extent, and methods that define the contemporary American experience follows historical trends in the wider discipline of archaeology. The following section offers a brief overview of the history of the archaeology of the contemporary world in an American context that will be developed more thoroughly in the subsequent chapters. Substantive and thorough surveys of the archaeology of the contemporary world have appeared recently (Harrison and Schofield 2010; Harrison 2011; Harrison and Breithoff 2017; González-Ruibal 2019), and these works have generally recognized their origins in an American context starting in the late 1970s, when American archaeologists took the lead in exploring archaeological approaches to contemporary material culture. Perhaps the earliest effort in the United States to conduct fieldwork on the contemporary world was Bill Rathje's Tucson-based Garbage Project, a significant and long-standing endeavor to which we will return throughout this volume. In 1981, Rathje made an important contribution to Michael Schiffer's and Richard Gould's edited volume *Modern*

Material Culture (1981), which stands among the first efforts to articulate an archaeology of contemporary American society. Subtitled "The Archaeology of Us," this edited volume includes contributions that situated the field amid a diverse range of perspectives, from historical archaeology (Leone 1981) to anthropology (Eighmy 1981), and Wilk and Schiffer reflect on how the archaeology of the present can positively impact the teaching of the discipline (1981). Rathje's "manifesto on modern material-culture studies" stands as the most influential and widely cited article in this edited volume. It emphasizes how an archaeology of the recent past can make four contributions to the field: "(1) teaching archaeological principles, (2) testing archaeological principles, (3) doing the archaeology of today, [and] (4) relating our society to those of the past" (Rathje 1981: 52).

Rathje developed these ideas over the course of his "Garbage Project," which he started in 1973, seeking to document the garbage from a number of neighborhoods in Tucson, Arizona (see Rathje and Murphy 1992 for the best summary of this long-lived project). By the mid-1980s, Rathje and colleagues had started to conduct systematic excavations of landfills. This work allowed Rathje to make a wide range of conclusions regarding modern discard and household behavior and also popularized archaeological approaches to assemblages of modern material adapted from well-established principles, methods, and practice. For Rathje, archaeological methods and principles could be separated from their focus on the past and applied to understand the present in new ways. In many ways, his approach framed the contributions in the second part of Schiffer and Gould's edited volume. This consisted of a number of case studies that applied archaeological approaches to contemporary America ranging from the discard of pennies (Rothschild 1981) to racial graffiti in Hawai'i (Blake 1981), the archaeology of supermarkets (Bath 1981), the use of space in modern houses in Texas (Portnoy 1981), and patterns of household reuse in Tucson, Arizona (Schiffer et al. 1981). As a general rule, these projects also recognized the ethnoarchaeological potential in the study of contemporary behaviors and formation processes, but rather than using modern material culture to explain past actions, they turned their conclusions on contemporary society.

In the decades following the inauguration of Rathje's Garbage Project and the publication of Schiffer and Gould, work slowly continued to appear in an American setting. Michael Schiffer, the founder of behavioral archaeology, produced a book-length study of transistor radios (Schiffer 1991), and Larry Zimmerman made the first probing reflections on an archaeology of homelessness (e.g., Zimmerman and Welsch 2006). Two books published at the turn of the twenty-first century stimulated renewed interest in the archaeology of the contemporary world. P.M. Graves-Brown's *Matter, Materiality, and Modern Culture* (2000) drew heavily on late twentieth-century interest in material and consumer culture that developed in sociology, history, anthropology, and elsewhere in the humanities (for a summary, see Hicks 2010 as well as chapter 3 in this book). Intriguingly, Michael Schiffer's contribution to this volume (2000) looked to behavioral archaeology as a way to critique the various interpretations used to understand the history of the early twentieth-century electric car. Consistent with emerging ideas of behavioral archaeology, he sought to integrate the study of material culture with an understanding of human behavior based on a range of historical and ethnographic sources. He showed that by studying the design of the cars, the advertising material related to their sales, and the history of their consumption, we could arrive at a more sophisticated and nuanced understanding of their histories. In the case of the decline in the electric car, Schiffer argued that gender and class influenced the adoption of the electric car in early twentieth-century society. Wealthy families purchased electric cars for short, household errands typically performed by women. The association of these vehicles with women and women's work limited their mass appeal, especially among consumers who wanted a single vehicle for both short- and long-distance trips. This, more than any limit in technology, accounted for the decline in popularity of these vehicles.

The second fundamental early twenty-first-century work is Buchli and Lucas's landmark publication *Archaeologies of the Contemporary Past* (2001), which included articles by Schiffer and Rathje, and also by Laurie Wilkie and the Ludlow Collective. Majewski and Schiffer (2001) describe their efforts to document modern material culture as an expansive archaeology of consumerism that explicitly linked the life history of modern objects to their place within the social and technological relations. They offer a case study grounded in historical archaeology of late nineteenth-century ceramics to ground the origins of contemporary consumerism within the production, distribution, consumption, and discard of these household goods. The contributions by Wilkie (2001) and the Ludlow Collective (2001) likewise locate their interest in the archaeology of contemporary American society in early twentieth-century material and the ways that nontextual artifacts served to articulate persistent notions of race, memory, and resistance. Rathje's article (2001), in contrast, returns to his "garbology" project, and echoing Schiffer, strikes a multidisciplinary and inclusive tone arguing for an "integrated archaeology" that brings together many of the key trends in archaeological thought of the late twentieth century, from New Archaeology to post-processualism. That said, Rathje's approach remains anchored in the processualism of the New Archaeology, with its emphasis on how the rigorous, quantitative analysis of contemporary garbage from Tucson could reveal behaviors that other forms of documentation would not.

Thus, despite this awareness of larger trends in the discipline of archaeology, American contributions to an archaeology of the contemporary world remained distinct in their effort to anchor this emerging subfield in the American form of historical archaeology. Historical archaeology in the United States developed in the 1970s and 1980s and focuses on the period from 1700 to the mid–twentieth century (Orser 1996). Methodologically, it combined commitments to systematic data collection and quantitative analysis with an interest in structural paradigms. This is especially visible in the work of James Deetz and Mark Leone (see Hicks and Beaudry 2006 and Beaudry 2007 for a discussion; also see chapter 3). The influence of these scholars and historical archaeology more broadly set the archaeology of the contemporary American experience on a rather different trajectory from its world counterpart (cf. González-Ruibal 2019). The archaeology of the contemporary world in Europe has tended to draw on post-processual approaches inspired by Ian Hodder and Michael Shanks and Christopher Tilley or the sociological studies of Daniel Miller and the so-called material turn (Hicks 2010). Shanks and Tilley's (1987) famous study of contemporary British and Swedish beer cans, for example, did less to consider the economic character of the beer cans, their contents, and their function, and more to look at the symbolic and social meaning of their design in the history of brewing, alcohol marketing, and social discipline in British and Sweden. This historically divergent trajectory manifests itself in the *Oxford Handbook of the Archaeology of the Contemporary World* (Graves-Brown, Harrison, and Piccini 2013), which included fewer than ten of the forty-nine contributions from an American context.

The divergent history of archaeology of the contemporary in the United States has not prevented scholars from engaging with their global counterparts. At the turn of the twenty-first century, the formation of the Contemporary and Historical Archaeology in Theory (CHAT) group brought together scholars from the United States and Europe to explicitly consider the role of theory in the rapidly developing fields of historical archaeology and archaeology of the contemporary (Hicks 2010). CHAT has produced a series of edited proceedings from their conferences that model theoretical and regional diversity. Driving this point home was the inaugural publication of the CHAT group, which featured a preface by American archaeologist Mary Beaudry and an afterword by Europeanist Victor Buchli (Buchli 2007; Beaudry 2007; McAtackney, Palus, and Puccini 2007). The volume consists of contributions from North America, Africa, the Mediterranean, and the UK, with contributors employing a range of methods and theoretical paradigms, from the quantitative approaches common to American-style historical archaeology to those informed by post-processual and phenomenological approaches developed in the UK. The chronological range of the contributions is likewise expansive, with research into nineteenth-century patent medicine advertisements and bottles in New England (Ryzewski 2007) rubbing shoulders with a phenomenological study of a contemporary shopping mall in the UK (Graves-Brown 2007). As the introduction to the volume points out, the contributions emphasize colonialism, conflict, heritage, and performance and practice despite the diverse range of methods and sites (McAtackney and Palus 2007). In CHAT, theory and method provide a common ground for considering the archaeology of the contemporary world.

The emergence of CHAT and the publication of volumes such as the *Oxford Handbook* demonstrate the convergence of archaeological practices and our awareness of the global scope of contemporary culture and society. On the one hand, the maturation of the archaeology of the contemporary world has established it as a recognized component of historical archaeology. The 2020 *Routledge Handbook of Historical Archaeology,* for example, includes a chapter on "Contemporary archaeology" (McAtackney 2020). On the other hand, the founding of the *Journal of Contemporary Archaeology* in 2013 may well mark the arrival of archaeology of the contemporary world as a field in its own right. It coincides with a growing interest among publishers in works that bring together approaches situated in both American and global practices in the archaeology of the contemporary world (e.g., McAtackney and Ryzewski 2017), and this has produced a steady stream of edited volumes, surveys, and well-regarded monographs on the archaeology of the contemporary world (including, I hope, this volume). As the chapters of this book will show, the global scope of archaeology of the contemporary world has emphasized the field's ability to trace trends and challenges common to our modern world. At the same time, the tradition of American historical archaeology offers a way to anchor the impact and significance of these global trends in the nuanced world of personal, local, and collective experiences.

The Organization of This Book

This book seeks to explore key issues in the archaeology of the contemporary American experience. My approach is anchored in two case studies that divide the book into two parts. The first part of the book unpacks the excavation of an assemblage of Atari game cartridges in the New Mexico desert in 2014, and the second part explores a decade of study associated with the twenty-first-century Bakken oil boom in western North Dakota with particular attention to workforce housing. Each part of the book constitutes a protracted and unorthodox case study that follows the deep and reflexive dive into the research that informed my analysis of the Atari excavations and the Bakken. In effect, then, the book is a case study both in the sense that it explores distinctive material assemblages associated with two contexts in the contemporary world, and also in the sense that it shows how these two assemblages open onto the development of the field. Because the archaeology of the contemporary world assumes the contemporaneity of the field itself and the objects of study, the following chapters go to some length to demonstrate the link between the way in which we use archaeology to study the present, as well as my own place as an archaeologist and participant in the disciplinary and cultural trends. I largely make these connections in brief preludes to each chapter that serve to reinforce my own "ego reference point" of the archaeologist in relation to the chapters.

My dependence on the case study approach also accounts for the unevenness of my coverage of the field. My justification for this approach is that it seems the best way to write a book on the archaeology of my own experiences as an American rather than a book on a period particularly bounded by a set of conditions (e.g., labor, race, consumer practices, incarcerations, urbanism, etc.) or a period distilled from a more distant past by generations of archaeological and historical practice. That said, I did my best to tease out the broader implication of my case studies and experiences both as an authentic reproduction of my decade-long study of these periods and in an effort to be fair and representative to the contributors the field.

Thus, the first part of the book starts at the edge of a landfill in Alamogordo, New Mexico, where a massive excavator removes domestic waste to unbury an assemblage of Atari games. The first chapter describes the stratigraphy of the landfill excavation in some detail, demonstrating that archaeology of the contemporary world can involve traditional methods of documentation. Chapter 2 locates the excavation of the Atari games within both a concern for the waste produced by American consumer culture and the tradition of the "garbology" instigated by Bill Rathje's Garbage Project. It traces how archaeology of trash started as a way to gain insights into discard practices associated with particular groups of people. Contemporary studies of garbage recognize that trash has the potential to tell transnational stories that speak to processes and the interplay between trash and individuals under various waste regimes. This more expansive view of garbology parallels recent approaches to elements discussed in chapter 3, which follows the Atari case study from childhood memories of wanting to buy the latest Atari game to the stinky mess at the edge of the Alamogordo landfill. This leads us to a more expansive consideration of things in archaeology and across the social sciences and points to how new attitudes toward agency complicate views of consumption and the production of culture and distinctive experiences. Chapter 4 completes the first case study by extending our reflection on archaeology of the contemporary American experience of media, starting with famous record collections, recording studios, and music venues, and continuing through archaeological investigations associated with various forms of digital media related to the Atari games we were excavating. Much like contemporary trash and consumer goods, these objects produce a distributed American experience that traces expansive networks of interrelated but contemporary experiences. The chapter concludes with a brief consideration of how archaeology as a discipline leverages these same networks and experiences to produce knowledge in the twenty-first century. Thus, the recursive relationship between the American experience and the emerging field of the archaeology of the contemporary world manifests itself in the tools and practices that archaeologists use to understand their world.

Chapter 5 begins the book's second case study, which focuses on the archaeology of contemporary oil production and labor in the Bakken oil patch of North Dakota. This chapter seeks to contextualize the experience of workers who flooded the Bakken region of North Dakota in search of jobs in the aftermath of a subprime mortgage crisis and resulting recession of the early twenty-first century. Their scramble for housing—which often included camping in public parks or living in RVs in the Williston, North Dakota, Walmart parking lot—revealed the connections among economic displacement, housing, and marginalization. In an effort to contextualize these experiences, chapter 5 considers the important work of archaeologists of the contemporary world on migrants, borders, and homelessness as a way to consider how borders, marginal places, and displacement contributes to the experience of contemporary American life. Chapter 6 is among the more discursive chapters of this book in that it considers the role that institutional housing played on military bases, college campuses, and residential schools. Like workforce housing in the Bakken, bases and schools sought both to promote orderly life and to obfuscate, whenever possible, signs of resistance or disorder. Archaeology of contemporary and historical sites has revealed the tensions between the carefully managed public appearance of these sites—which often take on a global scale—and the experiences of their residents. Chapter 7 continues to consider the interplay between the American and the global by considering topics important to the study of the contemporary city in both a chronologically broad American context and the geographically expansive transnational context. The ruins of the postwar and post-industrial American city speak to trends in the global economy that shifted manufacturing from American cities to cities in the "Global South." The remains of an industrial past form a dramatic backdrop for ongoing racial violence, protests, and various forms of urban redevelopment that draw on historical and transnational precedents. The final chapter of the book attempts to tie some of the threads introduced in chapters 5, 6, and 7 together in recent archaeological research in North Dakota's Bakken oil patch. While the work in the Bakken focused primarily on workforce housing with its connections to military, institutional, and urban forms, our time in the Bakken and our attention to human cost of the oil industry also forced us to consider issues that went well beyond the temporal and geographic limits of western North Dakota. Thus, the final chapter also introduces remarks on how the archaeology of the contemporary world has engaged with issues of global climate change. The chapter concludes with a brief discussion of the idea of the Anthropocene, which seeks to describe the human impact on the Earth in geological terms. The interest in the Anthropocene among archaeologists of the contemporary world offers yet another example of how the very notion of the "contemporary" defies tidy definition and how the American experience can be planetary in scope.

Because this book developed organically from the two case studies, it is in some ways limited in how it engages the field, and in other ways perhaps more expansive than one might expect. For example, the field of forensic anthropology or disaster archaeology largely stands outside the scope of my case studies, although it often involves research that would fall into the fuzzy chronological limits of "the contemporary world" (Gould 2007). Forensic anthropology and disaster archaeology, however, have also developed their own disciplinary discourse and methods over the last three decades (Powers and Sibun 2013). Archaeologies of race, gender, sexuality, and identity, while incredible fertile grounds for archaeological research in recent decades, do not appear in this book under distinct headings, although they form an obvious foundation to many of the chapters. As the archaeology of the contemporary American experience continues to develop as a field, I anticipate that it will contribute in significant ways to the archaeology of contemporary race and gender, but as yet, these important areas remain relatively unexplored when compared to the field of historical archaeology. My book also presents an American experience that extends well beyond the boundaries of North America and entangles traditional approaches to American historical archaeology with the flourishing field of archaeological contemporary world in Europe. This is in keeping with the approaches championed by groups such as CHAT with its European and American membership, and with my own sense that this is the best way to address pressing planetary situations such as climate change on a global scale. This has thus informed my decision to focus the potentially expansive remit of this book in the area where I have.

Of course, it is entirely possible that my reading of the field is wrong and that my oversights represent blinders imposed by my own sites, research priorities, and political anxieties. Some of these blinders are manifest in the book's appendix, where I present the gender bias in my citational practices. My blinders and biases will likely cause some readers to find this book inadequate or simply too idiosyncratic to be of use. My hope is that these readers will recognize that, despite its flaws, the book is but the first word in a rapidly developing field, which distinguishes it from many of the more narrowly situated works that have appeared in this series. I expect that future books on topics such as the archaeology of contemporary race, a queer archaeology of the modern American experience, and the archaeology of gender in the twenty-first century will fill in gaps, shift priorities, and consolidate the field in new and important ways.

I

1

The Alamogordo Atari Excavations

In this chapter, we return to the Alamogordo desert in April 2014 as I stood among colleagues and watched a massive backhoe excavate the town's landfill. The purpose of this stinky undertaking was to expose a deposit of Atari videogames dumped there in 1983. I was with a team of archaeologists who hoped to document this excavation. The team included Andrew Reinhard, who would popularize the concept of "archaeogaming" via his blog, articles, book, and, ultimately, in his 2019 dissertation that drew upon his experiences with the Alamogordo excavation (Reinhard 2015, 2018, 2019). Raiford Guins, the leading scholar on the material culture of video gaming, who had just published a book on the history and afterlife of videogames and gaming consoles (Guins 2014), was also there. Richard Rothaus and Bret Weber accompanied us as well. Rothaus, an experienced contract archaeologist and proficient and critical digital archaeologist, was the field director of the North Dakota Man Camp Project. Weber was the co-director of that project and a historian of the twentieth-century American West who worked with me in Cyprus. The team brought together years of archaeological field experience, a detailed understanding of videogames and digital media, and historical perspectives on the American West. Our team also had experience documenting modern material culture.

The story of Atari games in the Alamogordo dump had acquired the status of an American urban legend, which expanded widely in the early days of the internet (see Guines 2014: 207–236 and Reinhard 2015 for the basic narrative). Despite contemporary media coverage of the dump of Atari games, including a story in the *New York Times* (Section D4, Sept. 28, 1983), Atari fans composed a shadowy alternate narrative. The majority of games dumped by Atari, they reasoned, consisted of the poorly received *E.T.* videogame. This game was based on Steven Spielberg's 1982 film *E.T.*, and Atari executives had rushed the development of a videogame version of the plot to ensure it debuted in time for Christmas 1982. The game's developer, Howard Scott Warshaw, was a highly regarded programmer who had earlier in the year adapted another Spielberg film, *Raiders of the Lost Ark,* for a well-received videogame. The *E.T.* game, in contrast, received mixed reviews by critics, and gamers found it frustrating particularly because of the difficulty in extricating E.T. from pits, a common feature in game play. Despite selling over a million copies, the *E.T.* game started to appear on lists of the worst game ever released. This fueled speculation that Atari had dumped tens of thousands of *E.T.* games in the Alamogordo landfill in an apparent attempt to hide the game's poor sales. The burial also coincided with the beginning of the early 1980s "videogame crash," which not only crippled the industry but also forced Atari into bankruptcy. The location of the dump surely added to its legendary status. Alamogordo, New Mexico, was associated with the Trinity nuclear test in 1945 at the nearby White Sands Missile Range and the nearby town of Roswell with its history of UFO sightings. Alamogordo was also the site of the 1969 Huckleby poisoning when a local farmer accidentally fed his family pork from mercury-poisoned hogs with tragic results that garnered national media attention. In other words, the legends associated with the dumping of the games drew on a complex American tradition associated with the intersection of the nation's military and technological history, a tragic narrative of mercury poisoning borne of America's growing ecological consciousness, and the mysterious potential for the West as the backdrop for "close encounters" and unsolved mysteries.

The documentary history of the dump of the Atari games is less exciting but nonetheless speaks to the potential for archaeology of the contemporary world to complicate the contexts that shape the American experience. The dumping of the games in Alamogordo was not an effort to hide losses or obscure post-holiday returns but rather a financial decision to ship returned and remaindered games from Atari's El Paso distribution center to Alamogordo because its landfill charged less money for dumping industrial and consumer waste (Goldberg and Vendell 2012: 656–657). Despite numerous rumors, it was not the poor reviews of the *E.T.* game that caused Atari's demise. The recession of the early 1980s, the increasingly saturated videogame console market, the growing competition for games, and increased expectations for profits from Atari's new corporate owners, Time Warner, all combined to seal the company's fate amid an industry-wide slowdown.

The confluence of popular culture and contemporary archaeology offers a more significant context for the Alamogordo excavation. Rather than being a systematic and scientific excavation, such as those carried out as part of William Rathje's Garbage Project in Arizona landfills, a documentary film crew funded by Microsoft organized the excavation. Their goal was to make a film available exclusively via their gaming and streaming consul Xbox. The resulting film, *Atari: Game Over,* would use the footage of the excavations in the final part of the documentary, which would reconnect the game's celebrated developer, Howard Scott Warshaw, with his creation, the *E.T.* game. The New Mexico Environment Department (NMED) set most of the conditions and methods governing the excavation. As archaeologists, the filmmakers consulted our team before the project and interviewed us individually during and after the excavations. As the backhoe reached closer to the levels known to contain the Atari games, the local safety team allowed us under the safety tape to sort the trash removed by the excavator and to identify videogame cartridges. Andrew Reinhard and Richard Rothaus made the triumphant first identification of an Atari game. This moment presented the filmmakers with an opportunity for archaeological theater, with crowds assembled to watch the final day of excavation cheering each new discovery.

The commingling of narrative, objects, media, and practices in the excavation at the Alamogordo landfill provides a compelling view of archaeology's place in the contemporary world. This chapter provides the first intensive case study of the book, which subsequent chapters will contextualize in various ways. The goal here is to ground the archaeology of the contemporary world in one of the most basic expressions of archaeology: the excavation. We will attend to the planning, stratigraphy, deposition, and dating of the landfill and the deposit of Atari games. Attention to the archaeological detail will fill a gap in the existing literature on the excavations at the site (Reinhard 2015, 2018; Ruggill, McAllister, Kocurek, and Guins 2015). Moreover, this chapter provides a detailed perspective on one example of contemporary site archaeology, which, as noted in the introduction, often presents challenges to traditional archaeological practices and methods. As we will see, opening a landfill creates a wide range of environmental and structural problems that makes it difficult to document the process with the same level of detail as for a traditional excavation.

The dirt archaeology of this chapter introduces the first part of the book, which traces three major themes important to archaeology of the contemporary American experience. Chapter 2 will then focus on the unique roles that the archaeology of modern trash has in the archaeology of the contemporary. Chapter 3 then connects the Atari excavations to the recent turn to materiality and agency as part of both an ongoing interest in the role of

American consumer culture in defining experiences and identity and in the more theoretical work reconsidering the role of things in archaeological thought. Chapter 4 subsequently turns to media archaeology and archaeogaming, presenting a context for the Atari games as digital and media artifacts that increasingly contribute to our contemporary experiences. In other words, by combining archaeology's interest in discard with an early example of digital consumer culture in the United States, the excavation of Atari games in a New Mexico dump offers a quintessential archaeological window onto contemporary America. Further, it situates the excavation of the present in one of the fastest-growing regions of the United States. This juxtaposition commingles postwar American consumer culture, the growth of suburbia, and the global reach of U.S. military technology. It also offers a way to consider how consumer culture impacts fragile desert ecosystems, exacerbates growing racial tensions, and depends upon the continued marginalization of Indigenous communities. While the following four chapters will not explore all these aspects in equal measure, they contribute to a reading of the Atari excavation that embodies the plurality of the American experience.

An Archaeological View of the Atari Excavations

Our role as archaeologists on the Atari excavation project resembled the role of archaeologists on salvage excavations. Because a massive mechanical excavator was necessary to open the landfill efficiently, we primarily observed the excavations from outside a safety cordon (figure 1.1). Indeed, our efforts to document the excavation had to conform to access rules negotiated by the documentary film crew, the contractors operating the excavator, the NMED, and the City of Alamogordo. The excavation of a recent, if closed, landfill presented risks as well, ranging from the possibility of releasing flammable and toxic gases to the instability of the scarps of loosely packed household and industrial trash. NMED rules allowed us to approach the precarious scarps of the trench only on designated occasions and for short periods of time. In other words, the depositional processes and the nature of the deposit itself posed distinct challenges to how we observed and recorded the excavation.

The needs of the film crew, who was funding the excavation and invited us to be involved, further complicated our access to the site and to the excavations. The documentary team wanted to manage closely the reveal of the Atari games as a media event and to limit the circulation of information to

Figure 1.1. Excavator at work at the Alamogordo landfill.

a growing crowd of interested onlookers who had arrived in Alamogordo. The excavations generated global media attention fed by decades of online interest in the games themselves, their burial, and a deepening nostalgia for the first generation of home-gaming consoles. The excavation of this landfill exposed a window into the network of relationships that supported the distribution and discard of consumer goods that many see as central to the contemporary American experience. The documentary film crew, the media circumstances surrounding the excavation, and the resulting film emphasized how archaeology plays a significant role in the production and consumption of the recent past. Our presence on this project emphasized how archaeology can bridge the gap between the recent past and the present. The media excitement amplified the sense that, for many, the recent past was very much contemporary. While the subsequent report reflected many of the limits associated with salvage excavation, such as a certain amount of imprecision, it nevertheless demonstrated that excavating the contemporary world can follow a pattern quite similar to traditional archaeological excavations at a historic, or even prehistoric, site.

The setting for the excavation in the old Alamogordo landfill was largely indistinguishable from the surrounding desert. The city of Alamogordo stands in the Tularosa Basin near the foot of the Sacramento Mountains that form the eastern side of a wide valley. The city stands at over 4,000 feet (~1,220 m) above mean sea level (AMSL) at the northern reach of the Chihuahua desert. The 300-acre (~120 ha) landfill site was situated some 800 feet (~244 m) behind the commercial district of Alamogordo and accessed from a dirt road. The dump itself consisted of a level area where the trenches had been cut, filled, and graded. The low hills surrounding it consist of the fill excavated for the creation and maintenance of the landfill. The company of Souder, Miller & Associates (SMA) of Las Cruces, New Mexico, prepared the site excavation plan (2014a) and presented a careful description of the site. At time of excavation, low shrubs and grasses characteristic of the region covered the landfill area. The soil was fine-grained silty loam at the surface and sandier loam beneath. Because the landfill itself experienced several depositional events, however, we expected to find lenses of silty topsoil interspersed with sandier deposits beneath a covering layer of topsoil. The light and sandy soil combined with the loosely packed landfill to produce an unstable environment for excavation. The light soil also presented a challenge when driven by the high winds that the excavators encountered on the second day of the dig.

The stratigraphy in the Alamogordo landfill was fairly well understood prior to excavation. Conversations with the one-time operator of the landfill, Joe Lewandowski, and the material that he provided the film crew outlined the basic structure of the landfill deposit. The top soil covering the landfill was less than 1 meter in depth. Beneath that level was a 1-meter layer of trash deposited in 1986. This sat atop another 0.5- to 1-meter layer of sterile soil deposited when the first phase of landfill activity at the site concluded in 1983. The 1983 landfill deposit was approximately 5.0 to 6.0 meters (~16–19 ft) in depth and arranged in a series of columns along the length of an east–west trench or cell. The material in this level slumped at the bottom of each column as the weight of trash dumped from the top of the trench compressed and spread the trash at the base of the column. Unlike contemporary landfills that receive systematic compacting, the trash deposited in 1983 was relatively uncompacted. Beneath these slumped columns of trash was another distinct dumping episode that involved the Atari games, related material, and apparently some contemporary trash. This material was not deposited as a column but spread in a thin layer across the bottom of the cell and, according to some reports, the games were covered with a layer of soil and concrete. This layer was 6.0 to 8.0 meters (~19–26 ft) from the surface.

Planning

The planning for most archaeological projects takes many months, if not years, and represents an important occasion for ensuring strong relations among field methods, procedures, and research goals. The archaeologists were not significantly involved in the planning phase of the Alamogordo Atari Expedition. Lewandowski, the former landfill operator, expertly determined the location of the excavation through means of photographs taken at the time of the Atari dump. These photographs ultimately guided the placement of the excavation.

Since we did not work directly with Lewandowski prior to the excavation, our understanding of the planning phase of fieldwork derived largely from public documents and conversations with the production company. These documents reveal that the planning for landfill excavation began in August 2011, with Lewandowski and other interested parties communicating with city officials. Over the remaining months of 2011, Lewandowski secured preliminary approval to conduct a study at the landfill from the NMED and the Alamogordo city council with a nine-month window to secure the funding necessary for final approval from the city (City of Alamogordo 2011). Apparently, final approval for the excavation did not occur at the conclusion of this preliminary phase of the project as in May 2013 an exasperated Lewandowski returned to the city council in an attempt to learn the cause of the delay. The details of the situation in 2013 are obscure in official documents, but they reflect both the complexity involved in coordinating the project and the extensive efforts by Lewandowski and others to make this excavation happen (City of Alamogordo 2013a, 2013b).

Whatever the cause of delay, by 2014, the project had gained approval from the city, and the organizers had turned their attention toward receiving the necessary permission for the excavation from the New Mexico Environmental Department. In early 2014, the environmental and engineering firm Souder, Miller & Associates (SMA) reached an agreement with NMED to sample the site for potentially flammable and toxic landfill gases over both the cell where the games were thought to be buried and from another landfill cell some 20 meters (65.6 ft) south. The samples established that excavating the landfill would not expose the crew to toxic gases (Souder, Miller & Associates 2014a).

Shortly after this document was finalized, the production company corresponded with the archaeological team. Initially, they were interested in a method or a standard that would allow them to say definitively that the games were not present. Evidence of absence has always been a difficult task for archaeological work, and the size and complexity of the landfill presented a challenging context for ruling out the presence of a particular deposit. The best we could offer was to suggest a combination of coring with long slit trenches across the area most likely to produce games. We speculated on the basis of photographs taken at the time of the dump that the games were spread over a 45-meter × 10-meter area across the bottom of a 20-meter × 120-meter cell, but we proposed that we would like to thoroughly investigate only a 10- × 10-meter exposure. Since any vertical scarps associated with the silty loam of the Tularosa Basin and the loosely compacted landfill would be exceedingly unstable, they would have to be either gently slopped or stepped back if the plan called for archaeologists to enter the trench. In light of this situation, we proposed a depth-to-scarp ratio of 1:1.5, which echoed the recommendation by SMA (2014a: 5). Depending on the depth of the deposit, this would make it a time-consuming process to open a large exposure with a limited amount of heavy machinery.

From the perspective of archaeological research, we had hoped the trench could be open for a week, allowing us to document carefully both the context of the games as well as the deposit associated with the games themselves. Unfortunately, NMED and municipal authorities set a two-day limit for the time the dump could be open, and, once in New Mexico, it became clear that the work could occur at the site only when environmental and site safety personnel were present. At the same time, the film crew continued to make arrangements with SMA, Lewandowski, and NMED. Additional testing of the landfill by SMA in March 2014 appeared to indicate that the production team and Lewandowski had shifted the proposed location of the Atari games approximately 90 meters to the southwest of the location identified in the plan submitted in February. Then, in mid-April, another series of cores were taken from a cell further south, and these cores appeared to have marked the best guess for the location of the buried games (SMA 2014b).

On April 26, 2014, our team witnessed several bucket auger cores taken at 15-meter intervals along an east–west line following the course of landfill cell. The augur hole furthest east produced no cartridges. Two auger holes produced Atari games at the approximate depth of 8–8.5 meters (26–28 ft). The stratigraphy from auger holes was top to bottom: reddish soil, reddish soil and some trash, black soil with ash, and nearly 50 percent of the volume was trash. The auger holes reflected the basic stratigraphy of the site presented by Lewandowski and would guide the excavation on the next day. We were asked not to reveal the discovery of games.

Day 1

Day 1 of the dig introduced our team to the particular process of excavation, the limits to our access, and the challenges associated with excavating a landfill. A strictly maintained safety cordon with a single access-control point defined the excavation areas. Because an excavator with a 10-meter (32.8 ft) reach, a loader, and trucks to remove excavated material would be moving continuously during the dig, access to the work area was largely limited to essential personnel. Periodic breaks in excavating occurred to allow the archaeologists and members of the film production team to examine the trench. Most of our documentation work came from a base of operations set up immediately outside the safety cordon approximately 15 meters (49.2 ft) from the trench. We recorded regular observation in a field notebook and took photos and video of both the trench and the material excavated. This vantage point also allowed us to receive periodic updates from city employees, the production crew, and the foreman of the excavation contractors.

The instability of the landfill and the quantity of loosely packed overburden fundamentally shaped the excavation. The excavator had to move regularly to ensure a secure footing for digging. The regular repositioning of the excavator and limited number of trucks to move the trash to another landfill made the rate of work slower than anticipated. The pace and depth of the Atari deposit eliminated any hope for excavating a large, open area with sufficiently stepped or graded scarps to allow access to the trench or even clear views of the scarp during excavation.

At the start of excavation, a bulldozer scraped perhaps 0.2 to 0.4 meters (~0.65–1.3 ft) of soil from the surface to create a level space for the excavator and to remove some of the overburden above the first level of garbage. The excavator initially positioned itself at the north side of the trench, and from this position was able to remove approximately 3 meters (9.8 ft) of material that included both the highest level of reddish-brown soil, a level of trash, and then another level of reddish-brown soil. The second lens of reddish-brown soil represented an earlier surface associated with a temporary closure of this part of the landfill that was then covered by another round of dumping activity in the mid-1990s. Below that level was the trash deposited in the original landfill cell, which consisted of black soil and garbage.

After approximately 3 meters (9.8 ft) of excavation, the scarp seemed unstable and the trench was backfilled. The excavator then moved west along the south side of the previously excavated area. There it excavated a 2-meter-deep ramp that situated the excavator on what appeared to be more stable soil on the southern edge of the original cut made for the landfill. By noon, the new excavation was perhaps 3 meters deep, with no sign of Atari games. As expected, the stratigraphy of this new trench resembled that of the first. There were alternating levels of soil and garbage for the first 2 meters, and then a consistent level of black earth and garbage for 3 to 4 meters. Various members of the film crew and the contractors expressed a concern that the digger would not arrive at the Atari level by 6 o'clock that evening, or that the digger's arm would not be long enough to create an exposure at 8 meters below the surface.

The most visible material removed from the trench included fabric, plastic, and dense cardboard. Plastic tarps and lawn bags formed tangles torn by the excavator and connected pockets of discarded yard waste, household trash, and dirt. At one point, the excavator tore through a nylon parachute, which billowed in the wind to evoke the history of aviation in the region. The excavator unraveled spools of magnetic tape from broken cassettes and videotapes. As the pile of excavated trash grew larger, some of it spilled down the sides closer to the excavation, and when archaeologists were able to enter the safety cordon they documented an assemblage distinct to the 1980s. This group of materials included a glass Pepsi bottle, newspapers from the 1980s, and bills and check registers with similar dates. Amid the early 1980s detritus, a Donnie and Marie Osmond poster, probably associated with their successful late-1970s TV series, provided an intriguing reminder of use patterns in contemporary popular culture. It is tempting to imagine that the poster found its way into the landfill after a young person found the Osmond's wholesome brand of 1970s entertainment no longer appealing. By 6 o'clock that evening, the digger had gone as far as it could before daylight began to fade. It stopped excavating at about six meters below the surface. The digging would continue the following morning and for much of the next afternoon as the project searched for the games.

Day 2

Based on information from the cores and the dates found on material coming from the trench, we were reasonably confident that the excavator had stopped within a meter of the Atari deposit. It was also possible, however, that the production team and the excavator had breached the Atari deposit in the evening of Day 1 and simply did not divulge that information to the archaeologists. There was no visual indication that the Atari deposit had been breached, and no reluctance to allow the archaeology team to document the scarp prior to the start of excavation. The ragged scarp showed four clear depositional events consistent with our observations during Day 1: alternating bands of reddish-brown soil with levels of trash. Our slight distrust of the archaeological situation at the end of the first day of excavation reflected the questionable state of information moving between the production company and our team.

By the time excavation preparation began, over 100 people had assembled, awaiting entry into the landfill to watch the historic unearthing of the discarded Atari games. In preparation for a more public day of excavation, the production company set up a table near the safety fence. We also set up another two tables on the far side of the pit where we could document finds as the excavator recovered them. A closer scrutiny of the trash being removed from the landfill revealed the remarkable level of preservation. As William Rathje noted decades ago, the anaerobic conditions of a landfill offered a remarkable degree of preservation for organic material (Rathje and Murphy 1992). Even grass clippings, for example, remained green and vibrant after over thirty years of burial. More important to this excavation, however, was the degree to which newspaper and other paper documents were preserved. These allowed us to establish very precise *terminus post quem* for the household trash because we knew that the trash was deposited systematically with trash collected later deposited atop trash collected earlier.

As the excavator approached the expected level of the Atari deposit, we requested that the excavator dump every third bucket of material at the side of the trench for us to examine. We sampled this pile by filling a five-gallon bucket of material and sorting and documenting the contents. We did this efficiently with notes in a notebook, photography, and recording additional notes via a portable digital audio recorder. We sampled five excavator buckets of garbage and black soil removed from the trench and deposited in our sorting area. These first four buckets consisted of domestic garbage datable to December and November 1983. Amid the chips of broken plastic were a number of remarkably intact artifacts, including a Coca-Cola can, a candy cane, and a paper check dated November 7, 1983. The presence of discarded boxes from toys, the candy cane, and Christmas decorations suggested that the date in which the first buckets were deposited was near or slightly after the end of December 1983. It was impossible to discern whether this was trash dumped immediately above the Atari deposit or from the columns of trash dumped during the more systematic use of the landfill cell.

On Day 2, high winds and blowing sand bedeviled our entire operation, making it difficult, at first, and then impossible to prevent trash, our notes, and other debris from blowing about the site. Sustained winds of over 20 mph, with gusts of 40 mph, were recorded at the nearby Alamogordo airport. The light soil and dust kicked up by the constant movement of heavy equipment ensured that wind-whipped and billowing dust engulfed the entire scene. As a result, the first find associated with the Atari deposit was discovered by Tony Johnson, a visitor from Denver, Colorado: a rubber top to an Atari joystick, which had likely blown from the excavator's bucket over to the portable toilets. The producers introduced Tony Johnson and the find to the crowd over a public address system.

The excavator breached the Atari deposit in Bucket 5, but this load clearly included some of the later material associated with regular household trash (figure 1.2). This bucket included a newspaper article dated September 28, 1983, which implausibly featured a cover story on the dumping of the Atari games. By all accounts, the Atari deposit represented a single depositional process, made of a number of truckloads of Atari material dumped on the bottom of the landfill cell and below a level of domestic trash. The first Atari game discovered in that bucket was a boxed copy of *E.T.* The rest of the bucket contained other Atari cartridges and boxes, as well as paper manuals and inserts, plus an assortment of household trash. It would appear, then, that this level captured the contact between the Atari deposit and the later garbage. The absence of substantial quantities of concrete in the buckets from the Atari deposit indicated that the concrete cap was irregularly applied to the top of the Atari deposit, and our trench may well have encountered the easternmost part of the Atari dump beyond the edge of the concrete cap.

With the discovery of Atari material, the nature of the excavation—and the documentation of material—changed. The film crew had instructed Reinhard (who wore an earpiece and microphone for the day for crew

Figure 1.2. Bucket 5 from the Alamogordo landfill.

communications) to alert them on a private channel if anything significant was found. When the excavator produced a box that appeared to contain an *E.T.* cartridge, the documentary's director, Zak Penn, a soundman, and a cameraman arrived. They then placed the box in a bucket, and Reinhard and Penn walked over to present the artifact to the crowd and media. Reinhard unboxed the game for Penn. The box, beaten up from the landfill and extraction, yielded an intact *E.T.* cartridge, instruction booklet, and flyer for the *Raiders of the Lost Ark* game released by Atari in 1982.

Once the first Atari games were found, the team continued to examine the contents of each bucket-load, ferrying material to a set of tables further removed from the crowd and the excavator to unload, photograph, and record in a preliminary way. The team arranged the games and hardware on the table for videogame expert Raiford Guins to identify. We recorded his identifications in a notebook and photographed finds that were either rare or well preserved. The finds were recorded by title, contents, and condition before being returned to their five-gallon buckets. Special finds would be placed in banker boxes. The archaeologists were interviewed on camera during one recording session to describe the method employed and what was being found and saved.

As the crowd dispersed and the initial thrill of discovery gave way to the reality of standing in an open landfill during a sandstorm, the excavator proceeded more quickly to extract as much of the Atari deposit as possible. The bucket-loads of games and other debris were dumped outside of the trench, and we worked quickly to document the material as it was being extracted and before city employees collected it for removal, sorting, and storage. The quantity of blowing dust, the time constraints of the production and excavation schedule, and the irregular flow of information made the work on Day 2 chaotic and exhausting.

The Assemblage

There were three challenges associated with documenting the assemblage yielded by the excavation of the Alamogordo landfill. First and foremost, the excavation produced a massive quantity of material. The deliberate sampling techniques employed by Rathje's Garbage Project reflected his awareness that the contemporary world produces a tremendous quantity of discard every day. The second complication was the pace of excavation and the need to transport material removed from the landfill to a secure disposal site. The NMED simply would not allow piles of material from the landfill to remain exposed to the air and wind for any significant length of time. Third, because of the safety cordon around the excavation area, we had no consistent access to the discarded waste to allow for even superficial sampling. While these limits were frustrating, they represent distinct challenges associated with the documentation of sites of contemporary discard.

Since systematic sampling of the landfill was not practical (and perhaps not desirable), our observations on the character of the larger landfill assemblage will remain relatively general. The area of the landfill functioned as a dump site for over sixty years, with the earliest dumps dating to the 1920s and the landfill functioning as the official discard area for Alamogordo solid waste from the 1960s to 1989. The dumping of Atari games was not the only sensational event involving the Alamogordo site. In 1969, the contaminated hogs and grain associated with the Huckleby mercury poisoning were dumped into the landfill. During negotiations between the production company and the City of Alamogordo, several conversations took place relating to the risk of exposing the community to mercury contamination. City council minutes revealed that the site had also seen the dumping of 5,000 gallons of the pesticide malathion. These concerns had prompted a series of tests in 2004 by the New Mexico Environmental Department that revealed that soil and air at the site produced toxic chemicals at levels above federal limits (see SMA 2014a for reports on these tests). While all parties received assurances that the most toxic areas of the landfill would not be disturbed by the planned excavations, the general toxicity of the soil and air around the site represented an invisible component of the landfill assemblage. Tests before the excavation revealed that the landfill produced small yet detectable quantities of methane, carbon dioxide, and other volatile organic compounds in greater levels than exist naturally. The toxicity of the landfill also brought to the fore the logistical challenges of excavating a modern period site and the complexities of a modern archaeological assemblage that go well beyond discrete objects to include chemicals in the air and the soil. We became aware of site formation processes that saw the material content of the landfill transformed into less visible gases and contamination.

Despite the more sensational and concerning deposits in the landfill, most of the trash we witnessed during the excavation reflected a use history of the Alamogordo landfill that included significant quantities of local trash from the community. The billowing form of the parachute evoked the community's close connection to the military aviation. The bags of grass clippings reflect the spread of irrigation and the suburban lawns in the desert Southwest. The appearance of waste associated with national brands, from Coca-Cola to Stroh's beer to the Osmonds, reflects the ongoing integration of this community within national economic and cultural networks. The presence of Christmas decorations, cards, and empty boxes for mass-produced toys in the deposits immediately above the Atari levels reveals the rapid cleanup after the holiday season, the general prosperity of some segments of the community, and the commercial character of Christmas in the 1980s. The excavation of the landfill presented an assemblage reflecting the distinct character of both the experiences of life in the Alamogordo community and its discard practices, as well as the relationship between Alamogordo and broader national and global trends.

The initial assemblage of Atari games reinforces how the history of the landfill connected the local world of Alamogordo to the history of a national brand and its manufacturing and distribution networks. The games removed from the landfill in Bucket 5 presented an overview of the games found throughout the Atari deposit. The Atari debris can be loosely grouped into six categories: (1) paper artifacts including game boxes, instruction manuals, Atari Force comics, and catalogues, as well as assorted cardboard likely from shipping boxes that contained several boxes of games; (2) a significant number of games in boxes, ranging widely from plastic "clamshell" or blister packs that contained silver *Phoenix* and *Centipede* cartridges to cardboard packaging containing the silver *E.T.* game, as well as *Star Raiders, Asteroids,* and *Defender* games; (3) packages including price tags from Walmart and Target and, less often, return receipts and labels—some dated 1981 or 1982; (4) loose games, which tended to be the more unusual titles in the overall assemblage, such as *Indy 500, Baseball,* and *Golf,* which appeared only as loose cartridges dated 1980 or earlier; (5) *Star Raiders* video touch pads, which were sold with the games, and (6) several objects found throughout the assemblage that preserved small quantities of concrete adhering to the artifacts.

The structure of the assemblage collected in Bucket 5 provides us with the basis for some basic observations. First, the games were remarkably well preserved and intact, which speaks to their being exposed for only a short time before being buried under trash (figure 1.3). This also suggests the games were not compacted in a consistent way. Second, there is little evidence of concrete on the games, suggesting the concrete cap was either not extensive or not particularly robust. The presence of price tags and occasional return receipts from major retail chains indicates these games were either returned unsold or had been returned by unsatisfied buyers. Most of the games with price tags were released in 1981 or 1982, including *E.T.* (1982), *Centipede* (1982), *Phoenix* (1982), and *Haunted House* (1981). The presence of multipacks of games in boxes not designed for retail display, including a group of five *Asteroids* games without price tags, indicate that some of these games were either returned by the retailer before they were put on sale or never sent out to retailers. A handful of pre-1980s games, such as *Indy 500* (1978), *Baseball* (1978), and *Golf* (1980) were found as loose cartridges and did not appear in blister packs or boxes, suggesting these were residual games in the deposit that probably had a origin different from the majority of the material. The most common games, *Missile Command* (1982), *Asteroids* (1981), *SwordQuest-Earthworld* (1982), *Ms. Pac-Man* (1982), and *Defender* (1981), developed for the Atari 2600 and 5200 systems (1982), also appeared in boxes or blister packs. The presence of empty *Defender* and *Ms. Pac-Man* boxes and loose "*SwordQuest*" and *Missile Command* instruction manuals suggests that some loose games should probably be associated with these loose boxes and documentation. While this assemblage represents just a single sample from the massive quantity of games produced by the excavation, it is representative of

Figure 1.3. Recovered *E.T.* games from the Alamogordo landfill.

patterns present in the larger corpus of Atari material excavated over the course of the day.

As we hastily processed the first bucket of Atari material, additional material was removed and dumped along the side of the trench. We proceeded to document this material using digital photographs and taking quick notes as we looked through the pile of discarded Atari material. Of particular note in this assemblage was a quantity of wood both from pallets and from what appear to have been crates. Wood was not present in the first sample of material from the Atari deposit, and this probably reflects the first sample coming from the upper levels of the Atari deposit and the wood pallets being part of the lowest levels of the deposit. We also noted that the larger the sample from the Atari deposit, the greater the diversity of games in the sample. As already mentioned, however, the various titles present in the larger samples tended to be packaged in the same way. Older games were loose, and more recent games showed signs of being packaged for distribution or return. The larger sample also produced more game controllers, but there were few obvious indications of game consoles being part of this assemblage.

In short, the assemblage produced by the Alamogordo Atari excavation was not straightforward. Despite the challenges in documenting the Alamogordo landfill, doing so nonetheless presented a complicated image of both household trash and industrial and commercial discard. The presence of various toxic compounds produced by soil and air testing of the landfill revealed that the composition of the landfill did not remain static and extended to include small quantities of invisible and toxic gases. The removal of a substantial sample from the Atari deposit itself likewise reflected variation in the historical formation of the assemblage and its formation on site. The range of conditions of the games, their age, and the presence of price tags or packaging indicate that even the Atari deposit did not represent a single scenario, such as returned *E.T.* games or efforts to disguise surplus inventory. Instead, it appears that the deposit represented objects discarded at Atari's El Paso distribution center over the course of five years as well as in the run-up to the holiday retail season.

Conclusions

Few experiences are more American than standing in a New Mexico desert on an excavation funded by Microsoft watching corporate detritus being excavated from amid household trash associated with the holiday season. The landfill represented the literal embodiment of the growing commercialism of the 1970s and 1980s (chapter 3). This was not seen, however, as a cautionary tale of capitalism's excesses. In fact, the global media attention and the crowds who assembled to watch the final day of the dig made clear that the artifacts being uncovered in Alamogordo evoked nostalgia among a middle-aged, middle-class, white, male American audience who had grown up with Atari games, Steven Spielberg movies, and the pornographic capitalism of holiday catalogues. In fact, the documentary based on this excavation, *Atari: Game Over,* made this connection explicit by linking the history of Atari with innocent excitement of childhood. In the documentary, Atari's childhood comes to a crashing halt only when the videogame industry falters in the 1980s and Atari is acquired by Time Warner. That this trajectory of Atari as a company paralleled the upbringing of the filmmaker Zak Penn (b. 1968), most members of the archaeological team, and the vast majority of the enthusiastic crowd reinforced the sense that the American experience excavated in the New Mexico desert was contemporary with lives of those involved.

This assemblage of commonplace objects also gained significance from their geographic location. The urban legend that grew up around these games drew on narratives distinct to the American Southwest as a place abounding in mysteries, shaped by the United States' place in postwar political and military order, and suffused with the strength of the American economy. The games themselves and the decision to discard them in the Alamogordo landfill revealed traces of the global supply chain. The games were developed in California, manufactured in Asia, shipped to a distribution center in El Paso, transported to points of sale across the United States, and then returned to Texas before being dumped into a small-town New Mexico landfill. The well-traveled character of the games reflects the complex flow of capital and consumer goods. In New Mexico, the games mingle with domestic trash, other commercial and industrial waste, and contemporary individual and collective discard practices to form an assemblage that constitutes a toxic legacy of consumer culture.

The exceptional level of preservation of the material in the landfill made identifying and dating deposits far easier and more precise than most excavation allows. The preservation of paper documents, seasonal decoration, and the Atari deposit itself revealed precisely the point where the depositional character of the landfill changed from the daily dumping of local trash to the single episode of dumping associated with the Atari dump.

This point of contact defined the relation between these two assemblages in an obvious way and stood in contrast to the more complex chemical and historical relationships present in the old Alamogordo landfill. The tragic memory of the mercury pigs, the dumping of pesticides associated with agriculture, and the toxic chemicals released as part of decomposition contributed to an assemblage at the landfill that extended both into the past of local memory and into the future as discarded objects underwent transformation. Our experience at the side of the trench was as much informed by the objects that we handled that windswept weekend as the toxic and noxious fumes we breathed, the history of the region as the site of tragic chemical poisoning and atomic testing, and corporate America's capacity to transform crass consumerism into collective nostalgia for more innocent times.

2

Garbology and the Archaeology of Trash

Standing at the edge of a New Mexico town watching an excavator tear into a landfill may not sound to some like a particularly American experience, much less a transformational one. But for those of us interested in the archaeology of the contemporary world, witnessing the massive excavator work felt like a reenactment of the origins of the field. Hidden beneath an unassuming stretch of desert was a well-preserved assemblage of consumer waste that offered a window into 1980s culture, discard practices, and the construction of a modern landfill. The excavation exposed for a brief moment materials and practices that the community had so carefully hidden beneath the sandy loam of the New Mexico landscape. At the same time, working near an open landfill exposed us to the sweet stench of decomposing trash—an odor that permeated our clothes and clung even to the plastic cases of Atari games that stewed in the leachate produced by the landfill's upper layers. The buried landfill, the sickly sweet smell, and the rural location provided an experiential reminder of the hidden and marginal place of garbage and post-depositional processes that connect our experiences as American consumers to their persistent mark in the landscape.

Introduction

Archaeologists have always been interested in trash. The opportunity to observe and document the excavation of a landfill drew us (the team described in chapter 1) to New Mexico just as much as the search for the Atari games. This chapter locates an archaeological interest in contemporary trash in both trends in the discipline of archaeology and late twentieth-century concerns about a growing "garbage crisis." We will focus particularly on William Rathje's "Garbage Project" and trace the implications of his seminal work for the study of archaeology of the contemporary world and the study of contemporary garbage across a range of projects that looked to

Rathje's work for inspiration and methods. The chapter's final section looks at recent efforts to study garbage that go beyond Rathje's work, and which show how the study of garbage continues to provide a unique window into the contemporary American experience.

To claim that the discipline of archaeology depends on trash to understand the past is not an exaggeration. Indeed, the study of contemporary trash emerged alongside a growing interest in formation processes in archaeology in the 1970s that provided new ways to understand practices of consumption and discard in archaeology. Rathje's pioneering Garbage Project at the University of Arizona established him as both the father of "garbology" and one of the early advocates of the archaeology of the contemporary world (Rathje and Murphy 1992). His work paralleled that of Michael Schiffer, whose interest in ethnoarchaeology informed Rathje's interest in formation processes. Schiffer defined formation processes as the natural and cultural activities that produced the sites documented by archaeologists, and these processes reveal the material and technology that shaped human behavior in the past. Both Schiffer and Rathje taught at the University of Arizona in the 1970s and 1980s. They wrote a textbook together (Rathje and Schiffer 1982), and as we have seen, worked early on to establish an "archaeology of us." In an interview published in 2013, Rathje noted that garbology drew upon ethnoarchaeology, which used ethnographic techniques among contemporary populations to help understand past practices. Garbology likewise contributed to the emerging field of historical archaeology, which often looked to texts and documents to inform archaeological contexts (Rathje, Shanks, and Witmore 2013: 354–355). Thus, the archaeology of contemporary and past garbage presents an opportunity not only to understand discard behaviors in general but also to recognize that trash makes visible variable access to goods, the rise of industrial manufacturing, the changing character of consumer culture, and differing attitudes toward recycling and reuse. These processes and discard practices combine to produce distinctive assemblages.

While Rathje's work most famously focused on the systematic sampling and documentation of bags of garbage collected from contemporary curbsides, many of Rathje's most compelling observations concern the tension between responses on surveys and the analysis of trash from particular neighborhoods. For example, white Anglo and Hispanic households answered survey questions on the consumption of alcohol in very different ways. White Anglos tended to underrepresent the quantity of alcohol consumed when compared to discarded alcohol containers in their trash.

Hispanic households, in contrast, either reported no alcohol consumption or recorded their consumption quite accurately (Rathje, Shanks, and Witmore 2013: 366). Such research revealed the divergence between ethnographic and survey accounts of consumer practices and archaeological evidence for these practices. In this example, not only did the discarded objects associated with alcohol consumption offer a perspective on the role of alcohol in everyday life, but the incongruity of the information collected on the survey and physical remains suggests differing attitudes toward alcohol consumption.

The study of garbage also sheds light on often obscure processes that create dumps. Such studies can illuminate how objects transition from useful to useless. Garbology can also reveal the technological and natural processes that create modern dumps. Many of the more complex formation processes that produce assemblages at local landfills are not just materially invisible—they are socially invisible too. The growing attention to contemporary discard practices reveals the experiences of individuals and communities who work both within and around the modern system of solid waste removal in the United States. There has also been the recognition that discard and recycling practices have become a global phenomenon, and that archaeological inquiry holds the potential to reveal how the American experience of consumption and discard shapes communities, economies, and landscapes both in the United States and abroad. In this context, archaeology, with its interest in the relationship between the material and the social, stands alongside historians who have studied disposal practices in the past, sociologists and anthropologists who have explored cultures that exist around our contemporary waste management practices, and artists who repurpose trash in the service of social commentary.

It is fitting, of course, that both Rathje's garbology and the Atari excavation took place in the southwestern United States. As noted earlier, this region was the birthplace of America's nuclear arsenal, the shadowy crucible of the Cold War, and the setting for extraterrestrial fantasies that shaped the American experience. It is also a region that witnessed large-scale postwar demographic growth and the development of suburban sprawl. This demographic expansion and the ongoing government presence often placed both the state and white American society at odds with Indigenous residents of the region, taxed water and energy resources, and damaged the delicate local ecosystems. In the twenty-first century, the growing anxiety over undocumented migrants from Mexico and Central American has made the region a political, and at times literal, battleground crossed with long-standing racial and economic tensions. Thus the setting of both Rathje's Garbage Project and the Atari Excavation coincided with a significant arena for the American imagination, demographic and economic growth, military and foreign policy, and racial anxieties.

The History of Trash and Archaeology

While the setting of the Garbage Project speaks directly to its twentieth- and twenty-first-century American context, the study of contemporary or nearly contemporary trash is as old as the discipline itself. Dietmar Schmidt, for example, argued that preeminent German anthropologist Rudolf Virchow's accidental discovery of rubbish pits in Berlin represented a crucial moment in the understanding of archaeology as both a practice and metaphor for modern social science (Schmidt 2001). In the late 1860s, Virchow thought he had discovered the remains of an Iron Age pile dwelling in the middle of the Berlin, but he soon realized the deposit of bones, shells, and kitchen pots was discarded rubbish from the previous century. Despite his disappointment, he documented the deposits carefully and presented a number of papers arguing that this deposit of eighteenth-century kitchen waste revealed a good bit about the culinary habits of the German aristocracy and their predilection for oysters and mussels. When later in the century Virchow visited Heinrich Schliemann's dig at Troy, he commented on the discarded refuse in far more ancient contexts. More relevant to our interests here, Virchow's work led to periodic investigations of modern sewers and other nearly contemporary refuse deposits elsewhere in Europe. Schmidt suggests that Virchow's and others' interest in mundane trash over more aesthetically pleasing objects inspired Freud's use of the archaeological metaphor to characterize his exploration of the human consciousness. Both trash and Freud's construction of the unconscious represent objects that are hidden but also poised to reveal their formative and foundational influence on contemporary life.

An early twentieth-century examination of a garbage dump in the United States reveals how the study of contemporary trash informed archaeology's understanding of site formation as well as social differences and their impact on our modern psyche. In 1921, Alfred Kidder, best known for his systematic excavations at Pecos, New Mexico, found himself in Andover, Massachusetts, caring for his aging mother. Over the summer, he made regular visits to the local dump. He initially attracted the attention of the local police, who thought he was either a vagrant or an escaped resident from a nearby psychiatric hospital. While we have little direct records of Kidder's observations in the Andover dump, the various bits of information that Raymond Thompson gleaned for archival sources demonstrated Kidder's fascination with the depositional processes that created the landfill (Thompson 2002; Rathje and Murphy 1992: 93–94). Over the course of regular observations, Kidder recognized that the process of dumping material on the landfill mound influenced the distribution of artifacts, with such objects as baby buggies and garbage can lids rolling to the bottom of the slope. He also collected an assemblage of lamps during his observations at the dump and was able to develop a typology that anticipated the well-known Mayers-Oaks (1955) illustration of lamp seriation (Thompson 2002: 130).

As Rathje would discover fifty years later, despite the mundane character of the waste, Kidder's time in the landfill revealed aspects of the American experience that he would not have otherwise encountered in his daily life. For example, Kidder was initially unable to recognize a number of flattened metal bands, which his mother could identify as metal corset bones. Thompson observed that Kidder's study of the garbage dump offered insights into women's underwear, which he would not have had access to otherwise. The shift from whalebone to metal corset bones paralleled the decline in whale oil lamps and economic role of the whaling industry in New England. In more Freudian fashion, Kidder's time caring for his mother opened a marginal and often hidden world in the Andover dump. In fact, Kidder himself endured marginalization when the police misidentified him as a vagrant or someone escaped from an institution. This mistake linked the dump to individuals and situations ranging from the mentally ill to experts in the character of women's underwear that occupied the margins of his contemporary world.

Kidder's exploration of the contemporary Andover dump occurred amid important changes in attitudes toward household waste. As Gavin Lucas and others have shown in the late nineteenth and early twentieth centuries, awareness of the potentially harmful character of kitchen waste led to a rise in both disposable goods and manuals that advocated for their use in the name of sanitation and cleanliness (Lucas 2002; Melosi 1981). This attitude toward waste also contributed to the introduction of the municipal landfills in the first decades of the twentieth century across the United States so that trash could be sequestered from living spaces (Rathje and Murphy 1992: 85–86). The term "sanitary landfill" first appeared in the 1930s, and during World War II, landfills became the primary way in which the U.S. military disposed and sequestered waste on military bases (Rathje and Murphy 1992: 87).

The use of landfills for disposal in the interwar years was contemporary with changes in consumption practices. Michael Roller has tied the changes in the assemblages of household dumps to the U.S. government's efforts to encourage consumerism as part of a larger program of social, political, and economic engineering starting in the early twentieth century (Roller 2018, 2019). He argued that both industry and the U.S. government sought to encourage both the consumption and the discard of goods produced at an industrial scale. Support for new standards of sanitary practice rewarded the industrial elites, who developed a capacity for production that had outstripped the capacity for consumption. Encouraging consumption also promoted the development of a shared consumer culture between new immigrants, upon whom much of American industrial growth relied, and long-standing American communities. This involved stressing the need for sanitation among immigrant communities, which in turn encouraged reliance on disposable goods, which shaped both consumption and discard (Camp 2013). Thus, consumption and discard represented both economic and cultural strategies that recognized these behaviors not simply as formation processes that revealed an American experience but as the American experience itself. While Kidder's observations of the Andover dump produced a series of useful, if anecdotal, connections concerning deposition and particular habits of New England society in the recent past, the postwar interest in garbage that formed the framework for garbology regarded the disposal of waste as fundamental to the American experience.

This broader context made the study of contemporary garbage attractive for scholars interested in social critique, policy analysis, and cultural theory. Mid-century interest in garbage anticipated Rathje's Garbage Project. Vance Packard's influential work in the 1950s emphasized the close ties among consumption, the economics of production, and waste. Packard introduced his 1960 book, *Waste Makers,* with a series of fanciful anecdotes about "Cornucopia City," which manifests its abundance through fantastically cavalier attitudes toward consumption and destruction. Packard's city featured papier-mâché houses that residents simply destroyed when they required cleaning or maintenance, factories whose product went directly to landfills when demand slackened, and the ceremonial dumping of surplus goods at sea. Heather Rogers (2006) called the 1950s a "Golden Age of Waste" that emerged at the intersection of consumer culture and changing domestic attitudes toward sanitation. Packard, recognizing the accelerating pace of postwar consumption and discard, urged readers to return to earlier modes of thrift.

During the second half of the twentieth century, changing attitudes, practices, and anxieties surrounding solid waste disposal informed new attitudes toward urbanism and the rise of post-industrial cities. White flight, suburbanization, and the transformation of American cities provided the context for the late twentieth-century "garbage crisis." Not only did mid-century suburban sprawl require trash collection over a greater geographic area, but changes in the tax base and federal funding also complicated the financial situation of rapidly de-industrializing cities that made trash collection an often pressing matter of policy (Melosi 1981). Despite the growing urgency associated with the management of garbage across a wide range of American contexts, Rathje explicitly rejected the notion of a "garbage crisis" by making the first of his "Ten Commandments" of trash: "Don't think of our garbage problems in terms of crisis" (Rathje and Murphy 1992: 238).

Despite Rathje's admonitions, the concern about trash nevertheless contributed to the development of an "archaeological consciousness" in American culture. By the 1980s, this consciousness had materialized as an expression of a larger anxiety concerning the ephemerality and vacuity of consumer culture (Jelfs 2017, 2018). In 1986, the *Khian Sea* cargo ship filled with 14,000 tons of incinerated ash from Philadelphia found itself barred from entry to a range of Caribbean, African, and European ports, before dumping its cargo illegally in the Pacific and Indian Oceans. A year later, the *Mobro 4000* garbage barge wandered up and down the East Coast and the Caribbean filled with New York City trash, further pushing garbage to the forefront of headlines and nightly news. The growing public concerns for the quantity and character of trash in the postwar decades provided an inescapable cultural context for Rathje's work.

These events also sustained academic conversations centered on the movement of objects from household use to rubbish. Michael Thompson's *Rubbish Theory* (1979), for example, theorized a cycle that traced how discarded objects disappeared and then returned to a position of value in society. Thompson argued that objects circulate through various economic, social, and cultural contexts that assign or rob the object of value, but, in order for changes in value to happen, objects must at some point drop out of these contexts through losing all value and becoming rubbish. Thus, to become valuable, antiques and kitsch had to shed their functional value as household objects before returning to circulation as objects of nostalgia or historical significance.

Archaeology, of course, has leveraged this capacity of objects to return from discard and to regain value both as objects of art and as objects that inform how we understand the past and present. The term "garbology," which has come to describe archaeological interest in contemporary trash, first appeared in 1980 with the publication of A. J. Weberman's *My Life in Garbology* (1980). This book described Weberman's adventures in the trashcans of public figures, which often revealed hidden evidence for their private lives. The book popularized the term "garbology," which Rathje initially rejected in his own work because of the invasive and sensational character of Weberman's approach, but over time he came to embrace the concept[,] eventually making it his own (Rathje 2001: 63). As Joshua Reno has noted, Weberman's use of garbage presented to a popular audience the idea that discard reveals information about an individual that goes beyond what they present outwardly to society (Reno 2014). It paralleled the use of garbology as part of surveillance schemes enacted by the FBI in the 1950s. Like Thompson, Weberman's work emphasized that garbage gained importance because it lost all value when cast to the curb. Like Kidder's recognition of the hidden world preserved in the New England landfill, Weberman returned the hidden garbage to the public eye and created new value in these objects as a source of intimate information for the lives of celebrities whose garbage he documented. Without belaboring a simplistic Freudian interpretation, the tension between garbage being hidden in plain sight and its value revealing the reality of an individual's or community's experience follows a logic common to psychoanalysis and archaeology. The surface obscures a deeper reality; revealing the hidden creates new knowledge. Garbage is the first public expression of private consumption practices, and both past and contemporary research encourages us to dig beneath the surface to discover the roots of the American experience.

Garbology

A wide-ranging interest in garbage both within archaeology and in American culture in the 1970s and 1980s provided an important context for Bill Rathje's Garbage Project. Proximately, the growing concern about garbage in the context of the changing face of American urbanism intersected with a particularly dynamic time in the development of archaeological theory.

In the early 1970s, processual archaeology's emphasis on the relationship between the people and their environment had become increasingly concerned with how artifact assemblages reflected past human activities. This concern led to the development of "middle range theory," which drew archaeologists' attention to how the study of past and present human behavior could inform their interpretation of material culture. Michael Schiffer and Jefferson Reid proposed the concept of behavioral archaeology at the University of Arizona at the same time that the Garbage Project was taking shape (Gifford-Gonzalez 2011; Schiffer 2015; Rathje 1984; Reid and Jefferson et al. 1975). The idea that the study of contemporary behaviors could inform the study of material culture and vice versa provided a foundation for modern material culture studies that, in turn, offered a larger intellectual framework for Rathje's Garbage Project (Rathje et al. 2013: 376). Rathje was interested in studying garbage not only to demonstrate that people's behaviors were different from what ethnography, surveys, and public statements indicated, but also with the hope that revealing the disconnect between words and behaviors would motivate people to reflect on their actions and make changes (Lane 2011). In this way, Rathje was far from the abstract theorist parodied by Kent Flannery in his famous "Golden Marshalltown" article (1982). In fact, despite Rathje's urging us not to see public conversations about garbage in the 1970s and 1980s as a "crisis," his work was very much a practical response to such a situation. This contemporary, and distinctly American, context formed the basis of its contribution to various theoretical debates transforming archaeological thought at the time.

The study of modern solid waste disposal and eventually landfills offered an opportunity for Rathje to examine the behavior of contemporary communities. Archaeologists had long recognized the value of middens, rubbish pits, and other deposits of discarded objects. These deposits speak to both the material assemblages associated with everyday life as well as discard practices and attitudes toward what is valuable and what is not. For Rathje, the distinctive stability of waste removal systems, particularly in the United States, where trash is consistently and systematically collected and transported to landfills, created a relatively transparent lens through which to view consumption patterns at the level of both household and community (Rathje et al. 2013: 353–354). While subsequent scholarship has worked to complicate the relationship between discard and deposit in landfills and to interrogate more rigorously the multitude of processes that characterize deposition, Rathje's work defined garbage as a key resource for archaeological inquiry at a crucial moment in American history.

The immense body of scholarship produced by the Garbage Project makes it virtually impossible to summarize its reach and findings. A special issue of the *American Behavioral Scientist* published in 1984 presents a number of significant summaries of the project; a popular work coauthored with Cullen Murphy in 1992 supplies a broad, easy-to-read overview; and a consistent stream of articles extending into the twenty-first century trace the impact of this project. The first phase of the Garbage Project established its core methods and, as a result, is best known. Rathje's methods involved sampling, sorting, and recording garbage delivered by Tucson waste management to a special area of the municipal disposal site, at which time trash officially becomes property of the city (Hughes 1984). In most cases, his team sampled the garbage by census tract rather than by individual household, but in some cases, under well-defined rules designed to guarantee participant anonymity, they analyzed individual household trash in conjunction with paper surveys on discard habits. A set of codes enforced the systematic recording of household trash. Rathje admitted that, from the start, the project was open-ended, with no research question in mind beyond determining whether the study of household trash could inform archaeological interpretation (Rathje 1984: 12). Over time, however, the project adapted its coding to accommodate research goals often generated through collaboration with industry or federal research initiatives focused on particular patterns. For example, a collaboration with the USDA in the early 1980s focused on food loss. This initially led the project to document fat trimmed from beef to test assumptions regarding the number of calories from fat among beef consumers (Rathje 1984: 25–27; Rathje and Ho 1987). Over the course of its thirty-plus years of work, the Garbage Project was able also to map food waste to show that simpler diets with fewer ingredients produced less waste. Rathje called this the "first principle of waste," observing that households that consumed foods (and other products) regularly tended to waste less. In some cases, Mexican American households, whose traditional cooking practices often include fewer ingredients, produced less waste (Rathje 1995). Households that purchased more prepackaged meals tended to discard more fresh food. Similar studies that test and complicate these conclusions continue to occur globally (e.g., Mexico City: Rathje et al. 1985; Australia: Lehmann 2015). Rathje noted that similar patterns of discard appeared in an EPA-sponsored study of toxic household products in trash from New Orleans and Marin County, California. In this context, toxic products that households used regularly appeared in smaller quantities in the trash, and products used only periodically, such as paints and solvents, appeared unused in larger quantities (Rathje 2001: 74).

Throughout its history, the Garbage Project also selectively utilized surveys on which respondents recorded their discard habits. Unsurprisingly, these did not precisely correspond to trash collected from the same households. Alcohol consumption, for example, was under-reported, as was the waste of beef during the mid-1970s beef crisis (Rathje 1985). Rathje explains the latter as resulting partly from households stockpiling beef beyond their ability to consume it. In this regard, the Garbage Project contributed to Weberman's more colloquial "garbology" by confirming the tension between what individuals admitted in a survey and their behavior. The consistent demonstration of this tendency further justified the value of the Garbage Project for demonstrating the divergence between reports and practices that define the constantly changing expectations of our consumer age.

Among the more intriguing aspects of the Garbage Project is that, despite its origin as a methodological and theoretical exercise, it consistently displayed its usefulness for the public sector represented by the USDA, the NIH, the EPA, and other state and local organizations (Rathje et al. 2013: 356; Schiffer 2015). These collaborations demonstrated how archaeology of the contemporary world could inform policy decisions at the federal and local levels. The Garbage Project also prepared reports and conducted research for trade organizations like the American Paper Institute (Rathje et al. 1985) and for corporations such as Frito Lay, Oscar Mayer, NutraSweet, and Heinz (Schiffer 2015). Collaborations between academic archaeology and the private sector are hardly uncommon, particularly in the rapidly growing American Southwest, where contractors and developers often work closely with archaeologists to manage cultural resources in the face of large-scale construction projects. If the connection between the study of waste and consumer culture was not already clear in the patterns identified in the academic research coming from the Garbage Project, the interest of the major corporations responsible for a wide range of consumer goods makes this link explicit.

The work of the Garbage Project was not limited to using household waste to understand the character of consumer habits. Beginning in the mid-1980s, Rathje and colleagues excavated a series of landfills around the United States (Rathje et al. 1992). This component of the Garbage Project sought both to check the data gathered from curbside household trash against the material in landfills and to attempt to understand the formation processes associated with landfills. The latter interest continued and updated the more casual observations of Alfred Kidder, for example, who noted how trash was spread and tumbled down the mound of the Andover landfill nearly a century earlier (Rathje and Murphy 1992: 93–94). Rathje and colleagues were particularly interested in the volume of various materials in landfills, and they soon discovered that construction and demolition debris they had overlooked in their analysis of intercepted household trash accounted for a much greater volume of trash in landfills than they had realized. Another major component of landfills was paper, with the vivid description of paper phone books appearing in landfill strata like "currants in a cake" (Rathje and Murphy 1992: 104). Rathje was also able to push back against media claims in the 1980s that diapers and plastics and, in particular, polystyrene under its various trade names, including Dow's Styrofoam, took up a large and growing percentage of space within landfills. While polls showed that many people believed plastics and diapers made up over 40 percent of landfill volumes, the Garbage Project estimates revealed that the numbers were in fact under 5 percent (Rathje and Murphy 1992: 104–106).

The landfill excavations also produced more technical studies that focused on formation processes in the landfill. They largely challenged the assumption that waste in the landfill decomposed at an even or predictable rate. The Garbage Project's excavations revealed well-preserved foods, grass clippings, and papers with dates. In fact, as we discovered at the Atari excavation in Alamogordo, newspapers and canceled checks remained easily legible and provided precise chronological markers decades after they entered the anaerobic context of the dump. The project also tracked the presence of potentially hazardous chemicals in landfills, including lead, mercury, and arsenic, which are common in everyday consumer goods and used in a range of small-scale businesses whose waste ends up in municipal dumps. The Garbage Project produced data that demonstrated, in general, a higher than anticipated level of hazardous wastes in landfills. This finding had implications for the quantity and quality of leachate that landfills produced over time and their environmental impact. The potential of landfills to produce methane was also an issue of interest to the Garbage Project, with lab tests showing that most landfills produced less methane than expected. From an archaeological perspective, the study of North American landfills demonstrated the growing significance of chemical analysis in un-

derstanding the formation of cultural levels in late twentieth-century societies. As the chemical tests prior to the Atari excavations in Alamogordo
showed, site formation involving twentieth-century consumer waste is not
limited to the visible evidence of dumping and discard, but is also affected
by invisible chemical transformations taking place at the site. In many cases, this toxic output of discard is of particular relevance to policymakers.
That said, the range of conclusions produced by the Garbage Project at a
time of heightened concern for how our consumer culture impacted the
environment clarified the potential for archaeological methods to confirm,
complicate, and critique popular attitudes toward trash disposal. In this
way, the Garbage Project did more than analyze and interpret a contemporary American experience—it also embodied a growing ecological and
environmental awareness and critique of consumer culture.

A particularly compelling example of the long interpretative tail of the
project is an article coauthored by Rathje, David Platt, and Michael Shanks
on the removal of rubble and debris from the World Trade Center site after the 9/11 terrorist attack (Shanks et al. 2004). The work shows how the
removal of the debris from the World Trade Center site to the Fresh Kills
landfill and the recovery and display of personal objects presented a form of
utopian thinking. The objects selected from the untold tons of debris from
the site reflect a deliberate attempt to create an idealized and sanitized past.
The process of removing the debris and the construction of new buildings at the World Trade Center site represented efforts to overwrite the
past trauma and replace it with a new, unscathed, utopian vision with only
managed references to its history. For Shanks, Rathje, and Platt, archaeology plays a key role in constructing new visions of future by documenting,
winnowing, and curating debris not only from sites of monumental human
trauma but also from the everyday life of individuals and communities
over time. In this context, the Garbage Project presented not just a way to
uncover the everyday practices of contemporary households but also to
shed critical attention on the potential futures that these practices anticipated. This analysis stands in contrast to the work for forensic archaeologists, such as Richard Gould, who developed techniques to recover human
remains and personal effects from the massive scatter of debris produced
by the collapse of the buildings at Ground Zero (Gould 2007). The forensic
practices associated with Gould's approach to "disaster archaeology" are
fundamentally distinct from "garbology," but they too recognize the key
role archaeology can play in shaping the response to trauma in the present
and in the future.

The roles that both discard practices and archaeology play in antici-pating the future is perhaps nowhere more visible than in efforts to un-derstand the future for highly volatile and toxic nuclear waste, which can remain dangerous for 10,000 years. Rosemary Joyce's recent attention to the archaeological futures created through the disposal of nuclear waste foregrounds the ongoing discussions by two blue ribbon committees con-cerning how to mark the sites designated to receive tons of nuclear waste to ensure these sites are recognized 10,000 years in the future (Joyce 2020). The sites are conspicuously located in the American West, with the only operational facility, the Waste Isolation Pilot Project (WIPP) site in Carls-bad, New Mexico, less than 150 miles (~240 km) from Alamogordo. These committees sought to produce recommendations to the U.S. government for highly durable markings to discourage future generations from dis-turbing the site and releasing its radiation. Joyce's book pointed out that ar-chaeologists were not represented on either committee, despite their deep familiarity with sites of discard, and suggested that their absence shaped some of the committee's faulty assumptions about the persistence of mate-rials through time. For example, suggestions that the sites be marked with fired clay or granite objects revealed assumptions about the durability of these materials in archaeological contexts. Joyce points out, however, that past societies favored neither granite nor ceramic for their durability and, in fact, neither is especially durable. She notes that these assumptions re-flect a belief that the persistence of monuments and objects from the past reflected the intention of past builders. This misconception shaped how the two committees thought about communicating the present to future generations. In the context of this especially toxic waste, then, Joyce's in-cisive commentary shares Shanks, Rathje, and Platt's concern for how our identification and study of objects from the past, whether waste or objects used to commemorate our own situation, craft a utopian vision. The con-tinued study of waste, trash, discard, and garbage is more than just a way to gain insights into the past, as well as the present, but also has implications for how we seek to control our future.

Today's archaeological study of discard and trash extends well beyond the boundaries of the curbside and dump, illustrating a growing aware-ness that despite our efforts to produce utopian visions and to anticipate the future, the life of garbage extends well beyond our efforts to confine it. Evan Carpenter and Steve Wolverton's work at a number of sites along the Hickory Creek in North Texas deploy Schiffer's concepts of behavioral ar-chaeology and site formation to understand the distribution of trash along these estuaries (Carpenter and Wolverton 2017). They noted that different site formation processes shaped the distribution of plastics and other trash at these sites. The plastics present at the site of McNair, for example, arrived primarily via natural processes (or "n-transforms" in Schiffer's terminology) as the site was an "eolian trap" where wind-borne plastics accumulated. In contrast, two other sites, Hickory Creek and Country Club Road, saw more direct deposits of trash due to their proximity to roads and vehicular access. The different processes at play at the two sites meant that the McNair site would benefit from periodic trash cleanup, as lightweight plastic trash tends to enter the site and become trapped there before slowly releasing into the creek. The sites at Hickory Creek and Country Club would benefit from enforcement of littering bans and other techniques designed to encourage greater stewardship of the watershed because of their ease of access and the presence of trash clearly associated with opportunistic disposal from cars. If Rathje's original project coincided with a growing concern for the garbage produced by postwar American consumer culture, work like Carpenter and Wolverton's reflects an interest in how discarded plastics enter and remain within the wider ecosystem. This not only represents an intensified contemporary awareness of trash as a global challenge, as we will see in the next section, but also the particular challenge of plastic, which can enter diverse ecologies both through the air and water (e.g., see Schofield et al. 2021; Pétursdóttir 2017).

Garbology beyond Archaeology

As the Garbage Project had many stakeholders—from behavioral archaeologists to policymakers, from the private sector to activists—it also contributed to a wide range of interdisciplinary work that looks to garbage, trash, rubbish, and discard as a window into processes operating at the margins or beneath the surface of contemporary society. Opportunities to excavate landfills, however, remain rare and, as the extensive testing around the Alamogordo landfill excavations demonstrated, difficult to negotiate because of regulations, funding, and safety. As a result, surveys of garbage prior to its entering the landfill or recycling center have become a standard strategy to assess the effectiveness of recycling programs, the most cost-effective balance between landfilling and recycling, and attitudes toward waste management strategies at the local level (e.g., Lehmann 2015). Much of this work continues to focus on the relationship between consumer and waste and follows a template loosely consistent with the Garbage Project.

As noted earlier, Rathje's study of garbage and municipal waste sites relied partly on the relative stability of modern waste management regimes, which allowed the discarded waste to stand in for consumer practices without attending much to the processes associated with discard.

Recent scholarship has shifted from taking the stability and consistency of waste disposal networks for granted to studies designed to unpack the complexities associated with the practices, individuals, and flows that transport, process, and ultimately define our relationship to waste. In this work, the municipal landfill is less a destination for household waste and more a node in networks of individuals, attitudes, capital, infrastructure, and formal and informal practices. This perspective recognizes household and industrial trash as revealing the functioning of systems and the impact that these systems have on a wide range of individuals and practices. Household trash can be more than just a window onto American domestic life but can help us to consider the impact of the American experience as consumers on participants in regional, national, and global systems of waste disposal. As an example of this change of perspectives, studies of recycling have emphasized the role of formal and informal labor in the infrastructure of recycling on a global scale. In the twenty-first century, the term "waste regime" (Reno 2009; Gille 2007) has come to describe the relationships between waste and practice. The fluidity of waste regimes traces complex human, national, and economic networks and contrasts with the materiality of the waste itself, which has come to fortify the agency of objects in the waste disposal places in ways that go well beyond their value as representations of human choices and habits (see chapter 3). While many of these studies depart from the rigorous archaeological approaches pursued by Rathje, they nevertheless cite Rathje's Garbage Project as a landmark in understanding the relation between trash and twentieth-century society. Thus, despite their different theoretical perspectives, methods, and goals, they are descendants of the Garbage Project and reflect the transformation of the American experience from archaeology's interest in domestic behaviors to the functioning of global systems.

Much of the late twentieth-century popular literature on garbage and waste emphasized the "garbage crisis" as a way to critique the impact of our consumer culture. More recent work, however, has eschewed the rather narrow emphasis on household discard and municipal landfills in pursuit of a wider perspective on the impact of our trash on both the global environment and the society of communities who find themselves dealing with our garbage (Royte 2005; Humes 2012; Dondero 2019). Historians such as

Susan Strasser (1999) and Carl Zimring (2004, 2005) traced the development of these systems to the rise of sanitary standards in the late nineteenth and early twentieth centuries. These new standards created a kind of disposable culture that by the mid–twentieth century had become an issue of concern for the first wave of social critics of trash. More importantly, however, Strasser and Zimring showed that consumer attitudes toward sanitation and the practices of disposing unsanitary waste transformed the individuals who worked with waste. In the nineteenth century, individuals across a wide range of economic classes and ethnic and racial groups often recycled fabric (rags), paper, metal, and food for a wide range of purposes as a sign of thrift. This was often associated with women's role in maintaining an efficient and economical home (Strasser 1999). By the early twentieth century, however, Americans came to associate these same tendencies with groups who had yet to achieve "modern" status. Middle- and upper-class households concerned with cleanliness and sanitation looked down on the poor, immigrants, and other groups who recycled goods or collected household waste (e.g., Zimring 2005; Roller 2018: 154; Camp 2013). Moreover, the state came to view many of these practices as dangerous and undesirable. For example, social critics came to see scrap metal collecting as dangerous and the storage and sorting of rags as an unsanitary fire hazard. They perceived the level of skills necessary for these jobs as low and thus most suitable for immigrants and poor laborers. As a result, communities increasingly marginalized both the individuals and sites required for this kind of labor. In short, attitudes toward sanitation, consumer goods, and discard practices in the home marginalized individuals and groups who held onto earlier attitudes toward thrift and recycling or who performed such tasks on a large scale (for more on life around landfills see chapter 5).

The persistence of such social stigmas into the twenty-first century continues to obscure key aspects of the networks that handle our solid wastes. Both Jeff Ferrell and Ben Stickle have explored the social world of contemporary scrapper, scavengers, and metal thieves as part of the long history of individuals who deal with waste (see chapter 5 for further discussion of landfills as marginal spaces). It is worth noting that while neither scholar is an archaeologist, both immerse themselves in the same processes of discard that informed Rathje's Garbage Project. Ferrell's work (2006) documented his time spent as a scavenger in suburban Texas in an effort to understand the ways in which discarded objects retain value both in informal adaptation and reuse and through the sale of scrap metal and other objects of value found discarded in a suburban setting. He filled his house, his shed, and (in some cases) his wallet with the rewards of cruising the streets in affluent suburbs looking through piles of discarded objects set out for trash removal. Ferrell recognized that the value of discarded goods is far from absolute and much more aligned with the way individuals and groups see these objects. Stickle (2017) explore the shadier realm between the work of scrappers who sort waste for objects of value and metal thieves. The latter removed metal from what Schiffer and Rathje would call "systemic contexts," and Stickle demonstrated how the marginalized labor of the former often blurred into the illegal work of the latter. Notably, he observed that despite Ferrell's and Zimring's studies of individuals involved in the informal work of metal scrapping, no clear definition exists for these practices. While scholarship has continuously refined the definitions of trash, it continues to struggle to understand the complexity of actors present in these networks. This, in turn, reifies their marginal status by preventing middle- and upper-class Americans from articulating their own and others' experiences despite our participation in the same system.

A shift in emphasis from the objects themselves to the experiences of individuals who participate in the management of waste has led to several important studies of individuals who work at landfills. Joshua Reno's important work at the "Four Corners" landfill in Michigan likewise interrogates practices of finding value in discarded things. His work (2009) explores scavenging practices among landfill workers. Reno situates their practices within the larger discourse of value initiated by Thompson's *Rubbish Theory* (1979) and emphasizes how discard and reuse practices rely on complex networks of relationships defined not only by the objects themselves but also by social practices, economic status, and various political commitments. This shift of attention allowed Reno to show that the systemic and even automatic character of solid waste removal serves to obscure the relation between people and things and hide individuals involved in scavenging and salvaging. By working and doing research at the landfill, Reno succeeds in humanizing the "waste regime" and making individuals, experiences, and practices visible.

As our brief discussion of the fate of *Khian Sea* and *Mobro 4000* trash ships made clear, waste regimes are no longer purely terrestrial enterprises, which makes it all the easier to overlook the plurality of experiences associated with garbage. This realization motivated the MIT Track|Trash project to trace the movement of our trash not only through urban space of cities but also on a global scale (Offenhuber and Ratti 2017). By creating a unique GPS tracker that could move through the solid waste system and record its location periodically, the MIT project was able to demonstrate the national movement of domestic waste across the United States and, in some cases, marked its departure from American shores for processing in China, India, or elsewhere in the "developing" world. As a complement to Reno's work in the United States, a growing number of scholars have sought to document scavenging, recycling, and other forms of solid waste processing that occurs outside the United States. The export of discarded electronics, for example, to the Global South has fueled an growing interest in the human impact of this trade in waste, and e-waste in particular, on communities around the world (Lepawsky 2018; Alexander and Reno 2012).

The diversity of e-waste and the complex policies, rules, and regulations that define its movement and disposal has attracted significant attention in its own right. Josh Lepawsky's recent work is particularly significant in this regard as it emphasizes the comparatively small quantity of post-consumer waste being exported to the Global South in relation to the pre-consumer e-waste produced through the manufacturing processes behind contemporary electronics. His study charts the complex ethical landscape surrounding e-waste on a global scale and how the detritus of the American experience is now complicated by the multidirectional character of e-waste flows and the dense network of agents involved in its movement. In contrast to the often tidy definitions of waste and trash, Lepawsky problematizes the circulation of e-waste by pointing out the ontological problems in defining waste. His fieldwork emphasized how many objects that could be classified as "waste" are actually repairable and are repaired in economies throughout the developing world, which rely on these goods to keep their digital infrastructure intact. A significant quantity of the post-consumer e-waste exported from the United States and Europe does not go to landfills in Africa or Southeast Asia, but is instead repurposed, repaired, and sold. Lepawsky also notes that certain patterns in trade—including steeply discounted rates in backhauling on ships that had transported consumer goods from manufacturing areas in China and South Korea—shape the patterns of movement of e-waste. Atari's decision to use the dump in Alamogordo rather than elsewhere reflected just such an economic calculus. The dumping of returned and damaged Atari games in the Alamogordo landfill reflected the discard practices associated with the manufacturing and distribution of consumer goods that rely on low-cost and often marginal outlets for the waste inherent to these systems.

The global aspects of this economic calculus not only shapes the prevailing attitudes toward sanitation and sanitary practices that have greatly increased the amount of trash produced worldwide but also serves to marginalize individuals and communities who manage our discard practices. In cases like India, these attitudes combine with existing prejudices to reinforce the marginal status of individuals working with trash who make up an often vast and poorly understood informal economy. By exporting the experience of managing American consumer practices abroad, Americans have contributed to the vast expansion of landfills, informal dumps, and waste regimes as well as to the degradation of the environment at a social and economic cost for communities the world over. Francisco Calafate-Faria's work (2013, 2016), for example, among the scavengers and recyclers of Curitiba in Brazil show how strategies of the Global North, particularly the emphasis on environmentally responsible urbanism, intersected with the situation in the Global South. In Curitiba, migrants from rural areas found work in the city as *catadores,* whose labor has made both the city and Brazil one of the leading recyclers in the world. The contrast between growing mountains of waste, environmental and ecological policies, and the plight of dispossessed and marginal urban underclasses who labor in the shadow of the growing economies and gleaming cities of the Global South reflects how the American experience follows flows of global capital that pools in cities built to American (and European) urban standards.

In many ways, the recent research on garbology both from an American and global perspective provides a backdrop to the transnational experience of what Rob Nixon, in his classic work, calls "slow violence" (2011). Nixon's introduction begins with Larry Summer's infamous World Bank memo, which observed that "the economic logic behind dumping a load of toxic waste in the lowest-wage country is impeccable" (Nixon 2011: 1–2). The movement of European and American garbage, toxic or otherwise, to the Global South in the name of economic efficiency reveals the deep structural inequalities present in existing waste regimes. It also clarifies the potential for a garbology of the twenty-first century to reveal more than the complex character of household discard, also making visible on a global scale the relations among our experiences as consumers of goods, producers of waste, and arbiters of social justice. Nixon's sensitivity to issues of global environmental justice amplified earlier work of Benjamin Chavis and Robert Bullard (1990), who demonstrated that poorer communities—particularly African Americans, Native Americans, and Latino communities—were disproportionately impacted by the proximity of hazardous industrial activities, the dumping of solid and toxic waste, and the use of pesticides. Such patterns of discard reflect how the American experience depends on the reproduction of these diverse and asymmetrical encounters on a global scale.

While archaeologists have not necessarily contributed to these particular studies, they have started to look toward documenting trash at sea, for example, as a way to consider the impact of human activities on the environment and as a way to critically engage with the concept of the Anthropocene (see chapter 8). Much of this work, by necessity, takes place in a transnational context. The work of Arnshav and colleagues (Arnshav 2014) in the harbors of Scandinavia, for instance, demonstrates that the sea has long served as a dumping ground for both household and large-scale waste. Well-known sites, such as the Titanic wreck, are being increasingly strewn with modern trash, raising concerns about the integrity of these historical sites. Þóra Pétursdóttir's research on beach trash in Norway not only illuminated the global character of this garbage but also how this drifting discard refused to conform to localized notions of archaeological identity by being "unruly," "pestering," and above all "aggressively" present (Pétursdóttir 2017). The presence of beachside trash is not limited to any particular human actions; rather, these assemblages have emerged as part of the myriad coincidences of natural, material, and human interventions. This way of thinking about archaeological objects informs a more sophisticated approach to the archaeology of the American experience that surpasses the focus on domestic discard characterizing the earliest work of the Garbage Project. Recent work has offered new ways of "realizing the radical potential" of archaeology to understand how the American experience exists as part of a global system that includes a bewildering range of agencies, communities, practices, and objects (Pétursdóttir 2017). In this context, Rathje's closed system of domestic discard studied by the Garbage Project opens up into a vast network of relationships that characterize the often unclassifiable and invisible experiences of marginalized groups who handle trash, global networks that reinforce and rely on economic and political inequality, and the role of nonhuman agents such as wind, ocean currents, and chemical transformations.

Conclusion

This chapter began by locating William Rathje's famous Garbage Project in a broader cultural context. Far from being a methodological or theoretical exercised abstracted from the American experience or designed to document it, Rathje's project reflected changing twentieth-century attitudes toward trash that traced a broad swath through popular literature, archaeology, and history. This work documented the accelerated impact of a disposable culture informed by sanitary practices developed in the interwar years, but also increasingly concerned about the increase in garbage. Rathje's work traced the changing character of household discard practices while pushing back against the catastrophic perspectives on the rapidly increasing quantity of domestic waste promulgated by the fledgling environmentalist movement. His successors have increasingly shifted their attention from the study of garbage to the larger networks of social, natural, political, and economic relations that make up global waste regimes. At the turn of the twenty-first century, scholars have come to recognize that discard practices and the system of trash removal significantly contributed to the marginalization of immigrant groups, the poor, and minorities who managed the removal, processing, and recycling of trash well beyond the gaze of middle- and upper-class America. Attentiveness to the role of discard in critiques of the production, distribution, and consumption of household goods likewise traced the social impact that industrial and commercial waste have on a global scale. This parallels a growing interest in the potential of archaeology to recognize global systems and address global problems.

The excavation in the Alamogordo desert revealed both consumer waste from Alamogordo households as well as commercial waste from Atari's El Paso distribution center. The intermingling of the discarded Atari games with holiday trash, mercury-poisoned pigs, and barrels of malathion in a rural desert town demonstrates how these contexts and assemblages reflect tragedy, waste, celebrations, and everyday life made possible by our place within global systems. The discarding of this trash in a landscape perceived as marginal and adjacent to nuclear waste disposal sites, nuclear weapon testing sites, and other highly toxic situations contributed to both the mystery associated with the discard of Atari games as well as their designation as valueless rubbish. The recovery of the games, through a very unlikely excavation, led to the revaluing of these objects in a way consistent with Thompson's proposed "rubbish theory." In the next chapter, we will shift from considering how discard practices traced and projected the American experience both locally and globally to how our entanglement with things has come to shape the contemporary world.

3

Things, Agency, and
the American Experience

Standing at the side of the excavated Alamogordo landfill exposed me and the team to the hyper-abundance of things that constitute our contemporary American experience. From discarded holiday trash and catalogues, to beer cans, toys, broken cassettes and videotapes, table ware, and other household goods, the excavator's bucket revealed the complicated material lives of the community. The sweet odor of trash likewise reminded us that things changed in both visible and invisible ways. Even as the tests conducted prior to excavation revealed that the levels of toxic gas were within the safe zone, the smell of the open landfill revealed the ongoing transformation of objects not only from one form to another but also from one state of matter to another. At times, we recognized that when standing on the edge of an open landfill we were literally breathing *things*.

When the excavator began to remove parts of the Atari deposit, we witnessed another transformation. When I was a kid, Atari games were among the first things I wanted to possess. I'm sure I wanted other things earlier in life, but the coincidence of the rise of Atari in my preteen years and my growing awareness of how the market and money worked created an incipient awareness of how the consumption of goods gave me access to a particular form of cultural life. Owning and playing an Atari game such as *Raiders of the Lost Ark* or *E.T.* became a lens through which I could understand and, at least in my imagination, appropriate and re-narrate characters and stories that I witnessed in movie theaters. Moreover, these things created the basis for endless strategy sessions with friends, speculative conversations about the next round of games, and competition. In other words, for me the very Atari games being excavated from the Alamogordo landfill were not mere things but objects deeply entangled in my formative years. Just as breathing the sickly sweet smell of decomposing material led to discarded objects in the landfill literally entering my body, the excavation of the Atari games involved the excavation of parts of my childhood. This contemporaneity made me aware of how my presence at the excavation as much as the excavation itself represented a slice of the American experience derived from my own entanglement with discarded things.

As the excavation drew to a close and the Atari games were spread on the surface of the landfill, we witnessed city workers diligently combing through the trash to collect well-preserved games. The City of Alamogordo and the local historical society made these games available for purchase on eBay. Watching workers collect the games from the landfill transformed the games from discarded trash to cultural artifacts and made them, once again, commodities available for purchase. The city sold the games with a certificate that authenticated the stench and other signs of decades of life compacted at the bottom of a landfill. The materiality of their time in the landfill literally clung to the games. Like my experience of nostalgia on seeing the first Atari games removed from the excavation, their return to circulation as commodities reinforced the complicated interplay between their status as objects, the physical evidence of their age, the value associated with the context, and their ability to evoke nostalgia. In this chapter we will continue to unpack how archaeology's growing critique of things drew me to the edge of the Alamogordo landfill, and reflect on how our discipline's sustained interest in objects, materiality, patina, and agency intersects with the distinctive experiences of American consumer culture.

Things

The late 1970s represented a watershed moment for how archaeologists thought about things. In the United States, the postwar prosperity of the 1950s and 1960s encountered its first challenges in the oil crises of the 1970s. First in 1973, the members of the Organization of Arab Petroleum Exporting Countries (OPEC) enacted an embargo of oil exports in response to Western support of Israel during the Yom Kippur War. Then, in 1979, the Iranian revolution disrupted oil exports. The resulting shocks to the global oil market led to massive spikes in the price of gasoline and other petroleum-based products. This in turn led to slower economic growth and "stagflation," characterized by high levels of inflation and high unemployment. Ultimately, Paul Volker, chair of the U.S. Federal Reserve Bank, steeply increased interest rates in an effort to control inflation, while realizing this decision would increase unemployment. This move ultimately pushed the United States into the recession in early 1980s, which coincided with the rapid growth of Atari. At the onset of this crisis, President Jimmy Carter, in a now well-known nationally televised address, reminded the country that "we've discovered that owning things and consuming things does not satisfy our longing for meaning. We've learned that piling up material goods cannot fill the emptiness of lives which have no confidence or purpose" (quoted in Jelfs 2018: 37–42). Ronald Reagan's famous statement punctuated Carter's failed re-election bid a year later: "We don't have inflation because—as Mr. Carter says—we have lived too well." These contrasting attitudes, and Reagan's electoral victory, may well serve as an invocation for the famously acquisitive and materialistic culture of the 1980s (Jelfs 2018: 42).

The oil crisis of the 1970s and the associated recession triggered a national conversation about consumerism and the role of things in our everyday lives. This debate manifested itself in popular and literary culture of the "long 1980s" (see Collins 2006): the dirty realism of Raymond Carver's collection of stories, *What We Talk about When We Talk about Love* (1981), Madonna's "Material Girl" (1984), the brand-obsessed psychopath of Bret Easton Ellis's *American Psycho* (1991), artist Jeff Koons's *Luxury and Degradation* (1986) and *Banality* (1988) series, the meticulous materialism of Nicholson Baker's *The Mezzanine* (1988), and the weight of Tim O'Brien's *The Things They Carried* (1990). These works and others sustained a conversation about how things suffused American culture and offered critiques of consumerist society. The video for Madonna's "Material Girl," for example, concludes with Madonna rejecting expensive gifts from suitors before departing the scene in a beat-up pickup truck. The juxtaposition of materialism, poverty, and violence in contemporary rap and hip-hop music, perhaps best seen in the early 1990s work of Notorious B.I.G., provided a constant reminder that the benefits of consumer culture were experienced unevenly in the United States. Popular and literary culture made clear that access to consumer goods manifested the growing inequality characteristic of American society in the late twentieth and early twenty-first centuries.

Archaeologists of the contemporary world have become increasingly aware of how both our interests as archaeologists and the material that we study reflect our experiences as Americans. As we saw in the last chapter, the growing anxieties about trash in American society coincided with Bill Rathje's Garbage Project. In this chapter, we consider how the growing interest in things among archaeologists and anthropologists over the last forty years has coincided with an increasing awareness of the role of consumer culture and material possessions in our daily lives. Thus, at the same time that materialism and consumer culture were becoming topics of conversation in American political and cultural life, a series of important works emphasizing the role of things, material culture, and consumer practices came to influence archaeological work.

The publication of James Deetz's *In Small Things Forgotten: An Archaeology of Early American Life* (1977) not only stimulated the still-developing discipline of historical archaeology in the United States but also influenced British scholars seeking an approach to objects that went beyond the processualism of New Archaeology (Hicks 2010: 66; Hicks and Beaudry 2006: 5). Deetz's study of "small things" bridged the gap between the structuralist practices of New Archaeology and interests in objects as signs and symbols in anthropology (Hicks 2010: 46). In Deetz's hands, things occupied a vivid place in the daily and ritual life of eighteenth-century New England. His understanding of these objects, however, did not emerge from the work of excavation, or through other strictly defined archaeological practices, alone, but from the intersection of objects, texts, photographs, and informants. For Deetz, taking things seriously involved using them as evidence for the underlying culture that manifested itself through these physical objects (Olsen 2010: 143–145). In the next decades, a group of British archaeologists and anthropologists would continue their scrutiny of small things, but would stand Deetz's ideas on their head by arguing that things were more than mere manifestations of structures, attitudes, and "society," but instead actively contributed to the creation of human society and relations.

Deetz's interest in producing a richer context of things by acknowledging both their functional and symbolic meaning anticipated Schiffer and Gould's *Modern Material Culture: The Archaeology of Us* (1981), which appeared just two years later and, as we have seen, influenced a growing, global interest in contemporary things among archaeologists. Schiffer and Gould's work framed the study of modern material culture as ethnoarchaeological practice. The contributors in this book built on the work of Richard Gould over the course of the 1970s (e.g., 1978, 1980), as well as Michael Schiffer's interest in developing a middle range theory to bridge the gap between archaeological evidence and human behavior (Schiffer and Gould 1981: xv–xvi). As they acknowledge in their preface, any effort to apply ethnographic techniques to archaeological problems quickly comes to recognize that a "direct" relationship between modern behavior and past behavior in archaeology is impossible (xvi). Instead, as their book showed, archaeologists should look to the potential for indirect links between contemporary behaviors and the past, which could inform the nature of archaeological reasoning. In many ways, however, the approach developed in *Modern Material Culture,* and through Schiffer's later work both on contemporary objects (e.g., 1991, 1994) and behavioral archaeology (1995), continues to see objects as the manifestation of culture rather than productive or constituent agents in their own right (Hodder 2007: 202–203). Schiffer's later idea of material as "compound interactors" (Schiffer 1999; Olsen 2010: 136–137) demonstrates a growing willingness to acknowledge that things are not just markers of past situations but manifestations of the complex interaction between their materiality as artifacts, the actions of individuals, and certain nonhuman forces, such as climate.

The functional, symbolic, and ethnoarchaeological approaches that combine in the works of Deetz, Schiffer, and Gould found an eager audience in the UK, where anthropologists and archaeologists alike had read Mary Douglas and Baron Isherwood's *The World of Goods: Towards an Anthropology of Consumption* (1979) and recognized the appeal of ethnographic practices in understanding the place of things in both the past and the contemporary world. In the 1980s and 1990s, Ian Hodder, Daniel Miller, Michael Shanks, and Christopher Tilley took the ideas and methods presented in both Douglas and Isherwood's and Schiffer and Gould's books and applied them to a wide range of earlier and contemporary contexts. For an archaeology of the contemporary world, the relatively short analyses of punk fashion in Hodder's *Symbols in Action* (1982) and of Swedish and British beer cans in Shanks and Tilley's *Re-Constructing Archaeology* (1987) demonstrated the potential for the interplay of ethnographic, textual, and contextual critiques of modern material culture by archaeologists in the late twentieth century. In a 2007 retrospective on his edited volume *Symbolic and Structural Archaeology* (1982), Ian Hodder noted that despite the volume's generally unfavorable reviews at the time, alongside *Symbols in Action,* it demonstrated the potential of ethnographic practices to reveal how things play a role in relationships between both individuals and other things (Hodder et al. 2007).

These arguments made it possible to see late twentieth-century consumer practices as more than just slavish responses to cleverly constituted marketing campaigns or the manifestation of an uncritical herd mentality. Instead, consumer culture manifested the complex and often ritualized practice of identity formation and culture making. These ideas emerged in their most convincing form in a series of books published by Danny Miller starting in the mid-1980s. Drawing on Pierre Bourdieu's notion of *habitus*

(1977), Miller (1987) demonstrated how the interaction between individuals and objects created meaning both in past and contemporary societies. By grounding his assessment in the ethnography of British, Caribbean, and Indian society, Miller argued that the physical form and materiality of objects gives them a place distinct from language and other ritual practices in social interactions among individuals. Cellphones, cars, furniture, clothing, and other modern consumer objects produced social meaning and relationships in the same way that archaeologists had increasingly recognized for premodern societies (Mullins 2011: 6; Miller 1995). The massive increase in the quantity and diversity of things present in the modern world did not diminish their importance, but rather created an increasingly rich corpus of material for analysis. That said, Miller's attention to the essential role of cars in Trinidad or cellphones in Jamaica, despite its origins alongside the work of archaeologists Ian Hodder and Christopher Tilley, did not directly advance archaeological practices and methods when they confronted the daunting challenge of dealing with the late twentieth-century abundance of objects and consumer practices. Instead, Miller's work gave rise to the field of modern material culture studies and consumer studies, which has produced an impressive body of scholarship with relatively few contributions from archaeologists of the contemporary world in the United States.

It may have been that archaeologists found themselves more drawn to interpretative paradigms that centered objects over time rather than embedding them in complex, but sometimes static, networks established by ethnographic research. Thus, Arjun Appadurai's *The Social Life of Things: Commodities in Cultural Perspective* (1986) and, in particular, the chapter by Igor Kopytoff titled "The Cultural Biography of Things: Commoditization as Process" (Kopytoff 1986) continue to garner attention among archaeologists. Kopytoff's oft-cited essay proposed that things had biographies that could be tracked over time with productive results. In particular, he noted that objects could move in and out of commodity status depending on their exchange value in a society. Kopytoff argues that at some points in the life of an object, it may exist outside of commodity status and undergo singularization when it becomes the object of a wide range of social, ritual, and emotional values that extend beyond its value as a commodity. At other points, the object might acquire a hybrid status where it is both singularized and commodified to varying degrees. This not only represented a critique of Marxist views of fetishized objects as commodities but also provided a paradigm for considering the changing social meaning of objects over time. Unlike Miller's engagement with things in contemporary contexts, Appadurai's volume drew on a wide range of ethnographic and historical studies but avoided consumer culture in industrialized economies. Archaeologist Colin Renfrew, for example, participated in the volume and argued that the changing character of the objects excavated from the Chalcolithic cemetery in Varna, Bulgaria, stemmed from social processes rather than simply technical developments (Renfrew 1986).

While American archaeologists were not at the fore of the theoretical and largely European discussions of things, they continued to consider modern material culture in an American context. Michael Schiffer's 1991 book, *The Portable Radio in American Life,* for example, emphasizes the impact of the portable—and later transistor—radio on American life. He documents the history of radio technology starting with vacuum tubes and continuing through the use of transistors, ferrite rod antennas, multiple bands, various battery types, and gimmicks to show how the radio established a place within American consumer culture. He parallels the technologies used in radios with their role in American social life through the rise of radio shows such as "Amos and Andy," popular music and news programs, the use of the radio in politics, and of course, sportscasting. In the conclusion of this distinctly atheoretical book, Schiffer argues that in the 1980s Japanese companies like Sony rewrote the history of the technological and commercial development of the portable radio and claimed it as a Japanese invention. He argued that this misrepresentation of the history of the radio, which he calls corporate "cryptohistory," continues to have a significant impact on how American society and policymakers understand the development of technology. By tracing the history of the portable radio, Schiffer argued that by researching and re-narrating the origins of objects central to everyday life, Americans can free themselves from corporate narratives that overwrite the key role that inventors, tinkerers, and university researchers had in creating technology. It is worth briefly contrasting Schiffer's technologically focused narrative with Michael Roller's 2023 study of the role that high-powered commercial radio played in beaming a common consumer culture into the American home (Roller 2023). Roller combined evidence for radio ownership from the 1930 census with excavated evidence from a Pennsylvania coal mining town to argue that the way and degree to which the radio shaped American life varied. Interwar immigrant communities, for example, tended to show lower rates of radio ownership, which suggests different listening practices and perhaps different degrees of market penetration in the communities. In contrast, the rise of low-powered, unlicensed, pirate radio stations in the postwar decades created a platform of activists, community radio, and other forms of broadcasting that had the capacity to subvert radio's commercial commitments. Roller demonstrated that the technological aspects of radio that Schiffer explored to chart its growing impact on American society represent just one view of the role that radio—and mass media—played in creating a consumer society.

The rise and decline in electric vehicle ownership in the early twentieth century offered another example of how the study of things has contributed to how we understand technology, consumer culture, and American society. Despite their initial popularity, electric-powered vehicles failed to become the dominant approach to motor transportation. Schiffer argued that this had as much to do with their association with women and short trips in town on household errands as they did with any technological limitation (Schiffer 1994; Schiffer and Skibo 2008). His broader study on the history of practical electricity in the nineteenth century demonstrates how an archaeological and ethnographic approach to things can unpack development of technology in the modern period in ways comparable both to Bruno Latour's *Science and Technology Studies* (Latour and Woolgar 1979) and Appadurai's *Social Life of Things* (1986). Schiffer's work, however, remains largely an outlier in the broader field of American archaeology, finding more in common with recent works on the history of barbed wire (Krell 2002; Razac 2003; Netz 2004), twine (Evans 2007), pencils (Petroski 1989), and videogames (Guins 2014; Newman 2017) than with the approaches deployed by historical archaeologists.

Things and Consumer Culture

Standing at the side of the Alamogordo landfill, it was impossible not to reflect on historical archaeology's long and complex engagement with modern consumer culture. As any number of scholars have observed, all historical archaeology is inevitably about the emergence of consumer culture (Mullins 2011: 2–3). Starting in the mid-1980s, historical archaeologists began taking cues from Deetz, Miller, and Appadurai, as well as others (e.g., Campbell 1987). They explored the archaeology of consumer culture through such concepts as "consumer-choice" (Spencer-Wood 1987; Gibb 1996), Louis Althusser's concepts of ideology (Leone 1984, 2010), and world-systems theory (Hall 2000). This produced a dynamic body of work far too large to survey in a volume such as this (for a recent survey, however, see Mullins 2011; Heath et al. 2017). In general, however, much of this work has kept at arm's length the complex theoretical debates that have shaped the field of material culture studies and, instead, anchored their analysis in carefully contextualized excavations. They have nevertheless recognized the global context for modern artifacts, the utility of telling stories through and about individual objects, and a growing interest in the materiality of things (Martin 2017). In general, this extensive body of work has sought to explore how things defined social roles and American culture in the nineteenth and twentieth centuries. In this context, the excavation of an assemblage of Atari games in the New Mexico desert was more than just an effort to confirm an urban legend. Instead, this dig was an opportunity to excavate American identity at the very moment when things were rising to prominence in archaeological thought.

As one would expect, historical archaeologists have largely focused on material dating to the pre-1950s and derived from archaeological rather than systemic contexts (Schiffer 1972). As noted in chapter 2, however, broadly ethnographic comparisons grounded in critical attention to the systemic context of objects have often helped archaeologists to understand the practical, symbolic, and economic functions of artifacts in the past. For example, Paul Mullins in his survey of the archaeology of consumer culture introduced his book with a discussion of the Hummer SUV to demonstrate the complex ways that an object produces status in society (Mullins 2011). Elsewhere, Marlys Pearson and Mullins (1999) studied the development of outfits and accessories for Mattel's Barbie, from its introduction in the 1950s to the 1990s. They argued that the doll neither reflected a particular image of femininity nor a set notion of domesticity. Rather, the changes in Barbie's accessories revealed the instability of those notions in contemporary society and the changing realities of Mattel's financial situation. The Hummer and Barbie's accessories situated these objects within consumer culture and offered ways to understand both contemporary and historic social, political, and economic relationships.

The use of objects to negotiate racial identities provides a particularly valuable line of inquiry for studies of consumer culture in historical archaeology. Archaeologists have recognized the wide range of objects associated with various nineteenth- and twentieth-century ethnic communities: Chinese laborers (Voss and Allan 2008), Japanese Americans (Ross 2011; Camp 2020), Greek immigrants (Kourelis 2008), and Italian railroad workers (Wegers 1991). Maria Franklin's study of buttons from the nineteenth-century African American Freedman's town cemetery in Houston demonstrates how even the simplest of everyday objects, clothing fasteners and buttons, can shed light on strategies of self-presentation and the negotiation of identity in the segregated South (Franklin 2020). The individuals interred in the Freedmen's town cemetery revealed a community who wore similar clothing to white Houstonians despite the rise of Jim Crow laws at the time. Mullins's 1999 work, *Race and Affluence: An Archaeology of African America and Consumer Culture,* examined how African Americans in Annapolis acquired, used, and discarded consumer objects. Mullins unpacked the complex negotiations that marked out the desire both for affluence, social standing, and political power through access to goods associated with white respectability which the Black community also used to undermine and resist the racist character of the same white consumer culture (Mullins 1999). During World War II, efforts by interned Japanese American prisoners to resist the racist policies of internment manifest themselves in gardens that preserved memories of their previous homes, provided recreation for their fellow prisoners, and grew vegetables common to Japanese cuisine (see Camp 2020). Adrian and Mary Praetzellis (2001) have demonstrated that nineteenth-century Mexican Americans and Chinese Americans in California likewise used both imported and local objects to negotiate identities that allowed them to conform to expectations of Victorian gentility while continuing to preserve aspects of distinctive ethnic identities and practices. Mariano Guadalupe Vallejo's villa from 1852 featured traditional Mexican adobe architecture behind a Gothic facade; contemporary boarding houses for Chinese laborers destroyed by a fire preserved both imported Chinese ceramics and Victorian vessels common to white tables.

The archaeological study of consumer culture provided a framework for understanding how objects contributed to status, ethnicity, race, and citizenship in the nineteenth and early twentieth centuries. It located the negotiation of identity within the context of the emerging market economy and a notion of consumer citizenship established by shared material aspirations. The development of a taste for new goods and the latest fashion—"novelty" in the words of Lorinda Goodwin (1999)—in the eighteenth century infused older, more durable artifacts, heirlooms, with a "patina" of age that reinforced the traditional standing of the owners as members of a long-standing elite. The place of the North American colonies as important commercial ports and the access of a rising merchant elite to the latest goods from England and Europe created an opportunity for these communities to ascribe status to older goods. In this context, the patina of age evoked long-standing respectability. Recently, this notion of patina has been revisited, complicated, and significantly revised by Shannon Lee Dawdy (2016). Dawdy recognized in the patina on objects prized by some contemporary residents of New Orleans a way to critique contemporary attitudes and archaeological approaches to consumer culture.

Things with Patina

Patina on contemporary objects shows the passage of time and offers a visible, physical rebuke to a society and consumer culture preoccupied with innovation. Shannon Lee Dawdy located patina at the center of her landmark social readings of consumer culture in post-Katrina New Orleans (Dawdy 2016). Dawdy's work takes a critical interest in the concept of commodity fetishism in contemporary New Orleans and sought to rehabilitate the concept of the fetish in order to understand the role of things in creating social relationships in "antique cities." She expanded the concept of the fetish from its narrow use in Marx, who used the term to describe how certain objects obscure the labor and social relations necessary for their manufacture (Dawdy 2016: 138–139). In its place, she argued that the status of certain objects as fetishes serves not to obscure labor but to remove these objects from the commodified experience of consumer capitalism (see Wurst 2023 for a counterargument). This allows the patinated objects to acquire a special status. Following Kopytoff (1986), Dawdy drew on a wide range of interviews and objects to demonstrate that patina connected personal stories and histories to objects and that the physical signs of age— the literal patina in the book's title—allowed them to shed their status as commodities and reemerge as objects of singular value. Thus, fetishized antiques and "Granny-had-ones" stood out against the backdrop of the social displacement of post-Katrina New Orleans and helped to renew a sense of community in the face both of the profound destruction and the remaking of the city through new arrivals. A plain wardrobe owned by a longtime white resident of New Orleans was meaningful because it evoked the story of its purchase by the interviewee as a teenager as well as the physical characteristics that marked it as a piece of traditional furniture (129–130). The singular nature of this object paralleled the celebrated "throws" distributed by participants in Mardi Gras parades, which have themes and markings identifying them to particular years and groups (see also Wilkie 2014). These cheap plastic novelties are valued for their association with particular occasions but also serve as a blatant critique of capitalist culture when parading crews dispense them freely to crowds in such vast quantities that many longtime New Orleans residents fill garbage bags with thrown items from the parade season. While residents discard most of these objects, some of Dawdy's informants kept a few from each year as distinctive souvenirs of particular parades, themes, and experiences. For Dawdy, objects with patina in contemporary New Orleans show how commodities can escape, if even momentarily, from their commodified status, and offer an example of the kinds of "cracks in capitalism" that LouAnn Wurst and Attila Dézsi have recently argued are so important to archaeology that aspires to revolutionary action (Wurst and Dézsi 2023).

While archaeology of contemporary American culture has not necessarily excavated the racial dimensions of late twentieth- and early twenty-first-century consumer assemblages to the same extent of historical archaeology, Dawdy is careful to note the difference between white and Black attitudes toward the antiques and old objects. Her Black informants rarely had the same attitude toward old things as her white informants. The reasons for this were socially complex. On a simple level, Dawdy noted that both prior to and after Katrina, many Black residents had difficulty finding stable housing where they could collect, store, and display old objects. More subtly, she argued that remembering New Orleans' past did not just evoke the time before Hurricane Katrina but also conjured memories of slavery, Jim Crow laws, and other forms of systematic discrimination that negatively impacted Black New Orleans residents. Dawdy also recognized the difficulties associated with Kopytoff's comparison of the commodified object to an enslaved individual. Kopytoff argued that the movements of enslaved people into commodified status in the slave market was only temporary. He noted that enslaved individuals nevertheless continued to have agency, personalities, and individuality both in bodily form and in relation to others during their enslavement. Objects likewise have moments of commodification that then give way to more diverse and dynamic "biographies" that leave a physical imprint. Dawdy suggests that commodification of objects with patina that marks out their past life may evoke the experience of the slave market in ways that are deeply uncomfortable for New Orleans' Black residents (Dawdy 2016: 151).

The patina on objects from contemporary, post-Katrina New Orleans provided a material critique of consumer culture in ways that paralleled and complicated Goodwin's interpretation of patina on eighteenth-century New England heirlooms. The desirability of objects effaced by time and embedded with stories from the past subvert consumer culture by valuing the old and singular more than the new and improved. In a small way, the Alamogordo landfill bestowed its patina on the Atari games excavated from its depths and added to their value by establishing a particular context for their discovery. In both New Orleans and New Mexico, the fabric of old things preserves and communicates the evidence for their age and experiences and gives these objects a kind of material agency. The objects themselves refuse to obscure their life histories and remind us that objects exist within a dense network of relations between both individuals and things. The central role that such old things play in the fabric of New Orleans both renders the city a visible reminder of contemporary resistance to capitalism and also shows how the character of old things construct these cultural and social attitudes. The Atari games excavated from the landfill might not evoke a similar nostalgia, but the patina they developed from spending over forty years in a landfill nevertheless transformed them from functional objects (as we will explore in the next chapter) into objects encrusted with memories of the distinctively American experience of mid-1980s childhood.

Materiality and Agency

The development of patina clarifies how the passage of time transforms objects, whether they are subjected to the devastating impacts of a hurricane or the slow chemical reactions at the bottom of a New Mexico landfill. Dawdy's work stands at the intersection of American historical archaeology with its interest in capitalism and Daniel Miller's work on the place of objects in global consumer culture. By complicating and challenging Marx's idea of the fetish, for example, Dawdy demonstrates that things can be more than simply vulgar distractions meant to obscure the social working of labor. At the same time, her insistence that material culture in New Orleans represents a critique of consumer culture, rather than simply a distinctive expression of how things serve to construct social relationships, suggests a continued hostility toward things as expressions of contemporary capitalism. Patina, and other physical transformation of objects, manifests ongoing relations to chemical processes irrespective of human involvement. Patina also reveals that objects are complicit in marking the passage of time and the continuous emergence of the new and contemporary.

By foregrounding the role of objects themselves in subverting the demands of capitalism and marking time, archaeologists, historians, and anthropologists have come to recognize the key role played by both the materiality and agency of things. For example, in her book *Curated Decay*, Caitlin DeSilvey discusses her efforts to document the deteriorating remains of a recently abandoned, century-old Montana farmstead (DeSilvey 2017, 2006). Sorting through discarded objects, she observes the multiple processes and agents that shaped the assemblage of things associated with the farmstead. This included the cycles of human hoarding practices, as well as the work of nonhuman creatures preserved through evidence of the nesting habits of rodents and regular traces produced by hungry insects, alongside the play of humidity, microbial action, rust, and rot on the fabric of the farm and its contents. DeSilvey speculatively proposes the potential for collaborative curation with animals, microbes, and chemical processes that continuously transform the materials that make up our contemporary world. For archaeologists, DeSilvey's work is deeply familiar; anyone who has stepped foot in an abandoned building recognizes that the evidence of abandonment has less to do with the absence of human activity as with the visible presence of a wide range of nonhuman agents and processes. Miriam Rothenberg's recent work in the settlements destroyed by the Monserrat volcano in 1997 similarly stress the nonhuman aspects of site formation. Animal activities, tropical vegetation, and wind transformed the remains of houses, commercial buildings, and settlements in the exclusionary zones around the active volcano where human activity was rare (Rothenberg 2021). Back in Alamogordo, the distinctively sweet odor that emanated from the open New Mexico landfill similarly revealed the continued agency of discarded waste long after these objects retreated from regular human interventions.

DeSilvey's work offers a compelling North American example of recent efforts to consider the materiality of our world in ways that challenges the long-standing dichotomies between humans and nature and humans and things that have defined the social sciences and humanities for the last two centuries. Many of these approaches center on critiques of the working ontologies that allow us to group objects into categories of things. These critiques have often emphasized flat ontologies that reject the hierarchical divisions that rank humans, animals, and things at different levels. Flat ontologies, often loosely described as "object-oriented ontologies," offer a paradigm for understanding the interactions among things, between things and humans, and among humans as fundamentally similar. In this approach to objects, things have a kind of agency in their interaction with humans and other things. Archaeologists have introduced these and similar ideas in a diverse range of ways, from calls for a "symmetrical archaeology"

(Witmore 2007) to the concepts of "entanglement" (Hodder 2012; Hodder and Lucas 2017) and neomaterialism (for a survey of these approaches see LeCain 2017). Michael Shanks and Bjørnar Olsen, for example, stress that things are not a separate category (Olsen et al. 2012: 8–9). Other scholars invoke Donna Haraway's idea of the cyborg, in which the blurry division between humans and things extends to recognizing the heterogeneous character of objects in our everyday life (Haraway 1991; LeCain 2017: 80; Morgan 2019). Tim Edensor, like Caitlyn DeSilvey, observes that ruins provide a particularly vivid example of the blurred boundaries of human and nonhuman agency and make it impossible to keep tidy ontological divisions when confronted with elusiveness of human efforts to create order in the world (LeCain 2014: 64; Edensor 2005). Breaking down the purity of categories such as things and humans undercuts co-constructivist views in which things create society and, more importantly, provides a way to consider the commingled meshwork of existence that makes human life on Earth possible (Ingold 2011; Hicks 2016).

Timothy LeCain's study of the Berkeley Pit in Butte, Montana, demonstrates how some of these ideas can shape new understandings of the world (LeCain 2009, 2014). While LeCain is a historian, not an archaeologist, his attention to materiality and matter offers a compelling perspective for the discipline of archaeology and an opportunity to connect the discipline to environmental history. The Berkeley Pit was an open pit mine created by the Anaconda Copper Mining Company in 1955 after conventional mining methods using tunnels and shafts became less effective. The massive pit excavated by equally massive machines eventually extended 1,800 feet (~548 m) below the surface and was nearly 1.5 miles (2.4 km) wide (LeCain 2014: 71). In 1982, mining ceased, and when the pumps that served to keep the pit dry stopped operating, the pit filled with acidic water laced with a toxic combination of heavy metals. The copper mined from this pit served to conduct electricity, make guns, and produce components for TVs and Michael Schiffer's portable radios. It also provided jobs to generations of residents of Butte, Montana. On the down side, the pit changed the local landscape and introduced toxic chemicals to the water table. The toxic water interacted with residents and wildlife. LeCain started his 2014 article on the "ontology of absence" with the arresting story of a flock of migrating snow geese that landed in the pit in 1995 and were killed by its toxic waters. The interplay between the geese, the mining, the metals in the acidic waters, the rhythms of migration, and the weather conditions that night led to their demise. LeCain concludes with the observation that humans created the pit, and that its presence remains a persistent and independent agent in the global landscape, technologies, and even migratory patterns that shape our world.

Archaeologists and other scholars have increasingly recognized the interaction of various agents as assemblages and have drawn on a wide range of theorists to explore how interactions among various human and nonhuman agents create dispersed fields of agency. Unlike the traditional view of assemblages in archaeology, which may represent common types of objects derived from the same or similar stratigraphic or architectural contexts at the site, the assemblages proposed by Manuel DeLanda (2016) and Bruno Latour (2005), or developed through a critical reading of Deleuze and Guattari, constitute distributed arrays of agents that make any actions and situations possible (Deleuze and Guattari 1987). While these thinkers and those inspired by their works continue to debate how agency emerges from assemblages (e.g., see the discussion in the 2017 *CAJ*, especially Hamilakis and Jones 2017; Antczak and Beaudry 2019), archaeologists have come to recognize that the value of this more expansive definition of assemblage has the potential for tracing the significance of archaeological practices to things, people, and communities. Christopher Matthews, for example, has demonstrated that an emphasis on assemblages creates a method to analyze the people, identities, things, and places, as they serve as the locus of social change (Matthews 2019). In his work with communities of Native American and African Americas in a predominantly affluent and white community on Long Island, Matthews has proposed that engaging objects, places, and groups ensures the production of a socially meaningful past for all residents of this community. For Matthews, such attentiveness to the community as an active producer of archaeological knowledge has practical implications, especially for minority groups who have increasingly found their heritage threatened by the continued expansion of affluence and development.

Codex

In the final part of this chapter, we reflect on a recent multimedia project developed by artist Micah Bloom in Minot, North Dakota (Bloom 2017). Bloom's work, which was not archaeological in a proper sense, documented the aftermath of the Souris River flooding, which devastated the small city of Minot in 2011. The floods caused the evacuation of over 4,000 homes, the construction of almost 2,000 shelters by FEMA, and a final cost of over

$1 billion in U.S. dollars. Bloom captured the tremendous impact of these floods by photographing the books left behind by the receding waters over the course of 2011 (figure 3.1). He also collected some of the books and created an installation that traveled to several venues across the United States. In this exhibit, he arranged waterlogged and disintegrating books on shelves annotated with a series of inventory numbers. He paired them with the Tyvek suits, masks, plastic gloves, and scientific paraphernalia that his team used when collecting and examining the recovered books (figure 3.2). Finally, the installation featured a graveyard where Bloom arranged books in neat rows on a carpet of earth, awaiting burial. On the walls surrounding this cemetery hung photographs showing the find spots of these books with forensic clarity. The published book associated with this project included essays from a range of scholars who responded to his work.

Bloom is not the only artist approaching books and trash with archaeological sensibilities. In fact, a number of municipal waste disposal centers developed artist residency programs (e.g., in San Francisco and Philadel-

Figure 3.1. Books suspended in trees after the Minot Flood. Photo courtesy of Micah Bloom.

Figure 3.2. The Codex exhibition display of the recovery of books. Photo courtesy of Micah Bloom.

phia) as a way to capitalize on the long-standing recognition that everyday objects take on new meanings when discarded as waste and repurposed as art. Bloom's photographs of disintegrating books abandoned by the re-treating Souris River emphasizes the materiality of paper slowly return-ing to pulp when exposed to water. Their unnatural entanglement with the wooded banks of the river further suggests that the flood reversed the process of book manufacturing by returning the books to wood pulp and then to vegetation. The status of books as treasured objects (Prugh 2017; Sorensen 2017) carefully curated in libraries, homes, and institutions made these images of regression all the more haunting. By playing on books as personal things, always in the process of construction and decomposition (Liming 2017; Haeselin 2017; Kibler 2017), the disembodied state of the decaying books serves to illuminate the absence of humans. The absence of clear human intervention in the fate of these books offers a salient re-minder that agency is not limited to individuals. The interplay among the books, the flood, and their post-deluge deposition reveals evidence for the work of insects, animals, microbes, and the inherent fragility of any single material state.

Finally, Thora Brylowe's contribution to the Codex project recognized in this assemblage of books the interplay of forces on a global scale (Brylowe 2017). For example, the weather patterns that produced the 2011 Souris flood occurred as part of the larger El Niño–Southern Oscillation when the cooling waters of the equatorial Pacific created a La Niña weather pattern that caused a wetter than normal winter and spring in the Northern Plains as well as the East Asian drought. Climate change will likely make El Niño and La Niña events more intense, and the 2011 La Niña was the warmest on record. Brylowe notes that industrial practices—including paper production, which both removed old-growth trees from the landscape at a massive scale and relied on fossil fuels—not only allowed for the emergence of books as an affordable, personal commodity but also spurred global climate change. The entanglement of books, climate, humans, microbes, weather, and history demonstrates the dispersed character of agency across assemblages. This assemblage spanned not only continents but also centuries, emphasizing the immediacy of Bloom's photographs and installation as interventions that, like archaeology, seek to provide limits on how we see the interplay of objects.

Conclusion

This chapter began once again at the Alamogordo landfill, where the Atari excavations literally exposed both the detritus of twentieth-century American consumer culture and our personal histories as consumers of things in the mid-1980s. As archaeologists, our participation in the American experience as consumers of things, nostalgia, and scholarship encouraged us to reflect on both the history of the recent interest of things and how this has informed our view of things in the archaeology of twentieth- and twenty-first-century consumer culture. Thus, the place of things in the archaeology of the contemporary American experience in many ways reflects larger efforts to find our way and meaning in the abundance of "stuff" present in our everyday lives. My enthusiastic presence on the edge of the Alamogordo landfill reflected my childhood memories of Atari games as desired objects. By excavating this nostalgia and locating it amid the objects cast off from this New Mexico town, I came to recognize the tight connections between my academic interest in things as an archaeologist and the critical interest in consumerism that characterized late twentieth-century American life.

The interest in things and consumer culture extended beyond my personal attraction to the fate of discarded Atari games and included archaeologist's efforts to recognize the complex role of things in the construction of race, gender, status, and class in the twentieth century. This interest transformed contemporary objects from Hummer SUVs to Barbie Dolls into actors that both reflect and produce social relationships. The attention to things in the aftermath of loss—whether in the aftermath of Hurricane Katrina, the Minot flood of 2011, the Monserrat volcano, or the Alamogordo landfill—demonstrates both the persistence of things beyond sentimental human attachment and makes all the more clear the way in which nonhuman forces transform our material world. Patina, decay, and even the crushing weight of the Alamogordo landfill transform objects both physically and in their relationship to humans.

4

Music, Media Archaeology, and Digital Experiences

In this final chapter of the first case study, I return one last time to the edge of the Alamogordo landfill. Moments after the first bucket-loads of the Atari game deposit came to the surface, the film production team whisked them away to a prepared Atari 2600 console. With cameras rolling, the project's organizers inserted the game into the console to see if it still worked. As someone who recalled the frustrating gameplay of the *E.T.* game, I was amused at the prospects of reliving the experience of a game that some considered rather unenjoyable. I envisioned the scene where the recently excavated game cartridge came back to life and revived the frustrating challenge of extracting the blocky graphic representation of E.T. from one of the game's many pits. In my imagination, the filmmakers would use this moment to transport the viewer to a simpler time in the American experience, when charismatic game developers captured our adolescent attention by turning our televisions into a new form of participatory media. Unfortunately, this did not happen. The game did not work, but the moment highlighted the tension between the digital media and the physical character of the game cartridge itself. As we saw in the last chapter, scholars in the late twentieth and twenty-first centuries developed a more intensive appreciation for the nature of things. This chapter explores the emergence of digital and media objects over the course of the twentieth and twenty-first centuries and the way in which archaeology and the emerging field of media archaeology seek to understand the limits and potential of these new forms of objects. The first decades of the twenty-first century have made abundantly clear that the archaeology of the American experience is no longer limited to objects alone but must also acknowledge the relationship between objects and an expansive digital world.

Introduction

A distinct concern for things and materiality emerged in both academic and popular culture during the late twentieth century. These same years produced a growing interest in digital objects characterized by their seeming immateriality, ambiguous relationships to existing media, and capacity for generating significant cultural, economic, and social experiences. The ubiquity of television and radio over the second half of the twentieth century anticipated the digital revolution, which introduced home computers, videogames, and ultimately the internet to American households and communities (Roller 2023). These digital devices produced new forms of cultural artifacts that often sought to obscure their material form and complicate archaeology's traditional bias toward material objects. As a result, they pushed archaeologists to engage a wider range of media artifacts and to consider how immaterial digital objects informed our experience of the material world. The Atari games excavated from the Alamogordo landfill, for example, represented something more than just plastic cartridges encasing silicon chips. Despite the goal of the excavation to recover the physical manifestation of the *E.T.* videogame, the cultural significance of the game was grounded less in its physical form and more in its gameplay, which some critics considered among the worst ever created. Beyond that, the game was a transmedia artifact that relied on the prestige of the blockbuster film by the same name. Further still, digital giant Microsoft funded the excavations as part of a documentary that contributed to their effort to develop the Xbox gaming console as a streaming-media platform. In other words, the material objects at the heart of the excavations, the funding, and goal of the project situated the entire Alamogordo Atari excavation at the intersection of media and archaeology.

Music, Material, and Experience

Micah Bloom's Codex project (Bloom 2017), which we detailed at the conclusion of chapter 3, explored the fate of a distinctive type of physical media cast out of context by the Souris River flood in Minot. Bloom demonstrated how the topics and titles of the abandoned, damaged, and forlorn books created subtle ironies that both emphasized their abject state and communicated the intimate potential of media, even when found in disturbed contexts. In contrast, E. Breck Parkman excavated an assemblage of vinyl records recovered from the burned remains of Rancho Olompali, where the Grateful Dead had lived for two years in 1969 as part of a larger commune. This more controlled context, produced when a fire destroyed the rented mansion, produced a charred assemblage of LP records that offer a particularly vivid window into the recent past (Parkman 2014). This assemblage opened a window onto the band's collecting and listening habits, which included recordings by Judy Garland, Doc Watson, and Frank Sinatra, along with Broadway musicals and various jazz artists. The presence of lead and asbestos in the debris required extensive remediation before archaeologists could document and study the material. Like so many of the books recovered by Bloom's Codex project and the Atari games collected from the Alamogordo landfill, the records were largely unplayable, but nevertheless told the story of the "eclectic and contradictory" tastes of the commune surrounding the Grateful Dead. Parkman noted how the assemblage of records speaks to the diversity of tastes present in the Olompali commune in the late 1960s and complicates a narrow view of late-1960s counterculture.

Physical media, even when unplayable, can provide insights into the social and cultural experiences produced by late twentieth- and early twenty-first-century music. As another more contemporary example, John Schofield and Liam Maloney studied four archives left behind by prominent late twentieth-century disc jockeys in New York and Chicago (Schofield and Maloney 2022): Afrika Bambaataa, Frank Knuckles, Larry Levan, and Ron Hardy. These DJs and the record sets they played not only helped create the club culture in these cities but also shaped the development of hip-hop, house, and other musical genres that relied on sampling. Schofield and Maloney scrutinized the condition of records for efforts to mark or obscure their labels, wear patterns on the album sleeves, and various other indicators that might reveal how the DJs created the sets that made their performances so iconic. In other words, absent recordings of these DJ's performances, the physical marks on the records represent material surrogates. The traces of use in the record archives provide crucial evidence for the development of hip-hop, in the case of Afrika Bambaataa, and queer night club culture in the case of the other DJs. Schofield and Maloney's project remains quite preliminary at present, but they demonstrate a growing interest in using physical media to reconstruct and analyze experience of contemporary music culture.

Efforts to document and understand the traces of performance on the physical media similarly inform John Cherry's, Krysta Ryzewski's, and

Luke J. Pecoraro's work at the Sir George Martin's AIR Studios on the Caribbean island of Monserrat (Cherry et al. 2013). The studio hosted the recording of a number of famous albums from its establishment in Monserrat in 1979, including significant albums by the Police, Duran Duran, Dire Straits, Elton John, and The Rolling Stones. It was abandoned after Hurricane Hugo devastated the island in 1989, and in 1995, the eruption of the Soufrière Hills volcano blasted the studio with a pyroclastic flow, sealing its fate. Since then, the studio has stood in an exclusion zone surrounding the volcano and succumbed to vegetation and the elements. Cherry and colleagues explored the studio space in 2012 and documented its current condition and the dispersal of key elements of the studio—such as its bar, its recording console, and its sound system—around the island and the world. They also reflected briefly on how the studio's distinctive layout, design, location, and recording technology shaped the music that the studio produced. While their efforts to document the studio revealed no recoverable media or direct links to the studio's audible output, the archaeology did emphasize that the compact design of the studio and its location on a small island promoted a kind of intimate and intensive practice that contributed to its iconic standing in the music industry.

Much as the selection of records in the Grateful Dead's collection revealed challenges to our expected pattern of consumption associated with counterculture movement, the list of bands recorded by George Martin at the AIR studio is incomplete but nonetheless reveals the connection between this studio and the status of Monserrat as a British overseas territory. George Martin's locating of the studio on the island was possible in part due to British colonial expansion and its key role in creating the Black Atlantic as a political, cultural, and economic institution. The circulation of Caribbean music produced by Black residents of the British Caribbean and in the Caribbean diaspora in the UK led to its incorporation into the sound of punk and post-punk bands such as the Police, who by the 1980s traveled to the Caribbean to record their music. The appropriation of blues and R&B music by British bands such as the Climax Blues Band, The Rolling Stones, and Dire Straits further traced the spread of Black music beyond its origins in the United States through the sale of records. In the context of the AIR Studios, the genres of music and the lines of influence follow the recursive flow of Black culture through the Atlantic world and complicates the reading of the studio itself. If "sex, drugs, and rock 'n' roll" offered a compelling caricature of the excesses of the American society in the 1970s and 1980s, it is useful to remember that "rock 'n' roll" (like many of the more popular drugs of the same period) often traced long-standing colonial lines of exchange. These patterns of exchange also continued to appropriate the creative forces of the Black Atlantic for the benefit of colonial powers. The physical remains of Martin's AIR studio in Monserrat might ultimately become an important landmark in the island's late twentieth-century history. The media that this studio produced, however, traces a far more global reach and situates the studio in a longer and more complex history of colonial relations, appropriation, and power.

Domestically, Ryzewski's work at the Blue Bird Inn jazz club and the Grande Ballroom in Detroit has emphasized the role that venues play on the experience of music (Ryzewski 2022). The Blue Bird Inn was a Black-owned business that contributed to the life of mid-century segregated Black community in Detroit. As with most live music venues, it both shaped and was shaped by the dominant culture of the day as well as the city's changing economic fortunes. Notably, the Blue Bird Inn was significant for introducing Bebop to the Detroit music scene in the 1940s and contributing the flourishing of the city's distinct postwar jazz sound that integrated bebop with hard bop, blues, R&B, and rock influences. Ryzewski's team collaborated with the Detroit Sound Conservancy to evaluate and preserve the Blue Bird Inn jazz club, at which time they discovered an informal archive of invoices and a payroll ledger from the 1940s. These documents provided a window into the food, drinks, service, and music patrons at the club and the economic realities of running a live music venue. They also revealed how the Dubois sisters, who ran the bar, leveraged social and family networks to staff the inn and relied on regional trade networks to supply the bar with beer, soft drinks, and other mid-century comestibles. Thus, the mid-century music scene, regional commerce, and local and family ties intersected at the Blue Bird Inn to produce an experience for its often-well dressed and convivial patrons. As the city experienced demographic and economic decline and musical tastes changed, the Blue Bird struggled to survive after its mid-century floruit. Jazz venues elsewhere in the Midwest faced similar struggles, as Paul Mullins and Jordan Ryan described in their discussion of Indianapolis' Westside jazz scene (Mullins and Ryan 2020). Economic change, urban renewal, and the destruction of Black urban communities (see chapter 7) left venues and their vibrant culture to succumb to "a slow rotting death." Fortunately, in some cases, organizations such as the Detroit Sound Conservancy, which collaborated with Ryzewski's work, managed an intervention at the Blue Bird Inn, which removed the stage from the venue and its conversion into a display commemorating its significance in the city's music history.

The intimacy of the Blue Bird Inn contrasts with another Detroit venue: the Grande Ballroom. This much-larger performance space hosted big band and later rock acts for nearly a half-century until its abandonment in the 1970s. Today, the outer shell of the building remains a formidable structure in Detroit, but since the turn of the twenty-first century, the roof has collapsed and suspicion has grown that the building might be structurally compromised. Ryzewski's team surveyed the building and determined that despite the collapsing roof, the structure remained structurally stable (Ryzewski 2022). More interesting for our purposes were the traces of past concerts at the venue, including confetti and smoke bombs used to create the venue's famously psychedelic 1960s atmosphere. Ryzewski noted that the use of horsehair plaster in the ballroom's columns may have contributed to the space's distinctive acoustic character by absorbing some of the sound and reducing echoes. Thus, the materiality of the building as well as objects like smoke bombs and confetti shaped the experience of shows in this venue and almost certainly contributed to the fond memories of individuals who want to see the building preserved and revived. In the same way that a DJ's record collection offers a material manifestation of the experience of their performance, the archaeological and architectural evidence of the Grande Ballroom, the Blue Bird Inn, and AIR Studios demonstrate how the material used in the construction of the venues, the personal and commercial networks that supported them, and even global political relationships can leverage the effect of particular musical experiences.

Just as a preoccupation with trash and the interest in things in the wider American experience intersected with their distinctive role in archaeology of the contemporary world, so popular attention to the changing character of media likewise anticipated certain trends in archaeological thinking. As early as the mid-1980s, films such as *Blade Runner* (1982) and novels such as William Gibson's *Neuromancer* (1984) offered visions of the future world where the boundaries between digital media and the experience of a gritty urban reality blurred. Gibson, in particular, anticipated the development of the internet when he set his novel *Neuromancer* partly in a virtual reality world called the "Matrix" that contrasted sharply with the dystopian landscape of the near future. The interplay between futuristic digital culture and an urban backdrop characterized by decay, drugs, and violence created a foundation for the cyberpunk aesthetic. Gibson and

Bruce Sterling's *The Difference Engine* (1990) also imagined "steampunk" media worlds that looked to the past when they proposed an alternative history in which Victorian scientists created technologies based on Charles Babbage's nineteenth-century computers and the radically improved steam engines. The connection between Gibson's and Sterling's punk fantasies and the growing interest in media artifacts is nowhere more apparent than in Sterling's 1995 "Dead Media Project" that sought to document various earlier media technologies. Sterling's project reflected a growing interest in the contrasting styles, genres, and aesthetics between obsolete technologies and the modern digital world.

Archaeologists recognized the conceptual power of the familiar temporal contrasts between digital media and older technologies that often exist side by side in the present. Shannon Lee Dawdy recognized how the complicated interplay of time and media in the cyberpunk, steampunk, and less well-known "clockpunk" genres can inform archaeological thought (Dawdy 2010). She argues that juxtaposition of futuristic, dystopian, and nineteenth-century features at the core of the clockpunk aesthetic evoke Walter Benjamin's *Arcades Project,* which explored the ruins of consumer capitalism in the declining shopping arcades of Paris (Benjamin 2002; Dawdy 2010). Contemporary fiction writers shared Benjamin's interest in complicating the linear flow of modernity and progress and creating worlds where the past and the present intermingle. The attention to the temporal dimension of modern culture resonates both with claims that in the twenty-first century digital technology contributes to the ever accelerating pace of life and calls for "slow" practices in archaeology (Caraher 2019), science (Stengers 2018), and food (Petrini 2006). In other words, our experience of present and the tension between the rapid pace of the digital media and the slower more deliberate pace of the nondigital media create a heightened awareness of the various temporalities at play in the past and in the present.

As we have seen, contemporary critiques of technology and digital media informed popular literature, which shaped archaeological approaches to media. Works like William Gibson's *Neuromancer* and Neal Stephenson's 1992 novel *Snow Crash* trade in a paranoid style anticipated in the science fiction of writers like Philip K. Dick. This distrust for technology as a way to obscure the corrupt nature of capitalism, the modern state, and notions of progress becomes particularly clear in films such as *Tron* (1982 and 2010), *WarGames* (1983), and Terry Gilliam's *Brazil* (1985)—and more recently in the *Matrix* trilogy (1999–2003), the *Jumanji* films (1990–2019), and Steven Spielberg's adaptation of Ernie Cline's *Ready Player One* (2018; Cline 2011). These films pit individuals against technology and various powers that serve to use that technology as a method of control. While the plots, aesthetics, and degree of paranoia vary, they all blur the line between the digital and the physical world as characters are sucked into the mainframe in *Tron*, discover that a simulation on a hacked military supercomputer actually start the countdown to nuclear war in *WarGames*, and find that the search for a "Golden Easter egg" in a complex virtual reality game has consequences in the real world in *Ready Player One*. Thomas Pynchon's 2013 novel *Bleeding Edge*, set in the immediate aftermath of the bursting of the dot-com bubble in 2000 and the 9/11 terrorist attacks of 2001, combines a paranoid vision of the "dark web" with the uncertainty and fear in the immediate aftermath of the terrorist attacks. In the final pages, Pynchon's intrepid investigator Maxine Tarnow spends more and more time in an online virtual reality portal called DeepArcher, which draws from the deep web. As a result, she begins to experience "virtuality creep" as her physical surroundings begin to pixelate and reconfigure themselves as they would in DeepArcher's virtual landscapes. Media archaeologist Jussi Parikka noted that the immateriality of digital culture not only prompted growing attention to things as things but also a corresponding struggle to accommodate the ambiguity of digital objects, experiences, and encounters that work to obscure the very materiality that makes them possible (Parikka 2012: 84–85). As Raiford Guins has argued, digital technologies offer new methods for control (Guins 2009) and surveillance (Zuboff 2019), many of which are invisible to users.

While these films, works of fiction, and critiques may initially appear remote from conventional archaeological practices, as contemporary American culture becomes increasingly mediated by digital technology, archaeology has followed suit. As the examples from the Olompali Ranch and the AIR studies show, archaeologists have increasingly come to consider the role of archaeology in understanding the place of media in both the production and consumption of American culture. In the following section, we will explore how the field of media archaeology and the archaeology of media have contributed to our understanding the material manifestations of our digital world. The rest of the chapter will then consider how archaeology has deployed archaeological methods and practices to the study of digital media. The emergence of "archaeogaming," with its focus on the archaeology "of and in videogames," demonstrates how archaeological methods can serve to document the increasingly complex worlds developed in digital environments (Reinhard 2018). The nostalgia excavated alongside the Atari games in the Alamogordo landfill parallels the growing interest in media as both objects and experiences in our everyday experiences and in our practice as archaeologists of the contemporary world.

Media Archaeology

Over the last decade, the archaeology of the contemporary world has found parallels with "media archaeology," which emerged from the fields of media studies, communication, and cultural studies. Media archaeology as an approach has drawn more from Foucauldian notions of archaeology than from the practices associated with archaeology as a discipline. Foucault developed his use of the term "archaeology" to describe the unconscious rules that govern systems of knowledge and articulated it most clearly in *The Order of Things* (1966[1970]) and *The Archaeology of Knowledge* (1969[1972]). Foucault's methods encouraged media archaeologists to unpack the way in which particular media and technologies came to exist and function within society (Parikka 2012: 6). Siegfried Zielinski, for example, saw Foucault's archaeological approach as a way to discover the deep structures that will shape future media (Bollmer 2015; Zielinski 1996). Among German media theorists, Friedrich Kittler (e.g., 1999) and Wolfgang Ernst (e.g., 2016) encouraged the careful study and preservation of older and obsolete forms of media. This attention to the physical forms of media, especially in the English language work of Finnish scholar Jussi Parikka, found ready overlap with the archaeological interest in modern material culture. While he emphasizes that media archaeology is distinct from disciplinary archaeology, their shared interest in media, technology, and "the material manifestations of culture" (Huhtamo and Parikka 2011; Perry and Morgan 2015: 94) encouraged the cross-pollination of methods and ideas. Michael Schiffer's book on the portable radio (1991), for example, recognized the importance of media technology in both American national identity and economy as well as everyday life. Ian Hodder's early interest in punk fashion and identity in *Symbols in Action* (1982) and Shanks and Tilley's study of beer cans recognized the influence of media—music, television, and advertising—on contemporary experience.

In the twenty-first century, archaeologists of the contemporary world have continued to recognize the significance of media and have drawn on media archaeology to develop more sophisticated readings of the technology that shapes our mediated world. *The Oxford Handbook of the Archaeol-*

ogy of the Contemporary World (2014) included entries on mobile phones (Maxwell and Miller 2014), film (Watkins 2014), drawing (Wickstead 2014), and the internet (Cubbit 2014), authored by archaeologists and media theorists. In 2015, the *Journal of Contemporary Archaeology* included a 150-page forum titled "Media Archaeologies," which brought together media archaeologists and archaeologists of the contemporary world to compare methods and research questions. The contributions emphasized the materiality of our digital mediated world. Colleen Morgan and Sara Perry's "excavation" of a digital hard drive (Perry and Morgan 2015), for example, demonstrates how archaeological methods can serve to document both the hard drive itself as a physical artifact and, as importantly, its content. Perry and Morgan note that the hard drive as physical object lent itself to documentation practices typical to archaeology. The digital media derived from the files on the drive and, of course, from the files on the computer revealed a more expansive "landscape" that required a method more akin to intensive pedestrian survey and its attention to sampling.

The last twenty years saw a number of similar studies focusing on the material, cultural, social, and technological history of videogames. Influential works like Nick Montfort and Ian Bogost's *Racing the Beam* (2009), for example, paid particular attention to the relationship between code, hardware, and the social and cultural expectations of game play. They called this approach "platform studies," and much like media archaeology, the approach emphasized the relationships that create the experience of game play on a particular console. More recent works have expanded the social and physical context for videogames to include their place within notions of domesticity and the challenges associated with the material preservation of game consoles.

The shift of the game console from the public spaces of arcades to the domestic space of the home during the 1970s and 1980s transformed the impact of digital media. Michael Newman's book *Atari Age* (2017) argues that videogames underwent a process of domestication from the early 1970s when *Pong* was introduced to bars and video arcades emerged as the digital equivalents of gaming parlors in the later 1970s. Masculine homosocial bonding practices mediated by alcohol, competition, and often gambling dominated gaming parlors and bars. Game consoles by Fairchild, Magnavox, and eventually Atari brought both the games and the competitive practices associated with gaming parlors into the home. Videogame consoles originally entered the home as new ways to interact with the television, as the names of various consoles, such as the Fairchild "Channel F," suggest. Consoles like the Atari 2600 and the Magnavox Odyssey clad in faux wood finishes blended in with the wood-paneled family rooms and televisions of the 1970s and 1980s, locating videogames within the suburban, middle-class American family room (Newman 2017: 54). Once there, Newman argues that the relationship between the new gaming console and the television challenged the prevailing view of the television as a passive device with little cultural value often marketed to women. Domesticating part of the gaming parlor experience turned the television into an active device. This combined with the popularity of games associated with war (e.g., *Space Invaders, Combat*) and male-dominated sports to transform the television and the family room into a more masculine encoded space characterized by male, homosocial bonding over competition. Thus, both the material objects and the experience of digital media influenced the gender of domestic space. This paralleled the role that the backyard grill played in channeling the ruggedly masculine experiences of camping and outdoor adventure onto the home patio in the 1950s and, in part, created an acceptable way for men to participate in the domestic work frequently associated with the feminine space of the kitchen (Miller 2010). Archaeology of the videogames as both physical objects in a spatial context and as digital experiences contributes to understanding the transformation of domestic space in the postwar decades and anticipates the emergence of the television and gaming console as key components of the twenty-first-century man cave.

A more archaeological approach to the role that physical media played in our experience of digital games emerges in Raiford Guins's work *Game After: A Cultural Study of Videogame Afterlife* (2014). Guins considered, for example, the way in which the art on the cardboard packages of the game contributed to the game experience by clarifying and expanding the rudimentary graphics of early gaming consoles. He argues that to understand the experience of videogames, we must inhabit the intersection of the physical media and the digital experience of game play. While the digital content of games can be preserved to some extent through various emulators that allow for older games to appear on contemporary devices, Guins's study examined curated arcade game collections and the work of game restorers and stressed how the physical character of games contributed to how players experienced gaming. Perhaps the most compelling archaeological aspect of his analysis was his study of the wear marks on game consoles that showed the physical aspects of game play by demonstrating where players and spectators leaned against the cabinets to watch other people play. These marks emphasized the social practice of game play made visible through the traces of interaction left on the machines themselves. Guins was also attentive to the challenges facing museums and collectors in keeping their games working. CRT monitors are no longer manufactured, making it more and more difficult to restore screens. Key features of the devices like buttons and controllers have become increasingly rare, and circuit boards, microchips, and other aspects of the games' inner workings are essentially irreplaceable. Ironically, efforts to preserve these complex machines often limit access to the games, which may well help protect them from wear and tear but also further removes them from their dynamic social and cultural context.

The relationship between the physicality of the object and the expansive world accessible through the object also finds parallels in the study of mobile phones. Cassie Newland's pioneering master's thesis at the University of Bristol (2004) concisely explored relations among technology, legislation, practice, and even protests associated with mobile phones in the UK. Newland argues that mobile phones created new forms of social organization grounded in practices like texting as well as resistance to the encroaching of cellphone towers, for example, among groups concerned with the adverse impact of radio frequency radiation. Richard Maxwell and Tory Miller's (2014) chapter on mobile phones in the *Oxford Handbook* similarly emphasized the freedom associated with mobile phones, but also contrasts this with the new forms of surveillance possible through mobile technology and the environmental damage required to produce the range of materials present in each device. Moreover, mobile phones created new forms of social relations and practices in ways loosely similar to how digital games transported certain elements of the gaming parlor experience into the domestic spaces of the home. In all these cases, the experience of technology goes well beyond the materiality of the devices alone and requires an understanding of the often intangible digital media to recognize its social and cultural significance (see also Morgan 2022: 218).

The tension between the materiality of digital devices and the seemingly immaterial media is productive. Maxwell and Miller provide a depressing litany of environmental and social damage produced by mobile phones, ranging from increases in power consumption to the risk of cellphone towers to wildlife, the use of toxic chemicals in manufacturing, and the social and environmental damage associated with extractive industries necessary for our digital devices. Scott Schwartz's innovative *Archaeology of Temperature* (2021) describes how the ubiquitous public displays of temperature at sites throughout New York normalizes the role of numbers within our contemporary experience. Schwartz argues that converting the experience of heat and cold into numbers in the Early Modern period paralleled development of financial mechanisms that support contemporary capitalism. The effort to quantify risk, labor, experience, and eventually human life is manifest in the banal appearance of public temperature displays that draw our attention to consumer culture through their presence on billboards. The more sophisticated displays that include forecasts, such as those mounted on bus shelters in New York, rely on significant computer processing power, which not only depends on expansive networks of extractive industries with their obvious human and environmental costs but also constantly produce greenhouse gases. In short, numbers, code, and digital technology mediate the experience of being in contemporary New York. These same numbers and displays require and make possible global networks of physical and environmental exploitation.

Archaeological approaches that locate the contemporary American experience within a broader network of material, processes, and relationships coincide with a similar interest among media archaeologists. Jussi Parikka's book on the *Geology of Media* (2015), for example, considers digital media as both figurative and literal expressions of geology. Figuratively, Parikka plays on the concept of stratigraphy to understand how digital devices reflect layers of time and technologies densely superimposed on one another to create a functional surface. Literally, Parikka's emphasis on geology recognizes the complex cocktail of minerals necessary to make our digital tools work. Key rare earth minerals such as tantalum and coltan come from mines in Congo worked by children toiling under inhumane conditions (Maxwell and Miller 2014: 709). Lithium, gallium, indium, platinum, and other rare and expensive elements require large-scale extractive industries that function on a global scale and at a significant environmental and social cost. The microchips and cases are manufactured and assembled in factories that rely on dormitory labor in free-trade zones in China, which have their own history of exploitative practices, suicides, and abuse. Josh Lepawsky's *Reassembling Rubbish* (2018) makes the materiality of digital media even more explicit when he considers the weight of the internet. He contrasts the observation made in *Discover* magazine in 2007 that the internet weighed only "0.2 millionth of an ounce" (Cass 2007) with arguments that weighing the internet must take into account more than just the electrons that carry messages, but also the massive infrastructure that processes, transmits, powers, receives, and stores the digital data. Even the most immaterial media require a massive material infrastructure (Hodder 2014), and the weight of this infrastructure rests heavily on the American experience.

Returning to themes broached in chapter 2, we can consider how digital media nevertheless produce waste and byproducts associated with manufacturing, maintenance, and distribution of the networks and devices on a global scale. The materials themselves leave traces in bodies and landscapes both in the United States and around the world. Silicon Valley, California, has become synonymous with advances in digital technology and American innovation, and recent work has shown a growing awareness of the impact of digital technology on the landscape. Christine Finn's early archaeological study of Silicon Valley (2002), for example, emphasized how the growth of the technology industry in the region impacted land use with fruit orchards giving way to glass and steel corporate buildings, strip malls, and suburbs. Significantly, she also includes a chapter on the rise of businesses that managed the waste produced from the high-speed research and manufacturing cycle associated with digital technology. A decade later, Jennifer Gabrys's book *Digital Rubbish* (2011) starts with a discussion of the same landscape but emphasizes the twenty Superfund sites associated with former microprocessor manufacturing sites in the region. She demonstrates that the slim, convenient, and almost invisible digital devices that define our contemporary experiences produce a tremendous quantity of waste during their dispersed development and manufacturing cycles. Moreover, these devices, in some ways, are designed to become waste almost as quickly as they produce technological advancements. Devices scheduled for obsolescence move seamlessly from use assemblages into various states of provisional discard and global flows of waste.

If archaeology of the contemporary world has its historical foundation in the study of garbage (chapter 2) and consumption (chapter 3), then the archaeology of contemporary digital experience requires a global purview to understand relations among production, use, reuse, recycling, and discard. As Joshua Lepawsky has noted, however, tracking these flows of waste requires careful attention not only to the range of physical contexts where digital objects appear but also to the blurry categories that define their status. Efforts by global organizations concerned with the flow of digital waste from North America and Europe to Africa and Southeast Asia have revealed the complexity of these flows. Computers, for example, classified as waste in one context may reenter the market in other places after being reconditioned and repaired. Discarded technology might retrace the flow of distribution as ships arriving from China or South Korea filled with containers offer discounted rates for containers on the return trip. Devices slightly damaged during shipping or transported for repair may be classified as waste in one place even if they remain fully functional or can be easily returned to working order.

The complex character of the global flows of digital objects and media reflects the challenges associated with an archaeology of the intense connectivity at the heart of contemporary American society. In effect, archaeology of the contemporary American experience requires us to document and understand production and consumption practices on a global level. The modern middens produced from our industrialized, high-tech culture are as likely to be found in the heart of Silicon Valley as in garbage dumps in the developing world or in the New Mexico desert. By tracing the flows of digital technology at a global scale, we also recognize the complex temporal contexts that define modern technology. As Gabrys and Lepawsky have demonstrated, digital devices not only have complicated lives in which they can move in and out of blurry categories such as use, waste, discard, and reuse, but the devices themselves have multiple temporalities within them as old technologies like transistors function alongside microchips, and older standards—such as RCA—exist next to the latest protocols (Graves-Brown 2014). The simultaneous popularity of vinyl records, vacuum tube–powered amplifiers, complex new forms of digital encoding for media and music files and even more powerful processors, more precise clocks, and faster and more robust wireless protocols offers a model for understanding how contemporary audio combines technologies developed over the past century. In this regard, the spatial and temporal character of the media landscape requires an archaeological practice more akin to surface survey and its encounters with multiple temporalities existing on a contemporary surface. In this regard, media archaeology and the archaeology of media technologies parallels Rodney Harrison's call for an archaeology of the contemporary world that embraces temporal complexity (Harrison 2011).

Archaeogaming

The physical components of digital technologies may represent the most obvious object for archaeological research, but the hardware, circuits, cabinets, cases, infrastructure, and context contribute only one aspect to the place of videogames in the contemporary American experience. Videogames, in particular, represent a significant component of American culture. They occupy the increasingly blurry space as transmedia franchises in which films, book, and games develop interrelated plot lines, characters, and worlds that extend to toys, clothing, and other products. Games like *Mortal Combat*, for example, have inspired films, and film franchises like *Star Wars, Tomb Raider, E.T.,* and *Indiana Jones* have led to videogames. The beloved Danish toy company Lego has spawned both videogame and film tie-ins that involve iconic characters such as Batman portrayed through Lego blocks and appearing across multiple platforms. The increasing ubiquity of videogames in American life has given rise to a wide range of critical voices who take games seriously as cultural products—from Ian Bogost's widely read reviews of games (e.g., Bogost 2015) to treatments of games that consider their role in promoting certain values, practices, and notions of play (e.g., Dyer-Witheford and de Peuter 2009; Crogan 2011; Paul 2018; Muriel and Crawford 2018). Moreover, scholars have recognized videogames as art (e.g., see Clarke and Mitchell 2013), forms of literature, and film, with their own distinct narrative potential (Cremin 2016; Kerner and Hoxter 2019; Jayemanne 2018), and as unique ways of experiencing time and understanding the past (e.g., Watrall 2002; Champion 2015; Hanson 2018).

While videogames have received critical attention for decades, the role of archaeology in the study of videogames has emerged more recently. In part, archaeology's interest in games has revealed that any understanding of the material manifestations of digital media requires us to study digital media itself. This presents challenges that archaeology has long encountered in more traditional environments. Digital media, for example, have proven to be particularly ephemeral. As streaming music, books, and games becomes increasingly common, digital content can disappear from a consumer's collection without a trace. Archaeology has long cultivated methods designed to document ephemeral relationships, media, and experiences in the field. Archaeologists seek to identify even the faint traces of earlier formation processes, even as more recent processes work to obscure these traces. Archaeologists likewise concern themselves with recovering or, at the very least, attempting to imagine relationships among past technologies, practices, and experience. As Raiford Guins has shown, vintage cabinet games remain difficult to preserve and maintain. Further complicating our ability to understand and recover the experience of game play is that even older games remain valuable intellectual property. As a result, copyright restrictions often complicate efforts to preserve, maintain, or reproduce the code and the technologies necessary for gameplay. Recently, archaeological approaches to documenting digital media, particularly games, through careful description of digital worlds, landscapes and game play, attention to social and cultural context, code, and technologies have produced a small but thriving field of "archaeogaming."

Archaeogaming has sought to explore the potential of archaeology to document videogames. Andrew Reinhard (2018, 2019) has used a range of archaeological methods to document computer games as archaeological objects and spaces (see Rassalle 2021 for a recent survey). In his dissertation, he demonstrated the potential for using archaeological reasoning to disentangle the multiple strata of code developed to run the computer game *Colossal Cave Adventure.* Created by William Crowther in the mid-1970s, this early game, originally designed to run on a mainframe computer, has been continuously modified by programmers for over forty years. Reinhard used a suite of contemporary programs to explore the metadata, to compare the various bodies of code, and to quantify changes over time. In this regard, he embraced the work of computer scientists such as John Aycock who, in turn, followed the call of Ian Bogost (2011) to study computer code as a way to unpack the technological and social practices that produced these games (Aycock 2016). In his 2016 book, Aycock called this "retrogame archaeology" and situated it at the intersection of computer science and media archaeology. By following a similar method, Reinhard was able to identify some of the original code base that persisted despite the move to more modern programming languages necessary to make the game function on home computers and eventually on the web. He also situated the code socially by developing a prosopography of the programmers who developed the game. He noted that most of the programmers were males based in either the United States or Europe. He also recognized that the music programmed into early versions of the game remains relatively unchanged in terms of the code, but would have sounded quite different as computer audio technologies developed over time. The stratigraphy of code for *Colossal Cave Adventure* deployed archaeological sensibilities and metaphors and techniques from the digital humanities to understand both the development of a long-running game and the changing experience of game play.

The relationship between professional archaeological practices and those depicted in educational games such as "Adventures in Fugawiland: A Computer Simulation in Archaeology" (1990) or popular videogames like *Tomb Raider* and *Raiders of the Lost Ark* is relatively straightforward.

Professional archaeologists have debated the relative merits of glamorizing fictional characters who violated many of our discipline's core ethical positions by looting archaeological sites (Watrall 2002; Holtorf 2005; Meyers and Reinhard 2016; Reinhard 2018: 72–74) and the potential for games to simulate archaeological fieldwork or ancient landscapes (Morgan 2009; Mol et al. 2016). The ability to manipulate characters as avatars in videogames produces a sense of agency that allows players to encounter methodological challenges, architecture and objects, and, of course, to make decisions that reveal the limits both of the games themselves and of our understanding of archaeology. It became possible, for example, to play games in such a way as to subvert their intentions (although this does not always make for an entertaining game). Reinhard's critique of open-ended games like *Elder Scrolls Online* reveal how game designers understood the place of archaeology and museums. The museum in the game displayed objects relevant to the in-game narrative, and these formed the basis for various quests that users could choose to pursue in more or less ethical ways (Reinhard 2018: 83–86). Reinhard documents how engaging the quest in an ethical way by recovering relics and turning them into the museum reveals that the quest was a complex hoax and the artifacts worthless. The cynical view of archaeology presented in the game was apparent only to players who completed the quest in an ethical way by depositing the relics in the museum. Whether this is a commentary on the ethically complicated character of modern archaeological practices and museums remains unclear in the game, but Reinhard's description certainly leaves that possibility open.

The most ambitious effort in archaeogaming involved documenting a procedurally created world in the game *No Man's Sky*. This space-based videogame produced an almost infinite number of worlds populated with strange creatures, ruins, artifacts, and technologies. Moreover, various updates to the game, after some disappointing initial reviews, created a series of intriguing glitches where graphics associated with older versions of the game were visible or displaced in updated versions. Reinhard and a team of archaeogamers initiated a project dubbed the "*No Man's Sky* Archaeological Survey" and developed methods to document this virtual world through a series of surveys conducted on a number of the procedurally generated planets. This work prompted an ethical discussion on archaeogaming, which manifested itself as a code of ethics written by Catherine Flick and L. Meghan Dennis, published as an appendix to Reinhard's 2018 book (Flick et al. 2018). The relations among games as culture, the material culture in games, and the role of in-game rules, ownership, agency, and ethical judgment in games pushes archaeologists to consider both the definitions of archaeological practice and the context for ethical behavior in the discipline (Graham 2020). If a game is a site suitable for research, it also becomes a place to reflect on the ethics of archaeological practice as they relate to the intent of the game designer, the rights of other players, and disciplinary responsibilities to document, preserve, and report our work. To this end, Reinhard archived the results of his NMSAS with the Archaeological Data Service in the UK to ensure that the documentation of the game and its sites is preserved irrespective of the fate of the game itself (Reinhard 2019).

For now, it would appear that the larger implications of archaeogaming on the traditional haunts of historical archaeology remain unclear, but hints abound. For example, Angus Mol and Aris Politopoulos's recent article brought archaeology's scrutiny of colonialism and Eurocentrism to bear on Orientalist tropes in Sid Meier's popular *Civilization* series of videogames (2021). Similar work has critiqued the ethical standards advanced in games such as *Tomb Raider* (Dennis 2016) and celebrated the potential of games to overturn gendered perceptions of archaeologists (Hageneuer 2021). Such research demonstrates the potential of critical attention to games as a way to understand and perhaps even influence how videogames shape views of the present, the past, and the discipline of archaeology. Archaeogaming, then, takes seriously videogames as sites of material experiences, and this makes them susceptible to archaeological methods to document game play, games, and even code. This work contributes to the analysis and preservation of videogames as digital media and extends our notion of the built environment from the physical spaces of our material world to the graphic spaces of the virtual world. In the context of the Alamogordo landfill, the recovery of Atari game cartridges discarded in the landfill is only part of the story in understanding the place of videogames within the American experience. Archaeologists are only starting to develop the tools and approaches necessary to recognize the relationship between the material and immaterial world and to understand how this relationship defines our encounters with a growing array of digital technologies and media that shape our culture.

Digital Archaeology

Even if archaeogaming has only begun to contribute to the critical analysis of the contemporary American experience, there is no doubt that greater attention to media and digital technology has come to shape how archaeologists work. As noted in previous chapters, archaeology of the contemporary world embraces archaeology as both a method of studying the present and a window into contemporary attitudes and materiality. Thus archaeology itself is an object of study for archaeology of the contemporary world, and digital practices in archaeology reflect changing attitudes toward media. The scholarship on how archaeologists use media is vast, and expanding rapidly with the development of novel digital technologies and media (for recent surveys see Garstki 2020, Champion 2021, Morgan 2022). I will not attempt to provide exhaustive treatment but will highlight recent scholarship that demonstrates how archaeology as a discipline is taking media seriously. Sara Perry framed this conversation by calling for archaeologists to be more explicit, deliberate, and transparent in their use of media and recognizing how media—from photography to published maps, digitally manipulated images, and the latest 3D scans—play a central role in the production of archaeological knowledge (Perry 2009).

Archaeologists have long recognized that archaeological knowledge requires deliberate mediation, as information acquired in the field appears in articles, book, websites, databases, maps, plans, and reconstructions. Michael Shanks and his colleagues, for example, have emphasized media in archaeology as both an object of critical study itself but also as the vehicle through which traces of the past appear in the present. By turning attention to the creative processes associated with the mediation, translation, and distribution of the past, they encouraged archaeologists to become more critical and aware of the tools, technologies, processes, and techniques we use to represent traces of the past in the present (Shanks 2007). Yannis Hamilakis and Fotis Ifantidis (2015) called photography and archaeology "collateral devices of modernity" in recognition of the parallel development of the discipline and the media. This approach, in which media dictate the kind of knowledge archaeology can produce, has offered a key critical perspective on digital practices in the discipline as well. As Shanks and Chris Witmore (2012) point out in their long review of a 2011 book titled *Archaeology 2.0: New Approaches to Communication and Collaboration* (Kansa, Kansa, and Watrall 2011), digital technology continues this parallel trajectory with disciplinary practice by creating new conditions through which the past persists. Kevin Garstki and Adam Rabinowitz have noted that as digital 3D imaging of archaeological objects becomes easier, cheaper, and more ubiquitous, archaeologists have increasingly problematized the relationship between the digital model and the artifact

(Garstki 2017; Rabinowitz 2015). Issues of authenticity, for example, rest on understanding how 3D images produce a sense of pastness that makes the model a compelling alternative to the artifact, but also prevents the 3D image from replacing the artifact as the object of study. The preservation of information related to the creation of the digital model, the context in which the digital model exists, and the visual character of the 3D model all contribute to our reception of the digital object as a situational stand-in for the artifact itself. In other words, critical attention to media, digital and otherwise, is crucial not only for archaeologists interested in media archaeology or methods but for how the discipline understands and recognizes the past itself. Taken further, Leslie McFayden and Dan Hicks offer the provocative concept of "photology," "which collapses the distinction between media and object, and between photography and archaeology" (McFadyen and Hicks 2020). By eliminating the distinction between photography and archaeology, they reconceptualize archaeological practice as media rather than mediated. Critical attention to photography—and we can add the wide range of emergent digital practices from remote sensing, 3D imaging, and the construction of virtual and augmented reality—emphasizes how all media practices are irreducible elements of archaeology as a discipline. Thus "media archaeology," for all its claims of disciplinary independence, may be inseparable from archaeology itself.

The consistent appearance of visual essays in recent volumes dedicated to archaeology of the contemporary world suggests that archaeologists have come to understand the centrality media in producing archaeological knowledge, especially as part of an archaeology of the contemporary world (Breithoff 2021; De León 2015; Andreassen 2014; Camp et al. 2021). Micah Bloom's photographs of books in the aftermath of the Minot flood explored in the previous chapter represented an archaeological approach that did not rely on a formal archaeological method. My coauthor and I introduced a photo essay to our archaeological study of the Bakken oil patch (Caraher and Weber 2017) and collaborated with photographers and mixed media artists throughout our work of documenting workforce housing in North Dakota (Cassidy 2016; Holmgren 2016). The goal of working with photographers was to foreground visual documentation as diverse practices with distinctive outcomes that were in no way objective or separate from our creative and interpretative work. In effect, the photographs of Cassidy and Cullen (see Caraher and Weber 2017) and the mixed media works of Holmgren are set in parallel to our texts, not as supplements or illustrations but as alternate readings of the same situation. In many ways, this approach parallels Elin Andreassen's photographic work at the abandoned Soviet mining town of Pyramiden (Andreassen et al. 2010), her contribution documenting the harbor at Olsen and Pétursdóttir's *Ruin Memories* (2014), and Yannis Hamilakis and Fotis Ifantidis's use of photography as a form of ethnography and archaeology in Greece (Hamilakis and Ifantidis 2016; Ifantidis 2013). By minimizing the use of text in these works, the photographs invite and produce interpretative choices and views that superimposes the past in the photograph and the photographer's presence.

The renewed attention to media in archaeology extends to practice as well. Colleen Morgan (2016; Morgan and Wright 2018), Sara Perry (2014), and others (Leighton 2015; Mickel 2015) have shown how the move from analogue to digital recording, for example, revealed key changes in archaeological labor practices and the character of archaeological knowledge. For instance, the physical movement of the archaeologist when manipulating a tablet in the field, using a total station, GPS, or laser scanning rig, or appealing to a digitized map on a phone is a far different enterprise than trying to find oneself on a map flapping in the wind, measuring a building with tape and line levels, or drawing by hand on graph paper or mylar. The drive for efficient archaeological practices has created the potential for "slow archaeology," which explores the changes in archaeological work and analysis effected by digital tools and media. The changing character of embodied knowledge in archaeological practices as fieldworkers move from hiking across the landscape to mining LiDAR data and piloting drones will invariably shape the kind of research questions and results that the discipline produces. Likewise, the use of crowdsourcing, drone images, and other forms of distributed and remote data collection have led to new ways to produce archaeological knowledge at a large scale, but have also given rise to critiques of colonialism, exploitation of labor, and technosolutionism (see the special issue of the *Journal of Field Archaeology* edited by Van-Valkenburgh and Dufton [2020]).

Conclusion

The conclusion to this chapter also closes the first part of the book. In these initial four chapters, we have sought to unpack key concepts in the history of the archaeology of the contemporary world and to provide a context for the Atari games excavated from the Alamogordo landfill. The archaeology of contemporary garbage, the ongoing conversation about things and consumer culture, and the emerging significance of media both in and for archaeological work developed at the intersection of archaeology and contemporary American culture. These developments in the field both paralleled and interrogated significant moments in the American experience: the so-called garbage crisis of the 1970s, the growing critique of consumerism in the 1980s, and the embrace of digital technology at the turn of the twenty-first century. The recursive relationship between the American experience and the emerging field of the archaeology of the contemporary world means that studying the development of the field is every bit as significant for understanding the character of American society over the last fifty years as are the material and immaterial culture that the archaeology of the contemporary world takes as the object of its inquiry.

This recursive critique of the American experience provides a context for the excavation at the Alamogordo landfill. The excavation revealed the detritus produced by a small southwestern city, and, although we were not able to explore it systematically, the assemblage included artifacts consistent with late twentieth-century consumer culture. From celebrity posters to housewares, beer cans, catalogues, newspapers, broken household plastics, and holiday wrapping paper, the landfill itself embodied consumption practices of the city of Alamogordo that parallel the national markets. The material in this landfill, however, also spoke to the post-depositional processes that created unstable scarps, noxious smells, and harmful gases. These processes, ironically, made it truly difficult to study the landfill in a safe and responsible way. In short, the excavation of a contemporary landfill exposed us directly to the material challenges of doing archaeology of and in the contemporary world. The Alamogordo landfill's chemical and structural volatility demonstrated how the processes that remove post-consumer waste create spaces whose very materiality resisted analysis and interpretation. Sites like the Alamogordo landfill exist outside the American experience by design. As Michael Thompson's classic study *Rubbish Theory* postulated, the removal of the games from the experience of American life through their time in the landfill allowed them to acquire a new status that quite literally clung to their physicality. The smell, the damage done to the cartridges, and the certificate of authenticity all reinforce the provenience of the games, which enabled them to follow a trajectory from trash to treasure. The marginalization of modern trash deposits allowed the games to pass sufficiently out of mind and circulation, so that they could acquire a new value and cultural significance.

The use of the Alamogordo landfill as the dumping ground for Atari games also anticipated recent literature that has stressed how the disposal of e-waste is a global industry. Marginal spaces like a small city in the New Mexico desert became appealing sites for the bulk deposition of corporate e-waste for both economic and regulatory reasons. This coincided with a broader view of the American West as empty space suitable for the disposal of a range of toxic and radioactive waste. In this way, the practice looked ahead to dumping e-waste in South Asia and Africa in the twenty-first century where objects manufactured with material extracted from the Global South would return to the Global South when no longer useful. The deposit also revealed the international and national networks of manufacturing, distributing, and disposing of Atari games. The distributed origins of the American experience expanded from the regional networks that supplied comestible at the Blue Bird Inn to global networks of trade and manufacturing required to fill our offices, pantries, and homes. Objects such as the Atari cartridges represent relationships that extend well beyond the national borders. We can thus see how Congolese miners, Chinese assembly line workers, Filipino ship crews, midwestern retailers, and Nigerian landfill scavengers encounter and participate in a globalized American experience that supports our consumer culture. In the 1980s, the emergence of these global networks contributed to how Atari gaming consoles reshaped middle-class American domestic space. In the twenty-first century, the glass screen of the modern cellphone represents the best metaphor for this distributed experience. Designed to allow us experiences that are materially present in the palm of our hand and infinitely expansive through the images that appear on the transparent glass screen, they make manifest the distributed nature of contemporary culture. The Atari games excavated from the Alamogordo landfill, then, tell the story of how the supply chains, e-waste, and a small-town dump create the backbone of the late twentieth-century American experience.

Discard practices and the distributed character of American experience represent the material components of the Atari deposit in Alamogordo, and in many ways, this emphasis coincides with archaeology's traditional interest in things and materiality. When most of us think of Atari, however, we tend to think of the digital worlds that videogames created. Even with the comparatively primitive graphics of the *E.T.* game and its unforgiving gameplay, the Atari game allowed players in the 1980s to transform the passive experience of watching television or films into an active encounters with characters, plots, and settings. The emergence of media archaeology explicitly considers how the games themselves operated at the intersection of various media forms. This relationship between the games and the blockbuster films *E.T.* and *Raiders of the Lost Ark* amplified their significance and generated excitement in anticipation of their release. Moreover, the excitement surrounding these transmedia artifacts coincided with a growing interest in blurring of boundaries between media experiences and the physical world in movies such as *Tron* and novels such as William Gibson's *Neuromancer*. The excavation of the *E.T.* games in a project funded by Microsoft and streamed through the company's Xbox gaming console leveraged the nostalgia for Atari games to promote the latest transmedia platform. The work of archaeogaming specialists both at the excavation and in the wider field of videogame archaeology demonstrates how both the physical and digital artifacts associated with contemporary media co-constitute the distinctive experiences. Whether these encounters in digital space traced by the global reach of the internet are sufficiently spatialized in the physical world to constitute a distinctly "American experience" remains to be seen. What is more clear is that manufacturing, discard, and our interconnected digital world present new opportunities for archaeology to interrogate the present and future of physical and digital objects.

II

5

Borders, Migrants, and Homelessness
at the Edge of the American Experience

The first part of the book began at the edge of the Alamogordo landfill and explored the intersection of waste, consumer culture, and things in American society. In this second part, we step back from objects and their movement from things desired to things discarded, and shift our attention to the materiality of particular situations that define key parts of the American experience. The remainder of this book is an extended case study based on my work with the North Dakota Man Camp Project. This project documented the social and material conditions in workforce housing in western North Dakota's Bakken oil patch as a window into the history and archaeology of a twenty-first-century oil boom. Extractive industry booms represent a quintessentially American experience inscribed in popular culture, ranging from Upton Sinclair's novel *Oil!* (1926–1927, and its loose film adaptation *There Will Be Blood* [2007]) to the *Beverly Hillbillies* and *Dallas*. Over the last thirty years, however, images of burning oil wells set against the backdrop of the wartime desert and a growing surge of climate-change fiction have complicated domestic fantasies of abrupt wealth backed by spewing gushers.

The oil crisis of the 1970s served as a stark reminder that oil is fundamental to the American way of life (and, indeed, the modern world) while at the same time intensifying the global character of the American experience. Over the next four chapters, we will trace both the American and global situations that informed how we understood the phenomena witnessed in western North Dakota. These chapters seek to contextualize the contemporary Bakken oil boom, which peaked in 2014, amid ongoing conversations in archaeology, history, and the social sciences. Like the first part of the book, these chapters represent an extended case study that considers the Bakken both as a distinctly American experience and as representative of global trends. For example, our work in the Bakken examined how temporary and sometimes improvised workforce housing opened another chapter in the history of camps. Camps represent a distinctly modern form of settlement designed to accommodate, but also to control, groups displaced from more permanent housing. Historically, forms of temporary housing have served to impose order on members of the military, college students, guest workers, protesters, and migrants who occupy precarious legal, social, and economic positions. The proliferation of temporary housing reflects the growing mobility of populations and contributes to how we understand international borders, the transformation of American and global urbanism, and the creation of new forms of industrial and post-industrial landscapes. The growing archaeological interest in these issues, in turn, contributed to how we understood the Bakken as an example of an American experience and provided lenses through which we could disentangle the myriad objects that constitute the contemporary situation. The next four chapters will follow a trajectory similar to the first four but in reverse order. In other words, the next four chapters culminate in a description of our work in the Bakken. This approach begins not with objects recovered from excavations (no matter how unconventional) and instead starts with the more spatially and chronologically expansive contexts. Migrant and homeless camps, university campuses, and military bases provide diachronic surface assemblages that provide distinct insights into matters of control and resistance within the experience of contemporary American capitalism, nationalism, and society. Anchoring the second part of this book in the work of the North Dakota Man Camp Project will trace an argument that juxtaposes the American experiences with the global phenomena of climate change, the Anthropocene, and a post-human world.

Chapter 5 begins at the margins to consider how they play a role in defining the center of the American experience. In 2011, in the early days of the Bakken oil boom, many workers found themselves living around the edges of established communities in western North Dakota. Unable to find housing in the small towns already flooded by workers hoping for new jobs and a new life in the Bakken, workers lived in cars, in tents set up in parks, and in campers nestled into farm shelter belts. As housing caught up with the influx of workers, the formal workforce housing sites and RV parks set up for workers still stood apart from the towns and settlements of the region and reinforced the status of the precarious workforce as both temporary and outsiders. That said, local communities sought to control the number and distribution of workforce housing sites and, whenever possible, to encourage workers to buy permanent homes in the region. Workers, however, often arrived in the Bakken having been displaced from their homes in other regions by the subprime mortgage crisis of 2008. As a result, they lacked enthusiasm or the means to settle permanently. Moreover, they sometimes struggled to even afford an apartment or RV lot in the Bakken's overheated housing market. In the absence of more conventional housing arrangements, some workers tried to create a sense of community in RV parks and modified their RVs and trailers in ways that both accommodated the requirements of working in the Bakken and evoked an image of suburban life they had left behind or was out of reach.

To be clear, defining the mostly American workers who arrived in the Bakken and lived in temporary "man camps" as marginalized requires some qualification. For example, comparing these workers to the undocumented migrants, refugees, and the homeless runs the risk of confusing the similarities of form with similarities in situation. At the same time, the experiences of borders, migrants, and the homeless in some ways serve to define the limits of a normative national, middle-class existence that continues to characterize the "American Dream." In this context, efforts to manage movement across borders through increasinly rigorous border controls reflects a desire to control experiences that threaten to destabilize the idea of the nation by transgressing its borders. National borders contribute to both the idea of the nation and, even just by extension, some aspects of what it means to live an American life. Border controls can include holding undocumented migrants who defy borders without proper documentation in "states of exception," where they are outside and unprotected by any legal standing (Agamben 1995; De León 2015: 27–28; Hamilakis 2016). Communities often seek to deprive the homeless from the benefits of full citizenship as they develop policies designed to criminalize the visible presence of homelessness in urban areas and to limit access of the homeless to public space. For many communities, the visibility of homeless individuals complicates notions of prosperity, opportunity, and progress. Policing for vagrancy and loitering demonstrates how having a permanent place to live remains crucial for enjoying full rights and protections (e.g., Desmond 2016). In this chapter, we consider the archaeology of migrants and the homeless in an effort to understand how archaeology of the contemporary world can shed critical light on individuals whose place on the margins trace the limits to the normative American experience.

Introduction

It is commonplace to hear that digital technology and supply chain logistics have erased borders and linked the margins with the core through unprecedented levels of global connectivity. At the same time, the global refugee crisis has demonstrated that this digital, cultural, and economic connectivity is unequally distributed. It remains possible for the material present in a digital device to cross national borders far more easily than any of the myriad individuals associated with its manufacturing. As discussed in chapter 3, the miners for rare earth in Congo and the workers on the assembly line in China would find it difficult to follow the devices that they make possible on their global route. In fact, policies that allow goods and capital to flow freely on a global scale are often tied to policies that limit the movement of labor and work to create pools of poor, low-cost workers who can ensure high profits on the lower-cost goods enjoyed by European, North American, and Asian consumers. These barriers to the movement of individuals have created a crisis for undocumented migrants. Decades of warfare and economic sanctions, climate change, and the growing disparities of wealth precipitated the so-called refugee crisis, which brought new attention to the movement of people across borders on a global scale (Hamilakis 2016). In many ways, the plight of migrants at national borders throws into relief an American experience dependent upon pools of low-cost labor and the unimpeded flow of goods and resources. Moreover, the global refugee crisis is a manifestation of military interventions designed to preserve the nation-state as an institution and to support the extraction of resources. National interests and borders further exacerbate the environmental, economic, and social stress created by global climate change and generates both human and nonhuman migrants on a growing scale.

Attention to borders and, more importantly, the movement of individuals across these political boundaries reinforces Stacey Camp's assertion that the American experience goes well beyond the legal limits of citizenship (Camp 2013). In other words, you need not be American to partake of the U.S. experience. In fact, you need not even be in the United States. This realization has inspired significant work on the social, political, and material contexts of immigration, forced and undocumented migration, and refugees in North America. It has also coincided with a growing interest in borders and sovereignty among archaeologists, historians, and thinkers in globalization in the late twentieth century. Works such as Michael Hardt and Antonio Negri's *Empire* (2000) advanced new perspectives on the location of authority and capital in the twenty-first-century world when they argued that stateless entities ranging from terrorists to multinational corporations were poised to challenge the power of the sovereign nation-state. The American response to the 9/11 terrorist attacks in 2001 appeared to confirm some of Hardt and Negri's ideas of empire. These attacks triggered a period of heightened anxiety about immigration and border security in the United States manifested in the newly created Department of Homeland Security. Fifteen years later, President Donald Trump's campaign promise to build a wall along the Mexican border and, when president, his implementation of travel bans from a number of Muslim-majority countries further foregrounded the role of borders in divisive discussions of race, national sovereignty, and domestic politics. The racial tensions that erupted in protests and violence in the summer of 2020 provided vivid evidence of how borders intensify racial divisions that cut through American society and reinforce social, economic, and political inequalities.

These inequalities have contributed to the global increase in migrants and persistence of homelessness in the United States. Saskia Sassen has observed that domestic homelessness and global migrants as forms of "expulsions" are part of an assemblage of institutions, policies, and practices that exist at the heart of capitalism and the nation-state (Sassen 2014). On the global scale, expulsions frequently involve the combination of multinational corporate interests, various global financial institutions such as the World Bank and the IMF, and the military capacities of the nation-state. This assemblage of forces and institutions functions in different ways in different contexts. In some cases, these forces work to undermine local economies by introducing global standards or expanding the reach of international markets. In other cases, the state proffers military intervention to support extractive industrials like oil production or the route of an oil pipeline, as in the case of the Dakota Access Pipeline in North Dakota. The displacement of Syrians, Iraqis, and Kurds from the Middle East, for example, reflected the willingness of the European and American military forces to intervene on behalf of the global oil industry in the name of U.S. economic security. The displacement of people from Central and South America likewise reflects the intersection of the geopolitics of nation-states and global economic interests.

In the United States, the subprime mortgage crisis represented another example of how an assemblage of financial, political, and social forces led to the displacement of individuals through the mechanism of foreclosure (Sassen 2014). In this sense, Sassen's arguments parallel those of Matthew

Desmond, best known for his 2016 book *Evicted. Evicted* follows the lives of several individuals in Milwaukee, Wisconsin, as they endure eviction, homelessness, and transience and encounter structural and institutional barriers that prevent them from finding stable housing. Desmond argues that growing number of evictions traces a shift in attitudes toward housing in the postwar era from a right to an investment. This shift, in turn, supports the right of the state, financial institutions, and property owners to evict individuals and families for a wide range of reasons that go well beyond their ability to pay rent. Once evicted, many individuals have difficulty finding stable housing, which has significant impacts on their employment opportunities, access to education, and quality of life. The cycle of eviction intersects with the history of racism, the emergence of housing as an investment for individuals and institutions, and the willingness of the police, courts, and laws to support property owners at the expense of renters to create economically and socially marginalized groups within society.

Displacements caused by war, capitalism, and other socially and materially destructive forces have led some scholars to define our era as "supermodernity." Alfredo González-Ruibal (2008) has argued that our current supermodern era represents a period during which the scale of economic, political, and social change exceeds the scope of earlier modern institutions such as the state. The need to understand the American experience as shaped by supermodern forces has become a focus of archaeological investigation and critique. In the "supermodern" era, the globalized economy fuels populist anxiety concerning the limits of national sovereignty and has attracted the attention of archaeologists who recognize the significant part that historical archaeology plays in understanding the role of capitalism at the core of past and contemporary American society. LouAnn Wurst has recognized the key role that capitalism has played in the dispossession of workers in a historical American context, drawing on evidence documenting the struggles of workers at nineteenth-century tourist hotels in Niagara Falls and New Deal policies that led to the displacement of farmers from land in upstate New York (Wurst 2015, 2011; Wurst and Ridarsky 2014). In a more contemporary context, the work of Jason De León and his collaborators in the Undocumented Migration Project has shed significant light on the movement of people across the U.S.-Mexico border by applying archaeological methods developed in the American Southwest and Mesoamerica and ethnographic practices to document experiences of undocumented migrants (De León 2015: 10). The project also explores recent work on walls and borders and refugee settlements and homelessness in both a U.S. and global context.

Forced migrants represent just one of a number of groups and communities rendered invisible in contemporary society and attracting the attention of archaeologists. Archaeological methods have proven suitable for documenting the often ephemeral traces left behind by individuals who have sought to remain invisible. Archaeologists have also sought to make visible communities and practices marginalized by the dominant racial, economic, and political groups. For example, by bringing to light the workings and consequences of immigration policies and border control tactics, archaeologists have brought attention to brutality associated with state-sponsored efforts to preserve borders as symbols of political integrity and identity. When states encounter refugees or undocumented and forced migrants, they often detain them in secure "camps" located in marginal places, designed both to obscure status as provisional in the eyes of the state and to bring them back under state control and authority. Archaeologists have also directed attention to the homeless and the residents of temporary squats, who often find security in their invisibility while at the same time being systematically overlooked and ignored by many in society. The work by Larry Zimmerman and his students on homelessness in Minneapolis (Zimmerman and Welsh 2006, 2011; Zimmerman 2013) and Indianapolis initiated a global trend in the archaeological investigation of homelessness that brought together practices associated with historical archaeology and contemporary ethnography.

The work of archaeologists along what many suppose to be the margins of the state and society have revealed the mechanisms employed to maintain certain groups in their marginal and subordinate positions, as well as strategies adopted by these groups to avoid harm, mitigate their often harsh circumstances, and manage their daily life. As Alfredo González-Ruibal has noted, a fine line remains between acknowledging the distinctive practices of certain groups pushed by policies and politics to the margins and normalizing these practices and groups as legitimate and inevitable parts of the modern world (González-Ruibal 2019: 53–54). As Philippe Bourgois argued in his photo-ethnographic study of homeless drug addicts in Los Angeles, work documenting human suffering and abuse offers a way to reveal how individuals have internalized the structural violence so central to the supermodern experience of contemporary American life (Bourgois and Schonberg 2009: 11–19). Archaeology of homelessness, borders, and migrants can reveal the tension between individual agency and structural violence and creates opportunities for the discipline to function as political activism. Such socially informed archaeology both recognizes the diverse ways in which groups navigate the margins of society and works to inform policies both that can mitigate their situations and that created these conditions from the start. In this capacity, archaeologists of the contemporary world, especially when engaging with groups who lack conventional social and political power, have an ethical obligation in how they study, document, and present their research on the homeless or undocumented migrants. At the same time, this kind of archaeological work opens new possibilities for ethical interventions into public policy by making visible certain practices that the state and society have sought to obscure.

The archaeology of contemporary borders, migration, and refugees and the archaeology of homelessness have not only attracted serious attention in an American context but are also areas where work in a North American context speaks to global concerns in both contemporary society and archaeological practice. As our contemporary world is increasingly bound up in global systems that produce and require borders and rely on the preservation of surplus labor, homelessness and forced migration continue to impact marginal groups in peripheral situations and remain fundamental features of twenty-first-century capitalist society.

Undocumented Migration

It is hard to deny the strong connections among discussions of American identity, nationalism, and U.S. border policies in the public sphere. De León's groundbreaking work with the Undocumented Migration Project and its book-length publication, *The Land of Open Graves* (2015), provides a starting point for understanding archaeology's contribution to the experience of American borders (for a survey of this field see McGuire 2020). De León combined archaeological fieldwork in the Sonoran Desert with ethnography to document the experiences of crossing the U.S.-Mexico border. He demonstrates how a U.S. policy of "Prevention through Deterrence" uses the Sonoran Desert itself as a barrier to migrants seeking to enter the United States (De León 2015: 1–10). By hardening highly visible portions of the border near towns and major roads, migrants are channeled toward the more open but radically less hospitable terrain of the desert. He goes on to show, in brutal detail, the trauma inflicted on migrants who attempt to cross the desert, and the fate of those who died in their efforts. The unforgiving heat of the day and cold of desert nights, the absence of water, and the rugged topography filled with sharp stones, dead-end canyons, dangerous animals, and random patrols and surveillance by various U.S. agencies made the Sonoran Desert itself a remorseless ally in national border security. This policy not only subjects migrants to nearly unthinkable hardships in their efforts to enter the United States but pushes them into the rapacious clutches of "coyotes," who offer to guide migrants through the fraught desert landscape for a price. De León emphasized that the vast size and desolate character of the Sonoran Desert also serves to hide from the American public the fate of those who try to cross it. The marginal land of the Sonoran Desert renders invisible—and, indeed, marginal—the desperate individuals who brave its landscape. Just as a lack of documentation obscures migrants from most protections offered by the American legal system, so the Sonoran Desert removes their fate from the public gaze. Archaeology offers a view into an intentionally occluded aspect of the American experience.

The goal of De León's Undocumented Migration Project (UMP) is to make both the individuals and the crossing visible. While ethnography is central to De León's work, archaeological methods also play a key role. The material traces left behind by immigrants in their movement across the desert are ephemeral, especially in contrast to the massive state-sponsored infrastructure erected at official border crossings (McGuire 2013). The monumental efforts to control movement across the borders provides a counterpoint to the work of anti-immigration advocates who scour the desert of objects left behind by migrants. They regard the evidence of migrants' journeys as trash that contributes to the environmental degradation of the fragile desert, and evidence for failures of U.S. immigration policies (Meierotto 2015). In response, the UMP documents the evidence of migrants' movement through this landscape to show how ephemeral traces of human suffering are when subjected to the wind, sun, and occasional zeal of activists. The project's collaboration with forensic scientists, for example, revealed that human remains in the desert may quickly become subject to animal scavengers, which contributes to the underreporting of the number of migrant deaths (Beck et al. 2015). The UMP also recorded things left behind during the migrant crossing, from plastic water bottles to clothing to shoes, bags, graffiti, and more personal objects. Unlike more casual efforts to link discarded objects to migrant movement, the UMP sought to understand these objects in their spatial context. Over four years, the UMP documented almost 350 sites in the Sonoran Desert with over

30,000 artifacts that reveal the complexity of the migrants' journey, as well as strategies used by the Border Patrol to intercept migrants and by activists to provide them with aide. Regularly used camp and resting sites, informal migrant stations, water drops, Border Patrol installations, shrines, and pickup spots on secluded roads reveal a landscape of movement that illuminates the complexities of the migrant experience in the desert (Gokee and De León 2014; De León 2013). Many of the objects found in the desert reveal not only the strategies employed to survive the arduous journey, including water bottles, pain medication, first-aid for cuts and blisters, and religious objects, but also the objects necessary upon arrival, such as toothbrushes, deodorant, and clothes suitable for daily American life. The contrast between the overland routes of migrants and the clear-cut roads and hardened installations of the Border Patrol, for example, show not only different relationships to the physical environment, but also demonstrate that the U.S. government's efforts to control the desert landscape has had a much more dramatic and significant environmental impact.

More importantly, locating these artifacts in their context allowed De León and his collaborators to move beyond well-meaning efforts to display objects associated with migrants as a way to represent the migrants themselves (De León and Gokee 2019). The UMP's process of collecting and studying a vast number of artifacts bore witness to human suffering through their locations, wear patterns, and adaptation during the desert crossing (De León 2013; Gokee et al. 2020). Torn and tattered shoes, in one instance repaired with a bra strap, provide a vivid testimony to the migrant experience, especially when documented in tandem with the restraints commonly used by Border Patrol. Migrant backpacks recovered by the project became the basis for an installation that was part of the UMP's "State of Exception" exhibit at the University of Michigan. This installation, which also included video and still photography, revealed the ethical and political complexities associated with documenting migration and with curating objects associated with such traumatic experience. A follow-up exhibit called "Hostile Terrain 94" began touring in 2019, with plans to appear in 150 locations over the next several years. The centerpiece of this exhibit is a map of the Sonoran Desert showing the locations of over 3,200 known migrant deaths since 1994. Participants in the exhibit fill out toe-tags for each migrant body and affix them to the map. This creates a visually arresting display of the consequences of the U.S. "Prevention through Deterrence" policy.

Borders and Walls

Jason De León and the UMP represent part of an expansive, transnational, and transdisciplinary critique of borders. This work focused on how borders shape American life and global experience of sovereignty over the last fifty years. For example, Wendy Brown's work *Wall States, Waning Sovereignty* (2010) argues that as the forces of globalization have eroded the political and economic sovereignty of nation-states, nations have increasingly invested in walls and borders as the material expressions of their dissipating power (24). Reece Jones offers a similar argument in his 2012 book, which understood efforts to fortify the borders in the United States as part of global response to the early twenty-first-century war on terror (Jones 2012). The so-called border industrial complex (Dear 2013) and the militarization of borders formed a strategy of sovereign states to distinguish themselves from terrorists who, like global capital, are not constrained by the geographic limits of states. Materially, the construction of militarized borders between the United States and Mexico involved the redeployment of the "detritus of American imperialism," such as recycled Vietnam-era helicopter landing mats, concrete barriers developed to protect U.S. bases abroad, and leased drones and military surplus thermal imaging (Hattam 2016; Dorsey and Díaz-Barriga 2020). The material culture of the borders themselves, then, fortified colonialist political rhetoric, which characterized the residents of neighboring countries as military enemies. On the one hand, these material strategies dehumanized those on the other side of the border (Jones 2012: 26–52). On the other hand, the growth of the border industrial complex promises regular encounters with border security in airports, in the presence of Border Patrol offices, and in the border crossing themselves. These reinforce the place of the nation-state in the American experience, which occurs at the same time that our daily lives increasingly involves objects that trace global trajectories.

Randall McGuire's study of the Mexican-American border in the town of Ambos Nogales (2013) provided an archaeological perspective on how what was once a symbolic "picket fence" between the two countries emerged as a fortified expression of the United States' policy of "Prevention by Deterrent." Despite this change of policy, the border remains one of the most crossed borders in the world, and the economies of communities on either side of the border are deeply intertwined. Thus the border itself does less to deter crossing it and more to create distinct experiences for the individuals who must negotiate its presence. Attention to the experience of border crossings has informed the work of a number of scholars arguing that borders produce a distinct temporality (Little 2015; Papadopoulos 2020) and create an intentional sense of ambiguity (Dorsey and Díaz-Barriga 2020). The tactics designed to slow the flow of individuals across liminal zones creates confusion concerning the status of their rights as they exit one jurisdiction before entering another. The different rates at which individuals, capital, and goods move across borders heightens our experience of the strange temporality of border crossing. This is further exacerbated by the violence of sites associated with the indefinite detention of migrants, which represents a key theme in many of the critical studies of migrants in the contemporary world. The experience of borders also creates divisions on the basis of race, religion, wealth, and gender and other ethnic characteristics. White travelers find it easier to negotiate "violent borders," as their outward appearance reinforces nativist views of national identity. Non-white individuals, in contrast, often find the experience of moving across borders personally invasive, emotionally taxing, and consistent with a sense that racial identity complicates the rights of citizenship.

As the complexity and reach of border zones expand globally, the experience of borders becomes a more and more common aspect of our experience as Americans and global denizens. Archaeologist Uzma Rizvi's discussion of moving through checkpoints in Iraq in 2009, for example, emphasized the banality of these militarized interactions during which the sounds, objects, location, and practices of the militarized state contrasted with everyday conversations (Rizvi 2013). Like the border wall between Mexico and the United States, the check points constantly disrupted movement through the cityscape (496), and, more importantly, required the categorization of individuals by gender, nationality, and ethnicity. They also represented spaces where one's rights remain obscure as they imposed limits on Rizvi's ability to document these encounters and photograph the spaces. The mundane conversations that Rizvi recorded during the encounters belied the structural violence these spaces produced by reifying a limited range of identities and the expansiveness of military authority in the urban landscape. Her experiences of internal borders in Iraq paralleled the monumental "peace lines" erected in Belfast, Northern Ireland, which served both to formalize Protestant and Catholic claims to territory in the city and to reinforce the tense relationship between the communities where these walls stand (McAtackney 2011: 82–86). Returning to an American context, Setha Low's study of gated communities in the United

States opens with a striking childhood story of being denied entry to a playmate's gated home as a kindergartener both because he was Jewish and less affluent (Low 2003: 2). Zaire Dinzey-Flores's work in four gated communities in Puerto Rico similarly demonstrates how gates and walls contribute to the experience of race (2020, 2013). Gated, private, white communities have control over their gates and associate them with safety, property values, and affluence. In contrast, the residents of public, Black communities with gates monitored by the police see gates as part of the infrastructure of control, reinforcing state attitudes toward both their vulnerability and volatility. As McGuire and McAtackney have noted in their recent edited volume dedicated to wall-building in the late twentieth and twenty-first centuries (McGuire and McAtackney 2020), walls play a vital role in defining relationships both within and between various groups in our contemporary world.

McAtackney and McGuire's work, Rizvi's description of checkpoints in Iraq, and De León's work in the Sonoran Desert present distinct case studies of the kind of violence that individuals experience at borders. Reece Jones's book *Violent Borders* (2016) stresses that global borders inflict violence on individuals and communities both in the name of the state and in the service of capital. Distinct from Brown's reading of fortified borders as a rearguard effort to reinforce the relevance of the nation-state, Jones argues that borders remain a vital tool for creating pools of low-cost labor and limiting access to natural resources and other forms of wealth. Moreover, as De León and others have shown, borders themselves do environmental violence to the landscapes through which they run. Studies of migration seeking to compare archaeological evidence for migrations with contemporary migrations have likewise emphasized the role that environmental conditions and climate change have played in forcing groups of people to move across state boundaries on a global scale (Morrissey 2015 with citations in Baker and Tsuda 2015). Of course, as Morrissey noted in his study of migration in Northern Ethiopia, the Ethiopian state's highly centralized control over land and food aid has as much of an impact on the decisions of groups and individuals to move as the increased aridity of parts of the country. In short, the political, social, and economic contexts for movement contribute in a major way to our understanding of the material realities of migration and borders. Takeyuki Tsuda, for example, worked to unpack the complex factors that have produced a largely negative view of Mexican immigrants when compared to immigrants from Asia countries (Tsuda 2015). Of particular significance for archaeologists interested in the role of borders in the American experience is Tsuda's argument that the visibility of the border contributed significantly to a view of Mexican workers as disruptive to American society.

Despite the enduring and divisive character of borders in the American experience, archaeology has shown that borders are ephemeral and leave complex traces and meaning in the contemporary landscape. Anna McWilliams's study of Cold War border installations demonstrates how despite the massive and fortified appearance of contemporary borders, today they evoke nostalgia, especially for individuals who lived in the global shadow of the Cold War (McWilliams 2013, 2014; Schofield 2008: 166). The border installations, for example, in Czechia are now part of a large park. In the 1980s, the border between Czechoslovakia and Austria was not simply a national border but part of the "Iron Curtain" dividing the sphere of Soviet influence from the West. In the twenty-first century, much of the border installation has vanished into the woods and the paths once followed by border guards are now nature trails. The global scope of the Cold War, for example, produced a proliferation of walls, with the Berlin Wall and the "Iron Curtain" being only the most famous (Feversham and Schmidt 2007). These walls contributed to the prevailing sense of living on the "front lines" (Schofield 2008: 166–169), even when this border area is not geographically proximate to a national or regional boundary. The architecture vocabulary of the Cold War informed hardened installations—for example, across the UK, Western Europe, and even in rural North Dakota—that communicated the intercontinental threat of a Soviet attack. The materiality and architecture the Cold War contributed directly to the experience of U.S. borders and reinforced a view of the world divided between "us" and "them," which reminds "us" of the constant threat posed by the global "other." As the next chapter will show, the spread of Brutalist architecture in the 1950s and 1960s transposed the hardened concrete designs of the Cold War to such incongruous places as Boston's city hall and Washington, DC, metro stations. This is yet another example of how the experience of borders makes itself felt well beyond their literal limits to political sovereignty. The language of the border in its militarized banality suffuses contemporary American experience to such an extent that it can even evoke nostalgia.

Camps and Homelessness

Recent work on the archaeology of forced migration has invariably considered refugee camps an important locus for understanding the experience of migration and displacement. Archaeologists have joined architectural historians, anthropologists, and policymakers in an effort to understand how camps, squats, and other forms of migrant settlement contribute to the formation of migrant identities both within their communities and in their host countries. Dan Hicks's and Sarah Mallet's work at the migrant camp called "La Lande" and the Jungle at Calais in France (2019; see also Agier et al. 2018), for example, demonstrates through photography and argument how the border served as "a device for classification" (43). They see the creation of borders and camps as methods both to identify and to separate groups according to legal status as well as race, ethnicity, and wealth. The authors describe this "borderwork" as a way that nation-states attempt to manage the global impact of displacement and its relationship to complex phenomenon that often go far beyond a nation's control, such as foreign policy, military interventions, climate change, and transnational humanitarian activities.

Much of this scholarship, then, traces the growing anxiety surrounding the experience of the nation-state and its limits. For example, various forms of migrant settlements, whether defined by the borders of refugee camps or the more fluid spaces of squats and shelters, have become spaces where groups negotiate identities outside of the legal and territorial definitions of the nation-state. Recent studies by scholars from a range of disciplines recognize tensions in efforts to preserve distinct identities against the backdrop of globalized material culture and architecture of camps characterized by the ubiquitous presence of blue tarp (Hailey 2009: 377–382), barbed wire (Agier 2002), and cement (Abourahme 2014). The intensive work of M. Herz and colleagues in documenting the long-term refugee camps of Western Sahara (2013), however, demonstrates how these temporary encampments can take on their own organization and develop institutions and architecture to accommodate administration, commerce, culture, health, and education as well as dynamic forms of residential architecture.

In this regard, the work of archaeologists in understanding and documenting migrant experiences parallels recent work to document the ways in which homeless individuals create shelter as well as a sense of place, home, and identity. It is hardly surprising, then, that the work of Rachael

Kiddey, which initially focused on the archaeology of homelessness in England, has since shifted to study refugees as part of her "Migrant Materialities" project. Drawing on the larger "material turn" in migrant studies (Wang 2016; Basu and Coleman 2008), Kiddey published three portraits that contextualize some aspects of migrants in Athens, Greece: a collectively run squat in a former tourist hotel, a UNHCR-funded refugee settlement in another hotel, and a community center operated as a co-operative (Kiddey 2018). Her use of ethnography and archaeology in these contexts follows from her groundbreaking work on the archaeology of homelessness in the UK. Kiddey embraced a "translational" approach to her research, which proposed a view of archaeology that translated archaeological work and analysis into research of use to policymakers.

Kiddey's approach paralleled work in American archaeology that encouraged archaeologists to share their authority as a way to complicate the distinction between our status as archaeologists and the status of migrants or the homeless as the "other." Larry Zimmerman, Courtney Singleton, and Jessica Welch (2010) worked to show how these practices made it possible to connect the archaeology of the contemporary homeless experience to meaningful changes in attitudes and policy (Zimmerman et al. 2010: 444–446). While such activist archaeology hardly seems like a radical proposition in the twenty-first century (e.g., Barton 2021), the specifics regarding the methods, ethical consideration, and goals of these activist practices emerged from local projects with distinctive social and material contexts. For Kiddey, translational practice manifests itself in her close collaboration with members of the homeless community not only through the excavation, documentation, and interpretation of their material culture but also in their collaborative efforts to present it to both a wider public and an academic audience through lectures and exhibitions (Kiddey 2017; Kiddey and Schofield 2010, 2011). De León and his project, while not as collaborative in design as Kiddey's work, nonetheless shared its translational emphasis in its efforts to communicate their results through installations and exhibits and to produce a more politically aware society.

Ann Elena Stinchfield Danis's recent dissertation applied a translational approach to documenting the experiences of a community of people who built homes on a spit of reclaimed land called the Albany Bulb in San Francisco Bay (Danis 2020). The Albany Bulb was originally a dump site consisting of construction debris removed from rapidly developing Bay communities. The material dumped at the site, its relatively isolated location, and its spectacular views made it an appealing space for homeless individuals to build homes. When the city decided to turn the Bulb into a public park, they displaced the formerly homeless residents and destroyed their homes. Danis conducted an intensive pedestrian survey of the Blub and also collaborated with former residents to understand how they created homes and a sense of community in this space. Because many of the residents had signed legal agreements not to return to the Bulb in exchange for compensation for the destruction of their homes, Danis worked with them remotely to annotate maps, to produce digital catalogues and exhibitions of photographs documenting the spaces, and to record stories associated with the community there. In doing so, she emphasized that the residents of the Albany Bulb did not conform to a tidy definition of homelessness—because they had homes. Despite the Bulb's ambiguous status as reclaimed land, its residents not only created a community there but thrived. Danis recognized in the community on the Bulb a resilience that she defined using the term "survivance," which she borrowed from Gerald Vizenor's effort to describe the strategies employed by American Indian communities to both resist colonization and endure (Vizenor 1999). The neatly paved brick floor of one house on the Bulb, the carefully tended succulent gardens, the works of art constructed from material found at the site, the communal library, and ultimately, a sense of place transformed the marginal space of a landfill into new forms of private and public space that do not fit neatly into categories sanctioned by the state.

Danis employed a strategy of "re-presencing" to make the displaced community on Albany Bulb visible again to the public and policymakers. By drawing attention to the survivance of individuals traditionally defined as homeless, Danis, like Kiddey and De León, sought to make visible groups that the state tried to hide—in this case, the homeless and individuals who do not conform to the expectations of capitalism, with its emphasis on financialization of housing, engagement with the market, and promise of general prosperity. Collaborating with people identified by the state as homeless or migrants allowed these individuals not only to be visible in their own stories but also to produce new ways of understanding alternative lifeways that challenge conventional expectations that assume people without permanent homes or who live on the streets are simply failed capitalists.

In many ways, the origins of an archaeology of homelessness stems from Larry Zimmerman's work to document contemporary homeless lifeways. Zimmerman's efforts started as part of the efforts of the Minnesota State Historical Society (MHS) to renovate the gardens of the James J. Hill

House in St. Paul, Minnesota. When Hill and his wife died, the house and property passed first to the Catholic diocese and then to the MHS, who neglected the gardens. The location of the house near downtown and the secluded landscape became a convenient location for the homeless from the 1960s onward, and when work to restore the gardens began in 2003, archaeologists were confronted with a significant assemblage of material associated with homeless life there. Zimmerman folded research into the homeless occupation of this area into larger questions of the organization of the gardens, original use and iconography of the landscape, and reuse of the site (Zimmerman 2004). Using both survey and excavation, he identified relatively little material associated with the early twentieth-century structures on the site, but large quantities of material associated with the homeless occupation of the site over nearly forty years. He documented not only scattered debris but also several sites of repeated and intensive habitation, including the mushroom cave of the original Hill House gardens, which produced the kinds of middens familiar to any historical archaeologist. Zimmerman noted that the presence of drug paraphernalia produced some additional risk to excavators, but more importantly the contrast between the opulent 36,000-square-foot mansion and the abject poverty of the homeless encampments on the grounds made manifest the tensions inherent in a capitalist system that creates and requires concentration of both wealth and poverty.

Only after the excavations at the Hill House did Zimmerman and his team recognize the potential of using the material culture of homelessness to make the homeless visible. This initiated a more systematic and expansive survey of the homeless in Indianapolis, Indiana, guided in part by his collaborator Jessica Welch, who herself had been homeless and also volunteered at a local shelter (Zimmerman and Welch 2011; Singleton 2017). Zimmerman and Welch focused their work on assemblages associated with the homeless. They identified features common to homeless life, such as caches of possessions, and showed how these reflected a wide range of strategies necessary to preserve a sense of home and identity. Caches often included reading material, children's toys, efforts to create windbreaks, and other forms of shelter from the cold, hard surfaces of the city streets (Zimmerman and Welch 2011; Singleton 2017: 234–235). Also in Indianapolis, Courtney Singleton incorporated an ethnographic component to this approach. She showed how policies that treated homelessness as a situation addressed through providing homes for individuals living on the street also led to evictions, gates, and fences around areas used by the homeless for encampments. What these policies missed, however, ethnography and archaeology revealed. Homeless encampments provided a sense of community, stability, freedom, and even security for their residents and were often seen as a more appealing alternative to shelters or other more institutional forms of housing. In this way, archaeology demonstrated the limits to certain policies and certain public efforts to provide assistance. For example, gifts of canned food without can openers often results in improvised strategies to opening cans and the loss of food. Shampoo tends to require too much water to be of use to homeless individuals and is quickly discarded. Donations of shoes often frustrate the homeless because the shoes fit poorly and are often abandoned—but not before the valuable shoelaces are removed. True to their efforts at a translational archaeology, Zimmerman and his team often found ways to demonstrate how their research can provide insights to policymakers by making visible how the homeless adapt in unexpected and overlooked ways. Moreover, the rigorous documentation of material evidence associated with homeless life continues the traditions of historical archaeology, which have periodically set their attention on the archaeology of homelessness in the past (e.g., Baugher 2001; Casella 2007: 12–14 with additional references) and focused on the material culture as a way of making visible situations that have escaped the documentary evidence traditionally used in historical research. Significantly, Casella recognizes almshouses in the eighteenth and nineteenth centuries as part of the emergence of the "carceral society" that sought to distinguish individuals who were members of society from those who were not, in ways that paralleled the "borderwork" described by Hicks and Mallet.

Like Zimmerman's work at the Hill House and Danis's work at the Albany Bulb, Singleton's 2021 dissertation focusing on Pelham Bay Park in the Bronx revealed how systematic approaches central to historical archaeology—excavation, typology building, and surface survey—produce a more nuanced and sophisticated understanding of the homeless experience throughout the contemporary period. The park had a long history as a gathering place for not only homeless individuals but also seasonal campers, beach-goers, and local residents of City Island. From the 1960s to the 1980s, the dumping of New York City waste at a landfill site across the Eastchester Bay enticed people to use the park as a home base for scavenging at the landfill. This largely homeless population lived in the park until the 1980s when the landfill closed and the park management implemented a series of environmental conservation measures (Singleton 2021: 4). Singleton's work sought to efficiently document the material signature of these groups. Her work began with a systematic surface collection that revealed the patterning of drug use at the site, practices associated with personal hygiene, and other casual uses of the park. She argued that a dense scatter of discarded needles around a group of glacial boulders at the site revealed their use as a resting place for drug users. The pattern of small foam wedges of the type used to sample makeup suggested their reuse for feminine hygiene needs. Excavations traced the emergence of crack use in New York through the appearance of branded baggies in levels dated to the mid- to late 1980s. Earlier levels preserve signs of habitation at the site, including the reuse of part of a boat likely salvaged from the anchorages surrounding City Island. The earlier uses of the sites also produced artifacts associated with scavenging from the nearby landfill throughout its long history. Detailed construction of artifact typologies supported many of Singleton's conclusions and demonstrated how the careful scrutiny of objects recovered through survey and excavation revealed the ability of occupants of Pelham Bay Park to adapt everyday objects to new, if often ambiguous, uses.

Singleton's work relied less on direct ethnographic informants or collaborative practices of Welch, Kiddey, or Danis, but her analysis produced similar results. She demonstrated that homeless practices and lifeways manifest ambiguously in the material record. This in turn emphasized, on the one hand, how legal definitions of these concepts often fail to reflect the range of activities that constitute homemaking. On the other hand, the material from Singleton's work at Pelham Bay Park also made clear the deep engagement of the individuals who lived there with local, national, and global situations ranging from the New York City garbage "crisis" to the typology of bottles from nationwide beverage distributors and the global flow of cocaine and heroin. Set against the financialization of housing in New York City, the privatization of public spaces, urban renewal, and the nationwide eviction crisis, concepts such as homelessness have increasingly come to represent an economic or legal status rather than the more ambiguous criteria of access to adequate shelter. By making the experiences of the individuals who lived on the Albany Bulb or in Pelham Bay Park visible, Singleton and Danis not only expand how we understand the concept of home but also provide data and analysis with the potential to inform policymaking. This allowed these scholars to avoid the pitfalls articulated by A. González-Ruibal (2019), who observed that the challenge of the archaeology of migrants and homelessness is to document their situations without validating the social, political, and economic conditions that created their status. Danis, Zimmerman, and Kiddey attempted to make homelessness visible to a wider public, recognizing that awareness is a precondition for meaningful changes in policy. For Danis, this involved both digitally mediated and in-person exhibitions of their work at the Albany Bulb. Zimmerman led an ultimately unsuccessful effort to preserve for public view the graffiti left by individuals who had lived for many years in the Washburn flour mill prior to its reconstruction as the Mill City Museum in Minneapolis (Zimmerman 2013). There was similar reluctance to display an exhibit of artifacts that Kiddey and her homeless colleagues excavated from the Turbo Island homeless site in Bristol. The refusal to see the assemblages of artifacts associated with homeless as heritage, and the tendency to see many homeless placemaking practices, such as graffiti, vandalism, or, as in the case of migrants, trash to be cleaned up and hidden away, makes it more difficult to understand and prioritize the needs of these groups.

Conclusion

Archaeological attention to hardening of national borders and the increasingly restrictive maze of public and private spaces in the contemporary world highlights the tension between the experiences of displacement and expulsion in the twenty-first century and efforts to obfuscate the social and economic costs of these policies. Attention to the experience of crossing borders, in migrant camps, and at sites like the Albany Bulb or Pelham Bay Park demonstrates how the state deployed "devices of categorization" to define the nation, to classify various racial, ethnic, or economic groups, and to assert control in unstable spaces. The proximity of homeless settlements near landfills, for example, harkens back to our discussion of garbology in chapter 2, where we explored how our practice of discard marginalized both waste and individuals associated with its handling and processing. In the case of the Albany Bulb, the reclamation of the landfill as desirable public space involved the expulsion of a community, revealing the inconsistencies inherent in neatly defined categories of public and private. It is not hard to see in the transformation of Albany Bulb into a public park the kind of restoration of value proposed by Michael Thompson in *Rubbish Theory*, where discard is a precondition for objects regaining value. For the residents of the Albany Bulb, those in Pelham Bay Park, or migrants crossing the Sonoran Desert, efforts to remove their traces from public land serve to categorize their presence as intrusive and therefore not part of a putative "public." Archaeological projects that work to present and document these groups and their experiences not only mitigates efforts by the state to occlude these groups from public view but also reveals their remarkable capacity for resilience and survivance along the interstices of contemporary life.

Some of this scholarship, such as the two dissertations noted in the second part of this chapter, had not appeared when we started our work in the Bakken oil patch in western North Dakota, but early reports of workers sleeping in city parks, parking lots, and shelter belts led us to consider the archaeology of the homeless, the displaced, and migrants who adapted their housing and sense of community to their uncertain and often precarious situation. While scholars have rarely considered oil field workers to be displaced individuals, many made their way to the Bakken in the aftermath of the subprime mortgage crisis and encountered the need to adapt to the lack of housing in North Dakota, the challenging weather, and the need for a sense of community in remote and sparsely populated region. As subsequent chapters will show, migrant camps and homeless communities were not the only forms of settlement that informed our analysis, but efforts to negotiate a sense of place in situations where powerful interests often seek to control marginal spaces revealed strategies of survivance visible in the temporary housing of the precarious Bakken workforce.

6

Military Bases, Campuses, and Disciplining the American Experience

A casual visitor traveling the main arteries through western North Dakota at the height of the Bakken oil boom would be struck by the proliferation of workforce housing sites. The most elaborate forms of so-called man camps lined the major routes through the oil patch and presented neatly arranged grids of modular housing units surrounded by larger common buildings. They typically featured imposing fences, access-control points, and more often than not parking lots full of idling diesel trucks waiting for their drivers to return for the next shift. As the previous chapter suggested, the fences and control points associated with workforce camps bring to mind the security measures associated with borders and migrant camps. At the same time, the well-structured order of the camps evoked military bases. In fact, some of the same companies that provided modular housing for short-term workers in the United States provided the same kind of modular housing for military personnel deployed in the Middle East. When combined with the military-style uniforms of many oil field workers (complete with America flag patches that contribute to a general atmosphere of "petro-masculinity" [Daggett 2018]), it is hardly surprising that the landscape of the Bakken oil patch led us to compare these sites to military camps. The parallels between the global reach of the American military and reach of American extractive industries reflects changes in the scope of the American experience in the post–World War II era. In particular, our efforts to document workforce housing in the Bakken drew our attention to how the global character of the American military and industrial involvement informed local experiences in North Dakota. Just as hardened borders drew upon the architecture and material culture of the Cold War, the modular character of turn-of-the-twenty-first-century military bases in the Persian Gulf shared features with workforce housing in another oil rich region. Despite the geographic remoteness of life in the

Bakken oil patch, the experience evoked global trends in modular, temporary housing.

At the same time, nights spent in workforce housing in the Bakken invariably reminded us of our time on college campuses. The central place
of a dining hall, the dormitory-style accommodations, and the neatly arranged pathways and exteriors of the building emphasized an alternative
model of tidiness, order, and control. The interior space of workforce housing sites sought to promote efficient recovering from difficult and taxing
work, a degree of controlled camaraderie over meals, and limited opportunities for recreation. The external appearance of order was especially significant for the largest and most institutional camps as they sought to allay
the concerns of surrounding communities that the influx of oil workers to
the region would bring social disruptions, including an increase in crime
and violence. While the potted flowers, hotel-grade furnishings, and buffet
meals in the workforce housing sites we visited and stayed rarely reached
the level of contemporary college amenities, the sense of orderly convenience that pervaded these sites drew us to consider, from an archaeological perspective, the parallel between camps and campuses.

Both military bases and college campuses shared the orderly arrangement of housing, dining services, and access points, despite ostensibly
representing opposite poles on the contemporary ideological spectrum.
The similarities nevertheless reflect the shared concerns for shaping young
people in body and mind. This involves both laudatory efforts to celebrate
and enforce social cohesion, as well as more problematic strategies to suppress resistance and attempts to subvert conformity. Workforce housing,
military bases, and college campuses also tend to evoke concern from surrounding communities because concentrations of male workers, soldiers,
and young adults often appear as groups requiring strict controls to prevent anti-social, destructive, or violent behaviors. As a result of these internal and external pressures, camps and campuses regularly emphasize the
appearance of order and tradition. In fact, the appearance of order often
serves to both enforce conformity and to hide the complex realities of life
within these institutions. The archaeology of the contemporary world offers a method for exposing the activities, experiences, and processes that
these sites tend to obscure and for revealing more nuanced and dynamic
landscapes in places that privilege tradition and conformity. In this sense,
archaeology of the contemporary world offers perspectives of American
experience that extend beyond top-down views of institutional control,

emphasize the sometimes tragic consequences of dissimulation, and present new ways to recognize resistance and the limits of conformity.

Introduction

The archaeology of military spaces contributed in significant ways to the origins of the archaeology of the contemporary world. As early as the 1990s, archaeologists became aware of the ephemeral nature of installations associated with World War II in Europe. As these installations passed the fifty-year threshold for eligibility as heritage, archaeologists began to consider criteria that would determine their suitability for national landmark status. Evaluating these sites has proven challenging. First, the scale of World War II sites, which includes entire theaters of the war, such as the North Atlantic and the South Pacific, has made site definition difficult. Their functional and architecture diversity compounds the often irregular, hasty, or lost documentation associated with their construction. Finally, these sites were often repurposed or destroyed as necessary over their lifespan (Schofield 2002). These challenges of definition created a backdrop for a wide-ranging discussion across a series of academic conference and publications that explored the potential of military sites as both places of heritage and memory as well as contributions to our understanding of the war itself (e.g., Schofield, Johnson and Beck 2002; Schofield 2005, 2008; Moshenka 2013). While most of this work has focused on the UK and Europe, a number of projects documented the home front in the United States, particularly as it related to Japanese internment (e.g., Skiles and Clark 2010; Burton and Farrell 2001, 2019), prisoner of war camps (Thomas 2011), and matters related to the development of the atomic bomb (Kuletz 1998; McGehee et al. 2003; Schiffer 2013: 145–148).

These considerations of World War II monuments coincided with the end of the Cold War and, in particular, the destruction of the Berlin Wall and the complicated conversations related to the preservation of this monument (Dolff-Bonekämper 2002; McWilliams 2013: 45–65; Hanson 2016; Salmond 2011). Thus, archaeologists started to recognize that Cold War military installations existed in large numbers and could speak to late twentieth- and early twenty-first-century experiences both domestically and on a global scale. Taking inspiration from the work of Paul Virilio, for example, archaeologists have increasingly viewed the postwar and Cold War period as a time when the potential for nuclear conflict shaped both the extent and character of military installations as well as non-military architecture, objects, and material culture. In his iconic *Bunker Archaeology* (1994[1967]), Virilio argued that the World War II concrete bunkers and towers erected along the French coast by the Nazis were already becoming irrelevant in the context of aerial bombardment of German cities. Instead, they served to define the territory that could function as a new Nazi state. They marked out a space defined as much by the need to observe and communicate at the speed of modern weapons, aircraft, and vehicles as traditional definitions of culture or territoriality. The persistence of these bunkers during peacetime anticipated Virilio's arguments for "pure war" (Virilio and Lotringer 1983), in which expressions and experiences of the militarized state suffuse all aspects of life. In this way, Virilio's ideas echo those of Manuel DeLanda, who proposed in *War in the Age of Intelligent Machines* (1991) that military technologies, especially the rise of logistics, have shaped contemporary economic, political, and social life. As noted in chapter 5, hardened borders already extend the experience of militarized state beyond traditional theaters of conflict. Despite the monumental and intimidating expressions of state power, these contexts nevertheless obfuscate the emerging state mechanisms dependent on the far less visible technologies of communication, air power, and finance.

Our awareness of unconventional and less visible Cold War technologies of power has informed how we understand the life and work of universities in the United States. The postwar growth of American colleges emerged partly on the back of the GI Bill, which supported veterans seeking a college education. The military and the state also supported universities through federal agencies such as the National Science Foundation and NASA. These collaborations developed technologies designed to enhance the national defense portfolio as Cold War diplomatic, economic, and political objectives embodied in the space race advanced the technologies available to the military, civilian manufactures, and consumers. In fact, state support for education helped define the Cold War as a war centered as much on national economies as on technologically advanced weapons. College campuses often made this connection explicit through their adoption of concrete modernist and even Brutalist architecture that reflected the influence of efficiently produced and durable concrete buildings in military contexts. The interest in the orderly and efficient delivery of university education, which continues to shape political and education policies today, traces the convergence of military and civilian concerns for logistics that emerged in the postwar period. In short, the influence of the Cold War was particularly strong on college campuses, which further rationalizes the combination of military bases and college campuses in this chapter.

Military Bases

The archaeology of the military bases in the late twentieth and early twenty-first centuries offers a distinctive perspective on both the archaeology of the contemporary world and the place of Cold War and post–Cold War military installations in the context of American material culture. The growing trend toward hardened borders often incorporated elements of military architecture. This involved the liberal use of poured concrete structures, characteristic of Brutalist and large-scale mid-century military architecture, as well as occasional reuse of Vietnam-era military structures such as metal helicopter landing pads (Hattam 2016). The growing visibility of borders and walls illustrates but one way in which military architecture has come to the fore in twenty-first-century American society. This process has echoes in Virilio's attitudes toward the visibility of World War II installations in Europe through which military values, attitudes, and forms increasingly entered all aspects of European life. The growing visibility of military priorities in the public consciousness is perhaps nowhere more obvious than in the late twentieth-century "space race," which paralleled Cold War competition in science and technology and the development of rockets for space flight as well as the delivery of ballistic missiles (Gorman 2019). In the twenty-first century, military technologies touch on nearly every aspect of daily life, from the use of military-style GPS technology to such diverse expressions as nuclear power, the militarization of police forces, and even the internet. In sum, many daily American experiences— from our cars' GPS navigation systems to border crossings to government and university architecture to surfing the web—rely on the long "tail" of military technologies, which continues to shape our lives.

From an archaeological perspective, then, the significance of military installations and research sites extends far beyond the military sphere. Indeed, many challenges associated with documenting and preserving significant structures on military installations speak to issues common to such work in a range of contexts in postwar and twenty-first-century America. John Schofield, for example, noted that military installations frequently consist of the "teeth" and the "tail" (Schofield 2009: 29). The teeth are structures that served military purposes, such as fortifications or missile silos, and resist repurposing because of their specialized design and often massive and hardened forms. These structures thus tend to persist in the landscape even after they no longer serve their intended function. The so-called Nekoma Pyramid (more properly named the Stanley R. Mickelson Safeguard Complex), for example, in Cavalier County, North Dakota, was part of an abortive nuclear missile tracking system constructed in the early 1970s and abandoned after only four months of use (figure 6.1). Until its sale to a local Hudderite colony in 2013, the site stood empty and unused on the northern prairie for nearly forty years (Hanson 2016: 61–62; Hubbs 1992). A similar fate awaits the various ICBM sites scattered across the Midwest, as well as specialized research facilities and nuclear testing sites across the American West. The tail, in contrast, includes buildings of less specialized designs that could be easily repurposed over their lifetimes in ways that make understanding their original functions and subsequent history difficult. Schofield notes that guidelines established in the 1990s in the UK encouraged "sympathetic reuse" for buildings associated with the "tail" (*sensu* Schofield 2009: 29).

Both the neglect of military sites and their repurposing present challenges associated with their preservation and documentation, but also speak to the contrasting aspect of their contemporary character. Modern, postwar architecture, for example, often privileged the adaptability of design, which allowed buildings to be easily reconfigured for new purposes. At the same time, the use of reinforced concrete, steel, and more specialized, synthetic materials present new challenges for maintenance and restoration work, as well, which are then compounded by the often massive scale of late twentieth-century military sites. Caitlin DeSilvey's study of the closed military facility at Orford Ness in the UK emphasized the way in which the decay of the reinforced concrete structures interacted with the natural surroundings to create a distinctive landscape. When the National Trust acquired the property as a wildlife preserve, they decided to allow the military structures to continue to decay (DeSilvey 2014; Bartolini and DeSilvey 2020). This decision, however, has recently been met with some ambivalence from heritage authorities, who have become interested in preserving the site as part of the UK's military heritage (DeSilvey 2014: 87). As another example, Todd Hanson described the challenges associated with preserving the Trestle, a massive entirely wooden structure designed to test weapons that used electromagnetic pulses to disrupt electronics at the Kirkland Air Force Base near Albuquerque, New Mexico. Because the structure is entirely made of wood, preservation costs would be prohibitive even in light of the unique character of the structure. As a result, when the

Figure 6.1. The Nekoma Pyramid near Grand Forks, North Dakota. Historic American Engineering Record, 1968.

Trestle went out of use in 1991, Hanson documented the site on behalf of the military, and then it was left to deteriorate in the New Mexico desert (Hanson 2016: 81–85).

The vast scale of mid- and late twentieth-century military sites likewise offers a challenge to archaeologists seeking to document, understand, and preserve them (Schofield 2005: 24). John Schofield, Wayne Cocroft, and Marina Dobronovskaya have stressed the transnational character of many Cold War sites and argued that national criteria for their preservation often overlooks the dispersed and global scope of this conflict (Schofield et al. 2021). An archaeology of the Cuban Missile Crisis, for example, requires research both in the United States and around Soviet missile sites in Cuba (Burström et al. 2009; Burström et al. 2011). The experience of the Cold War from an American perspective extends to airbases in the UK and Germany, where American soldiers were stationed, and could include local responses to the base, as we will see in chapter 7. A transnational view of the broader Cold War experience must also include their Soviet counterparts on the other side of the Iron Curtain. This kind of archaeology and heritage work, moreover, must contend with regional and national attitudes toward the Soviet past both in Eastern European countries of the former Warsaw Pact and in Russia. In this context, efforts to document American installations associated with the Cold War represent only a narrow window into what was a vast, geographically dispersed, transnational (if not global) phenomena.

Even in the United States, Cold War sites often spanned vast areas. The Nevada Test Site (NTS), for example, extends over 1,360 square miles in southern Nevada and witnessed close to 2,000 tests of nuclear devices from its opening in 1951 to implementation of the Comprehensive Nuclear-Test-Ban Treaty in 1992. The site itself includes a wide range of landscapes, monuments, and artifacts associated with the development of the United States' nuclear deterrent. As a number of commentators have noted, for most of the twentieth century, the NTS represented a major front in the Cold War, where the United States demonstrated their continued commitment to nuclear weapons and peace through strength. Efforts to document key areas of the site have revealed not only the development and use of this important installation over time but also a wide range of post-depositional processes that have shaped the assemblage across this massive installation. Archaeological work at Frenchman Flat, an area of almost 100 square miles that saw nuclear tests throughout the 1950s and 1960s, revealed an area with 157 buildings and structures, most of which were eligible for the National Register of Historic Places (Beck 2002; Hanson 2010; Johnson et al. 2000). The most unusual of the sites recorded in this area was the wide range of features erected to test the effects of nuclear devices on typical American homes, businesses, and landscapes. The construction of temporary forests, realistic suburban dwellings, various types of bomb shelters and, in one instance, a massive metal safe in the blast area served to test the ability of various structures to endure a nuclear explosion. In many cases, the remains of these features continue to stand on Frenchman Flat as enduring reminders of the site's role as an active front in a Cold War arms race. The presence of ersatz civilian structures in military surroundings offers an inverted image of Virilio's concept of "Total War," which traced the spread of bunkers, walls, and installations throughout Europe and North America (Virilio 2008: 18). They appear to anticipate the rise of Cold War suburbs in the vicinity of the CIA headquarters at Langley and the Pentagon in Northern Virginia to house many of the men and women responsible for maintaining American political and military strength (Friedman 2013).

The work at the vast Nevada Test Site also included the documentation of Camp Desert Rock, which functioned to house soldiers and officers associated with the nuclear tests in the 1950s. The study of the camp revealed how the space was adapted to accommodate changing functions over the its short, six-year history (Edwards 1997; Hanson 2015: 87–94). Moreover, Edwards's survey of the site showed how the archaeological study of relatively recent military installations identified changes in the camp unreported even in the copious archival records of the modern military (Hanson 2015: 91–92). Upgrades to toilet facilities and hospitality areas for officers and officials, for example, may speak to changing expectations regarding postwar domesticity and sanitation both in the military and in the civilian world. A similar trend is visible in the development of purpose-built communities to house American soldiers stationed in the United States' myriad foreign military bases. These bases frequently followed templates established by postwar suburbs that housed military leadership at the Pentagon or members of the intelligence community who shape American policies (Friedman 2013; Gillem 2007).

The undocumented aspects of military installations likewise inform Valerie Kuletz's 1998 study of the "Science Cities" in the American West. Her work, which is not strictly archaeological, nevertheless embodies attentiveness to materiality and landscape-scale thinking, situating the presence of vast military research operations developed in the 1950s, 1960s, and 1970s in the western deserts of the United States. She documented how the construction of these facilities relied on the misperception that the American west was empty, unoccupied land (Kuletz 1998). This justified the use of these facilities to conduct dangerous, toxic, and secretive research during the Cold War. In fact, much of the land surrounding these sites forms either Indian Reservations or the wider range of Native American groups. Thus, military bases established during the Cold War represent not only a front in a global conflict but also a late phase in the United States' internal efforts to colonize Native Americans by using their sovereign and traditional territories as "outdoor laboratories" and as sacrifice zones in the name of a global conflict. The clearly delineated and secured borders of these sites often belie the wider impact of their presence. The detonation of nuclear devices upwind from Native American communities and the mining and release of toxic and radioactive material into the air and water inflicted lasting damage on the people, livestock, and environment (Witmore and Francisco 2021). At the same time, the neatly defined and often covert character of these science cities inscribed the landscape with the specter of colonial power that obscures and protects both systems of colonial domination and individual scientists from the complicated consequences of the global conflict.

The use of ostensibly "marginal landscapes" as theaters for the Cold War conflict similarly appears in Alice Gorman's (2019) understanding of the science city at Woomera village in South Australia. This site served the scientists, technicians, and their families who worked at the Woomera rocket range. The range remained an important Cold War research site from its founding in the late 1940s through the early 1970s when the UK and their European allies shuttered the Europa missile program. In the twenty-first century, the Australian government used the remote desert location as the site for a migrant detention center (Gorman 2019: 98), making explicit the transnational legacies of the postwar era.

At its extreme, the transnational character archaeology of the contemporary world extends well beyond the terrestrial realm. Gorman and Justin Walsh and colleagues have explored the archaeology of space, which includes both terrestrial sites and those in space, including the International Space Station. Access to the technical and classified areas and material associated with contemporary military activity or space exploration (as well as secure corporate research sites) presents a challenge. The archaeologists associated with the International Space Station Archaeological Project have turned to the systematic study of publicly available photographs of the interior of the space station to document not only daily life on the station but also ways in which the international team of researchers and scientists represented their national and ethnic identities. For example, Salmond, Walsh, and Gorman show that the display of Orthodox Christian religious icons, national heroes of space exploration such as Yuri Gagarin, and flags on the walls of the Russian module in the space station paralleled the resurgence of the Russian church in the post-Soviet era. These images expressed both the astronaut's personal piety and their national identity even in the deliberately transnational context of the collaborative space station (Salmond et al. 2020). The connection of national identity—especially through displays of earlier heroes of the Cold War space race—and technological prowess in the space station reflects the persistent postwar links among space exploration, national pride, and international competition. The explicit interest in the contemporary ongoing social and even ideological aspects of space exploration contrasts with earlier space archaeology, which tended to emphasize the technical and even forensic aspects of archaeology to document "relics" of the recent past (e.g., Capelotti 2009,

2010). The use of photography to document remotely the subtle shifts in how the space station's residents work and live in space evokes the use of spy photographs to attempt to analyze and interpret changes at secretive military installations (Walsh and Gorman 2021).

The use of public photographs released from the ISS demonstrates the potential to use public data to provide windows into the fragmentary and often secret archive of U.S. military operations. Adrian Meyers used public imagery made available through Google Earth to map the development of Camp X-Ray, Camp Delta, and attendant facilities at the U.S. installations at Guantánamo Bay in Cuba (Myers 2010). The careful study of Google Earth imagery exposed the rapid increase in buildings associated with the secret detention facilities between 2003 and 2008. Meyers traced the expansion of the Guantánamo installations as evidence for the speed with which the war on terror intensified. Many of the first structures at the various detention camps were portable units imported from off site to accommodate both a growing number of detainees and personnel. The United States later replaced these portable units with more permanent concrete-style prison buildings. By tracing these changes in architecture at the site, Meyers was able to see the growth in capacity at the various camps and understand the increase in inmates either realized or expected at the site. This served to make visible the secret workings of U.S. military installations and also to preserve a record of change at the sites to compare to declassified archival material in the future.

The use of archaeological methods as a medium for critiquing military activities by making them visible extends to efforts to document protest sites that developed alongside Cold War military installation. For example, work to document the Peace Camp site outside the main gate to the Nevada Test Site demonstrated the extent and character of protests against nuclear testing, the eviction of the Western Shoshone from their traditional land, and the environmental impact of military activities on the fragile desert ecology (Beck et al. 2007; Beck et al. 2011; Hanson 2015: 100–105). Ironically, the camp's iterative development in some ways paralleled the adaptable character of the various Guantánamo Bay camps and the development of Camp Desert Rock. The early versions of the camp were largely ad hoc and loosely organized, aside from some fire rings and small tent pads. Subsequent iterations of the camp reveal greater structure and formality, with neatly delineated spaces for activities ranging from sleeping, cooking, meditation, art, and the sanitary needs of the protesters. Unlike the hierarchical organization of Camp Desert Rock, where VIP visitors and officers had increasing creature comforts, the Peace Camps took pains to appear egalitarian in organization.

In the following chapter we will further consider the archaeology of protest and activist sites, such as the series of camps that emerged as a response to the installation of cruise missiles at the Greenham Common Airbase in the UK (Schofield and Anderton 2000; Schofield, Beck, and Drollinger 2008) and the annual gathering of activists and artists at the site of Burning Man in the Nevada desert (White 2020), but it is worth noting here some recent work at the site of Slab City in California's Colorado Desert. Slab City stands on the site of the World War II Marine Corps training base known as Camp Dunlap. After the military decommissioned the base and returned the land to the state of California, the squatters occupied the site drawn to the network of concrete slabs left behind after the military removed the buildings from the base. Rechristened "Slab City," the site has hosted a community of permanent and seasonal occupants drawn to the public land in the desert as "the last free place on Earth" (Hailey and Wylie 2018). Most residents embrace a spirit of creative anarchy at the site, which lacks water or power. Many embellish their campsites with art; collaborate in support of a lending library, religious institutions, and social events; and negotiate a fragile balance between community and solitude in the desert. The interplay between the remains of the military installation and the anarchic character of the squatter community reveals the "disciplined, yet ephemeral transience which has endured over seventy-five years" (Hailey and Wylie 2018: 9). While the site has yet to attract systematic archaeological work, the reuse of a military installation offers a metaphor for the long "tail" (*sensu* Schofield 2009) of military sites and Virilio's arguments for the persistence of postwar militarism in shaping the material culture of the contemporary world. The same materiality that often works to obscure the character and extent of military bases and their discipline can leave its traces inscribed on the landscape for the future. In this way, bases continue to shape the experience of individuals who seek to reuse their "tail" in much the same way that Cold War installations and technology have infiltrated everyday life.

From Military Camps and College Campuses

Christopher Tilley and Kate Cameron-Daum in their study of the East Devon Pebble-bed heathlands noted that this unique landscape served well the rigorous training undertaken by the Royal Marine Commandos (2017).

This landscape plays a key role in shaping the body of the soldiers as they endure grueling weeks of training activities set against human and natural features in this distinctive environment. From copses of trees and hills to paths, foxholes, and water features cut into the hard pebbly ground of the heath, the experience of training in this unforgiving terrain contributed to the sense of camaraderie among Royal Marines as well as their tactical abilities (Tilley and Cameron-Daum 2017: 84–123). Like the Nevada Test Site and the Woomera rocket range in South Australia, sites such as the East Devon heathlands formed part of the sprawling battlefield of the Cold War, which evokes both nineteenth-century aspirations for imparting military discipline on mind and body and the totalizing context for the twenty-first-century War on Terror.

The second part of this chapter explores the similarities between the archaeology of military installations and schools and university campuses. Like military bases, these institutions sought not only to impart discipline but also to demonstrate their effectiveness to a diverse audience. As a result, camps and schools tend to present attractive and well-ordered campuses, and often have a vested interest in obscuring or obfuscating the limits to institutional control. Archaeology thus offers an opportunity to reveal both the methods of control and evidence for student resistance. Moreover, college campuses have long served as useful training grounds for student archaeologists. Campus archaeology programs seek both to introduce archaeological methods and to produce a more nuanced understanding of the contemporary campus and their past. The architecture of control present on American university campuses has unfortunate parallels with the design of schools established to impart white, European discipline on the bodies and minds of Native American students. Recent archaeological research into the character of Native American residential schools in the United States and Canada has revealed abuses obscured by tidy military-style discipline as well as evidence for resistance and survivance among Native American students. As many of these schools remained active into the mid–twentieth century, research has involved former students and their descendants who have collaborated with white and Indigenous archaeologists to unpack the complex histories of these institutions. While the origins and development of Native American boarding and residential schools fall outside the main chronological range of this book, the significance of these sites and others like them affords these schools an ongoing relevance for understanding the contemporary trauma of internal colonialism experienced by Native Americans.

American college and university campuses in the postwar decades shaped a generation of citizens. In some cases, their experience on college campuses created opportunities to reinforce and critique the Cold War rivalry between totalizing views of democracy and capitalism and those of communism. As Laurie Wilkie's brilliant study of the fraternity Zeta Psi on the University of California's Berkeley campus has shown, fraternity life played a key role in shaping the white, male, upper-class identities of the fraternity's brotherhood (Wilkie 2010). Through a careful and creative reading of material culture, architecture, and documentary sources, Wilkie traced the role that Zeta Psi played in shaping the identity of its brotherhood and amplifying the larger social situation of American university life and culture in the late nineteenth and early twentieth centuries. Her excavations of the two generations of Zeta Psi houses that had become the property of the University of California in the 1950s demonstrated the potential for archaeological work to reveal a nuanced and deeply human image of fraternity life that navigates a complex middle ground between the dystopian visions of fraternity life present in the mass media and the utopian aspirations of their founders (Wilkie 2010: 7–8).

The history of excavations on campus largely follow the development of historical archaeology with work at Harvard (Stubbs et al. 2010) and the University of South Carolina (South 2010) beginning in the 1970s. While the focus of campus excavations has varied, many projects have sought to reveal more about student and private life on campus. The results of such fieldwork invariably complicate the relationship between often-pious official histories of the campus community and evidence for the lived experience of student and faculty life (Lewis 2010). Like archaeological work associated with military bases, records preserved in official documents and correspondence tell only part of the story. For example, on Brown University's campus, Andrew Dutton's discovery of bullet casings in excavations that date to the end of the nineteenth and early twentieth centuries suggest that students did not heed gun bans on campus (Dufton et al. 2019: 307). Similarly, work at the former Zeta Psi house produced a significant number of alcohol bottles from the era of prohibition, indicating that house residents illegally consumed alcohol (Wilkie 2010: 195–199). These kinds of disjuncture between official policies and rules and practices are common in historical archaeology. In general, attention to the archaeology of the contemporary university and college campuses has focused on periods, buildings, and activities prior to the mid-twentieth century. This is consistent with the often conservative attitudes toward both campus life and the physical fabric common at American universities. The emphasis on tradition as a way to produce memories shared across generations of students creates an environment where archaeology would complement the larger mission of the university in presenting its own past and image of persistence.

In addition to these practical and ideological motives to explore campus archaeology, campus excavations reflected a desire to create an affordable and accessible field school. Wilkie's work at the Zeta Psi fraternity house, for example, involved students, and generations of students have cut their teeth on various excavations at Harvard (Stubbs et al. 2010) and Brown (Dutton et al. 2019). The awareness of accessibility and inclusivity in the field represents an important trend in the discipline (Skowronek and Lewis 2010). Campus field schools offer more inclusive opportunities for students and provide opportunities for outreach to the campus community, whose support is often vital to the sustainability of programs (Klein et al. 2018).

Despite the roots of campus fieldwork in historical archaeology, few projects have focused more narrowly on the archaeology of contemporary campus life. In the early 1980s, Wilk and Schiffer, for example, proposed a class that used the material culture of the University of Arizona as the basis for studying and documenting the archaeological formation process, stratigraphy, survey, and hypothesis building as well as a more acute understanding of modern material culture (Wilk and Schiffer 1981). They started by introducing students to evidence of wear patterns in campus buildings, architectural stratigraphy, and discard patterns across campus through a material culture tour. Students were encouraged to develop hypotheses for these patterns and eventually document them on their own. More recently, Stacey Lynn Camp's Campus Trash Project at the University of Idaho integrated some of the lessons of William Rathje's garbology project with contemporary environmental and conservation concerns on the university campus (Camp 2010). Like most campus archaeology projects, part of the goal of Camp's work was to train students in methods of intensive archaeological documentation. Camp's project also sought to inform policy decisions and propose better ways to manage discard on campus. This shaped their focus on the distribution of contemporary trash across campus, the discard practices associated with regular events like tailgating, and the impact of trash on ecologically sensitive landscapes. In a similar project, G. Logan Miller developed an archaeological methods class designed to document the distribution of cigarette butts on the Illinois State campus (Miller 2017). The decision to document cigarette butts, at a time when many campuses were going smoke-free and smoking appeared to be in decline, demonstrated that archaeology can challenge the "hegemonic narrative" found in the documentary records. Miller and his students showed that high-traffic areas produced the greatest number of cigarette butts, but also that most of the butts were over a month old and likely had been moved from their original location of discard. This attentiveness to site formation, time, and distribution created a context that allowed for more refined analysis of the dataset. The simple conclusion that smoking continued to occur at measurable levels on and around campus contributed to the larger trend in campus archaeology seeking to complicate traditional narratives of campus life.

On Stanford University's campus, Timothy Webmoor and his colleagues studied Building 500 during a phase of abandonment prior to its repurposing as the Stanford Archaeology Center (Webmoor 2014). Their work applied a wide range of experimental techniques that sought to capture the complicated interplay between materials and objects associated with this building. From the start, they recognized in Building 500 a common type of structure on university campuses. It was neither a ruin of the kind that has attracted photographers to places like Detroit in pursuit of "ruin porn" (see chapter 7), nor was it a building in active use. The indeterminate state of the building, perhaps evocative of the process of revaluation described by Michael Thompson in his "rubbish theory" (Thompson 1979; see chapter 2) obscures its status as a ruin as it undergoes continuous transformation into new, useful, forms. The constant regeneration of buildings across university campuses reflects the practical realities of these fixed investments and finds a parallel with the processes that encourage the refitting of buildings that make up the "tail" of military sites. Moreover, it produces "transitory ruins" that preserve signs of abandonment, ruination, reuse, and adaptation that complicated conventional archaeological practices and emphasized the ontologically blurriness of ruins as a category. For Webmoor and his team, this encouraged holistic practices of documentation that challenged archaeology's traditional commitment to metrology and dividing the whole into parts as a means of complete documentation. Instead, Webmoor employed overlapping approaches to documentation that included both conventional practices such as photography and textual description as well as a range of video techniques, audio recordings, maps, illustration, and list making designed to represent the messiness and complexity of this building. For Webmoor, these approaches reflected an interest in understanding the materiality of the building as not simply a passive object awaiting documentation but as an active participant in the archaeological process. The fluid responsiveness to the ruins themselves produced methods of documentation that emphasized a care for objects and their role in creating our shared world.

The application of these techniques to a building on a university campus is more than just an exercise in convenience. While Webmoor stresses the proximity of ruins in our daily lives, campus architecture represents a distinctly dynamic assemblage of buildings and experiences. Not only are campus buildings regularly adapted and repurposed to serve the needs of a changing group of students and faculty, but, perhaps paradoxically, they represent the material backdrop for students during a key transitional time in their social lives. This sense of attachment is manifest in the fondness of Zeta Psi members for their former house on campus and their concern that the new house has compromised the sense of brotherhood among more recent fraternity members (Wilkie 2010). Despite the significance of architecture to the experience of campus life, buildings are also continuously falling in and out of ruin and abandonment as they are repurposed to serve different functions and to maintain pace with the changing expectations of research, learning, and student life.

Boarding Schools, Violence, and Resistance

The dynamic character of campus buildings and the tension between the promise of disciplined bodies and the realities of resistance, decay, and change over time, provide a crucial backdrop to recent work on twentieth-century boarding and residential schools. From the late nineteenth century, these schools often used military-style discipline as a means of social control over often involuntary subjects. In the case of boarding and residential schools aimed at Native American populations, the well-ordered appearance of schools reflected the promise of an orderly transition to a way of life in keeping with white European standards of bodily and social discipline. On the other hand, the appearance of student discipline, the tidiness of the school grounds, and the arrangement of campus spaces often served to hide the messier and deeply traumatic side of student life and to prevent and obfuscate efforts at student resistance. It is in this context that the archaeology of educational institutions plays a key role in not only unpacking the methods that the schools used to communicate and enforce social expectations but also as evidence for student resistance. In the following section we will look at recent archaeology done at Indian residential and boarding schools, which explicitly considers how these places sought to suppress and hide student resistance to their mission. While the history of these institutions often falls outside the narrow chronological scope of this book, I justify including them because of their continued operation into the late twentieth century and their ongoing personal and cultural relevance to these communities. The examples explored in this section will also consider how their ongoing significance shaped fieldwork associated with these institutions and the efforts by various stakeholders to commemorate their role. The final example involves the tragic research into the remains associated with the Arthur G. Dozier School for Boys, a reform school in Marianna, Florida, with a long history of abusive practices toward its wards.

The legacy and history of Native American residential and boarding schools is complex and often tragic. Introduced in the late nineteenth century, these schools represented a strategy designed to force Native American and First Nations children to abandon their Indigenous identities and adopt settler-European ways of life. The origins of these schools was in the nineteenth-century shift from military and political efforts to colonize Native Americans as external enemies of the state to twentieth-century efforts at internal colonization that sought to eradicate Native American groups through various forms of assimilation. The military origins of these practices persisted in the organization of boarding and residential schools where federal and state authorities sent, sometimes by force, Native American children for re-education. In general, these institutions, such as the Carlisle Indian School founded in 1879, provided basic instruction in English, reading, writing, and math, as well as vocational training military drills and discipline. In practice, these institutions prepared Native American children for manual labor and domestic service after their schooling and sought to undermine their connection to their Indigenous languages, traditions, and lifeways. While most of the research has focused on the origin and early twentieth-century history of these schools, many of these schools continued to function in various capacities well into the late twentieth century. More than that, the often traumatic experiences associated with time spent at these schools continues to shape Indigenous identity in the United States and Canada today.

Archaeology has shed particular light on the strategies used to enforce discipline, promote gender roles common in white society, and deter resistance among the pupils. Sarah Surface-Evans's study of the Mount Pleasant Indian Industrial Boarding School in central Michigan offers a useful example of this approach (Surface-Evans 2016). This school functioned from 1893 to 1933 and drew students not only from the adjoining Saginaw Chippewa Reservation but also Menominee, Miami, Mohawk, Ottawa, and Potawatomi Tribes. The architecture and design of the campus imparted European standards of order through its use of symmetrical neoclassical architecture, and also strictly segregated the boys' and girls' sections of campus according to educational and social expectations. Girls' dormitories stood proximate to buildings dedicated to domestic science, the hospital, and the laundry, whereas boys' dormitories stood adjacent to vocational education buildings, athletic fields, and a wooded area of campus where boys had considerable freedom to roam. Surface-Evans showed that the degree to which students adhered to these formal divisions remains difficult to determine in the archaeological record. In fact, her excavations suggest that students circumvented school policies in various ways, such as by developing their own currency comprised of clay tokens and beads. Moreover, it appears likely that a student set fire to a dormitory and the school's laundry, both of which stood on the girls' side of campus, suggesting student resistance was perhaps not limited to boys.

A similar pattern of discipline and resistance appeared in Owen Lindauer's work at the Phoenix Indian School dump site. He documented over 100,000 artifacts associated with turn-of-the-twentieth-century life at the Phoenix Indian School, which drew students from Navajo and Hopi communities throughout the American Southwest (Lindauer 2009). The school continued to operate until 1990, although excavations at the school's dump produced primarily artifacts from the early twentieth century. Lindauer argued that the artifacts from the dump revealed the use of military discipline at the school, including the buttons from military-style uniforms, but also showed how students resisted this discipline. The appearance of manufactured objects adapted through traditional tool-making techniques indicated the persistence of Native American craft practices, suggesting that students did not entirely embrace the emphasis on mechanized and industrialized production skills. The presence of nonlocal pebbles and clay effigies of animals and birds hint at continued Native American religious practices at the school despite efforts to suppress them.

Not all work at Indian schools involves excavation, and many recent projects by archaeologists prioritize archival work, ethnographic methods, and historical and commemorative practices that reflect sensitivities to the trauma experienced at these sites. Davina Two Bears's 2019 dissertation documented the Old Leupp Boarding School on the Navajo Reservation. The Old Leupp school functioned from 1909 to 1942, when it was converted to a Japanese Internment Camp before being destroyed in the 1960s. Because the Diné consider excavation to be problematic, Two Bears developed an archaeological approach that drew on archival material, oral histories, and her own familiarity with the site. Consistent with the results of archaeological work by Lindauer and Surface-Evans, Two Bears showed that students at the Leupp School continued Diné practices associated with kinship and gender roles, cosmology, and language despite the sometimes violent efforts to suppress Indigenous ways of life. Her work is especially significant because it both develops and relies on an archaeological practice that respects Indigenous understandings of material remains and presents a complex and nuanced understanding of the experience of childhood at the Leupp School. In this way, Two Bears's work provides another significant example of Gerald Vizenor's concept of survivance (2008), which we saw deployed in Ann Elena Stinchfield Danis's study of community on the Albany Bulb in chapter 5 (Danis 2020). Two Bears understood, for example, that the role of older girls protecting younger or small boys at the school, as well as girls' roles in pilfering additional food at night, preserved Diné attitudes toward kinship and gendered practices outside of the formal structures of education practices. At the same time, she demonstrated how it was possible to subvert the expectations of contemporary archaeological practice with its emphasis on excavation and other materially invasive practices. Her dissertation demonstrated how it was possible to approach the archaeology of the Old Leupp school in ways that respect Diné attitudes toward the past while still rigorously documenting both trauma and stories of resistance.

The emphasis on resistance and survivance at Native American residential and boarding schools should not serve to paper over trauma and physical violence associated with these places. As recent work at the Brandon Indian Residential School in Brandon, Manitoba (Nicols 2015, 2020), and at the Kuper Island Industrial School in British Columbia (Simons, Martindale, and Wylie 2020) have shown, the existence of unmarked burials at these schools reflects the level of crass disregard for the communities they sought to serve. Archaeologists working closely with First Nations communities have sought to make visible the horrible toll of these schools on students and families despite efforts to hide physical cost associated with colonialist practices. The violent dislocation of children from their families, the often inadequate provisions for their well-being and health, and the willingness to conceal the failings of institutions claiming to prepare Indigenous children for a better life reflected a system that required the appearance of control and domination. In such situations, archaeology becomes an approach that can provide a foundation for contemporary Indigenous communities to understand and regain ownership over their own past and, when possible and appropriate, find closure and articulate terms for reconciliation.

The archaeology of Indian residential and boarding schools has benefited from collaborative practices with former Native American students, survivors, and communities. Field schools at the Stewart Indian School in Carson City, Nevada, for example, modeled a multivocal collaborative approach that included Native American archaeologists and communities with college students and white academic archaeologists (Cowie, Teeman, and LeBlanc 2019). The school, which operated from 1890 to 1980, initially drew students from the local tribes and advanced a typical curriculum focused on assimilation of Indians to European culture. In the mid–twentieth century, however, the school adopted more lenient policies to Indian culture, and over the course of its long history garnered a reputation for academic quality and produced both positive and negative memories among former students. Archival work, ground-penetrating radar, and test trenches sought to shed light on the early history of the school and its transformation into the late twentieth century. Test pits not only produced artifacts associated with military-style discipline at the school such as uniform buttons and buckles, but also student behaviors including hunting and games. In many ways, the objects excavated at the school were consistent with those found at other Indian schools in the United States. The military discipline, well-kept lawns, and carefully ordered spaces of the schools belied evidence of student life that resisted neat categorization. The more significant contribution of this project, however, was the project's deep commitment to collaboration with the Native American community in the field. This resulted in the project reburying Native American objects dating to before the school's founding in ways consistent with Native American beliefs that objects should be returned to the earth. The publication also featured reflections by white and Native American contributors on the project, its methods, and its goals. Adopting practices such as prayers and smudging prior to the start of excavations each day reinforced the character of this project as a collaboration designed to recognize the past and chart the future of this school and its legacy. The project's emphasis on ethical collaborative archaeological practices reveals the crucial interplay between archaeological work as a method for complicating historical narratives of domination and resistance and as a component of preserving these narratives for future generations of both white and Native American communities.

The work at Native American residential and boarding schools paralleled the excavations at the Arthur G. Dozier School for Boys in Florida by archaeologists from the University of South Florida (Kimmerle, Wells, and Jackson 2016; Jackson 2016). This work revealed over fifty burials dating to its time as a reform school. The excavations at the site were in response to a committed chorus of voices describing the physical, emotional, and sexual abuse at the school and the shady history of undocumented and poorly documented burials at the site. The excavations focused on a small cemetery at the school, where an indeterminate number of burials existed beneath a grid of thirty-one white-painted crosses erected only after the school had closed its doors in 2011. The excavators argued that the poorly maintained records and cemetery reflected an effort to hide the number of deaths at the school and the long-standing abuse of students in its care. Excavations revealed fifty-five burials at the Boot Hill cemetery at the school, and these included at least fifty-one individuals. The remains of at least ten individuals who died in a 1914 dormitory fire were commingled and spread among seven graves. Most of the other burials belong to children whose remains will never be reunited with their families and who leave only tragic traces in the school records. The most recent deaths occurred in the 1950s and early 1960s. Kaniqua L. Robinson's dissertation focused on efforts to ensure that these children receive proper memorialization and considered how issues of race, political power, and religion shaped the negotiation between survivors of abuse at the Dozier School and stakeholders with various interests in the school. Race shaped the experiences of survivors, for example, because prior to desegregation, the school grounds were divided according to race, with Black students and white students living in separate dorms and attending classes in separate buildings. The ultimate decision to erect two memorials, one in the Dozier School chapel and one in Tallahassee, embodies the diverse stakeholders in the development of narratives that memorialize the abuses at the school. These memorials, as well as the regular gatherings of survivors and the careful archaeological work by the USF team, disrupted the historic efforts to obscure the abuses on the Dozier campus and the deaths of students in their care by making visible activities at the school that school administrators sought to hide.

Conclusion

Studying military bases and school and college campuses may seem quite a stretch from workforce housing sites in the Bakken, but both campus and camps represent two contemporary examples of landscapes of control. These sites, however, tell more complex stories when subjected to archaeological investigation. Just as the archaeology of border crossing, forced migrants, and the homeless reveals traces of lives obscured, the archaeology of military installations, protest camps adjacent to bases, research sites, and the tidy spaces of the "ivory tower" and boarding and residential schools demonstrates how systematic fieldwork can reveal hidden complexities even amid the most controlled and well-organized spaces of our contemporary world. The way that the persistent grid of cement pads at Slab City continues to order the squatter community at the site offers a particularly tangible example of the influence of military architecture on the American landscape, which has come to characterize our national borders, our internal landscapes, and even our expansion into outer space. The neat records and arrangements, however, often serve to hide the long-term impacts on military activity in the landscape or the creative efforts to adapt military plans to the new needs and functions. In other cases, the archaeology of college and school campus reveal how students experience sometimes defies military discipline and the architecture of control. Tragic events at Indian boarding and residential schools and the Dozier School for boys show how the orderly external appearance of schools can obscure horrors. At the same time, efforts to document student life on campus and at boarding schools have revealed myriad ways in which studies resisted control, preserved their cultures and identities, and undermined efforts to produce discipline bodies. Thus, archaeology of the contemporary world lays bare the disconnect between strategies of control and resistance in the past and provides a basis for understanding and commemorating both invisible impacts of military activities and survivance of groups and individuals whose experiences shaped their lives.

Efforts to document military bases and school and college campuses might appear at quite a remove from our efforts to document workforce housing in the Bakken oil patch of North Dakota. This work, however, provided us with a model for understanding the tension between efforts to produce outward expressions of order, through controlled access points, tall fences, and the tidy uniformity of corporate workforce housing sites, and the realities facing workers in North Dakota as they seek to balance the brutal winters, the difficult housing markets, and their own desire for autonomy in an environment defined by efficiencies and profits. As subsequent chapters of this book will show, understanding the limits to control is often the basis for organized protest as well as a significant contribution to the development of informal urbanism that shaped certain elements of workforce housing in the Bakken as well as urban growth on a global scale.

7

The City, Ruins, and Protests
in the American Experience

The orderly arrangement of workforce housing camps illuminates one pole in our experience of the Bakken oil patch. Our efforts to understand the character and influences on workforce housing in the region compelled us to engage with not only unfamiliar forms of urbanism and settlement but also a vast industrial landscape. This led us to research the archaeology of camps and campuses, as discussed in the last chapter, and also the archaeology of contemporary cities and their ruins. As we engage with the rapidly growing body of scholarship, we expand our perspectives from comparisons with the tidy and controlled appearance of some workforce housing sites to the more chaotic and ad hoc forms of domestic space across the Bakken more broadly. The range of housing forms present in western North Dakota during the oil boom offered a poetic parallel to the aspirations for the orderly extraction of oil and the sometimes unruly and reticent character of the Bakken formation itself.

In this chapter, we will consider the intersection of the archaeology of industrial ruins, protests, and the contemporary city. As we crisscrossed the Bakken oil patch documenting houses, we also attempted to follow the routes of oil and gas pipelines and to understand the relationship between pipeline and tank farms, marveling at the sudden appearance of gas compression stations, wastewater disposal wells, and rail unit yards. In doing this, we shared experiences of urban explorers who marveled at the complexities of Detroit's abandoned industrial landscapes and hidden infrastructure in Los Angeles. Much like these urban landscapes, the Bakken landscape was diachronic. We noted evidence of the past boom and anticipated the future ruins of the early twenty-first-century frenzy of oil exploration and extractions (figure 7.1). The intrinsically diachronic character of these landscapes served as a useful reminder of the limits of the

Figure 7.1. Abandoned oil pump in the Bakken. Author photo.

contemporary as a chronological period narrowly focused on objects and situations originating in the last fifty years.

Reading scholarship on the archaeology of the contemporary city while witnessing the 2020 protests following the killing of George Floyd similarly revealed the limits of our Bakken case study as a window for understanding recent work on the past and present of the contemporary city. This chapter thus indulges the same discursive tendency as many other chapters in the book and tests the limits of a case-based approach to defining the field and the chronological boundaries of the contemporary world itself. This indulgence, however, seems appropriate, if not necessary, to understand the archaeology of contemporary settlement. Urban, suburban, and ex-urban landscapes often epitomize the juxtaposition of the physical traces of past and present experiences and push the archaeology of the contemporary world to recognize the complexity of contemporaneity, as noted in the introduction to this book. Recent protests remind us that the past is very much present in the contemporary world. The entanglement of the past in the present helps us understand the protests surrounding the route of the Dakota Access Pipeline and transformation of monuments dedicated to Confederate leaders in Richmond, Virginia. While this chapter originated amid the drill rigs and tank farms of the contemporary Bakken oil boom, it will go beyond the questions of extraction, industrial production, and urbanism to show how archaeology of the contemporary world shares historical archaeology's commitment to critiquing capitalism, colonialism, and racism. Scenes of protest set against the dystopian scenes of abandonment, decay, and toxic history trace the uneven social landscape at the blurry boundary between the past and the present.

Introduction

Since the 1980s, if not before, industrial and urban ruins have fueled the popular imagination. The post-industrial ruins of Los Angeles, Detroit, and Philadelphia created a dystopian backdrop for movies such as *Blade Runner* (1982), *RoboCop* (1987), and Terry Gilliam's *12 Monkeys* (1995). The use of power stations, abandoned factories, and urban decay as the setting for the future leveraged obsolete industrial spaces as a gritty critique of technology's anticipated failures. The popularity of these settings echoed the rise of "industrial" rock music that literally drew inspiration from the sounds of late twentieth-century machines and the acoustics of empty and abandoned industrial spaces. Bands like Joy Division, Chrome, and, perhaps most famously, Nine Inch Nails connected punk rock's urban despair to the grinding sonics of abandoned industrial sites in cities such as Sheffield, Detroit, and Cleveland (Wright and Schofield 2021). In this way, films and music popularized an aesthetic cultivated in the science fiction of J.G. Ballard and Philip K. Dick in the 1960s and 1970s, which looked toward the future with skepticism (Jameson 1982, 2005; Caraher 2019).

Decaying industrial landscapes continued to attract attention into the twenty-first century. "Ruin porn" photography emphasized the failure of modernity by focusing on the rusting hulks of modern structures (for a review of the term see Lyons 2018). Factories, schools, train stations, and even entire neighborhoods formed a Gothic backdrop of despair. The interplay between the abundant light, shadow, sharp edges and angles, and the presence of trash, discarded objects, overgrowth, rust, decay, and disorder embodied the tensions between our persistent optimism in science, economic growth, and progress and our growing awareness of the failures of capitalism, its uneven benefits, and the looming cost of its ecological and environmental blind spots. These associations likewise made abandoned buildings appealing backdrops for artists' exhibitions, theater, and music performances that sought to complicate arguments for rigid boundaries between work and play, science and art, capitalism and gifts, and the past and the future (e.g., Murray 2020). The transgressive character of these industrial ruins proved irresistible to urban explorers who found ways to infiltrate abandoned buildings. Urban explorers found in these ruined, urban, and industrial spaces opportunities for the kind of unstructured play that generations of campers, hikers, and suburbanites found in nature (Edensor 2005). Of course, the experience of ruin porn photography and "toxic tourism" peddled to well-healed voyeurs commodified the tragic aesthetic of these transgressive spaces (Pezzullo 2007). The cities of Detroit and Athens, for example, have become known as much for the impact of contemporary economic struggles on their urban fabric as for their past glories. In a contemporary context, abandoned and decaying buildings suffused with human suffering present cautionary tales.

Modern ruins also attract positive associations, as Tim Edensor (2005) brought to the fore in his book on industrial ruins. Ruins offered a counterpoint to structures designed to channel human behavior into predictable, formal, and productive outcomes, replacing them with spaces that seemingly embraced chaos, imagination, and freedom. The potential of industrial and urban ruins as unstructured places for imagination, play, and transgression found formal expression in projects such as Richard Haag's Gas Works Park in Seattle (1972; Whitehouse 2018) and, more recently, Latz and Partner's Landschaftspark in Duisburg-Meiderich in the industrialized Ruhr Valley of Germany (1991; Edensor 2005; DeSilvey 2017). These projects transformed abandoned industrial ruins into municipal parks and recognized industrial ruins as historical monuments, aesthetically interesting structures, and opportunities to bear witness to the re-naturing of industrial landscapes. Caitlin DeSilvey's study of the Landschaftspark in Duisburg-Meiderich emphasized that industrial ruins are not static but always undergoing change. She parallels the ongoing decay of the park, with similar processes at play, with the Orford Ness military installation. Over time, the decay of these former industrial and military structures produced a convivial home to significant plant and wildlife species (DeSilvey 2017; Edensor 2005). The blurry line between the human and the natural environment finds echoes in Jeff VanderMeer's fictional Southern Reach trilogy (2014), which combines an abandoned coastal town and lighthouse with runaway nature in an apocalyptic landscape. Anna Tsing's *Mushroom at the End of the World* (2015) describes how matsutake mushrooms, which have a particularly prestigious position as gifts in Japan, thrive in the denuded environment of industrial forestlands. In these contexts, ruins are generative.

The prominence of ruins at the center of contemporary critique should not imply that industrial landscapes and urban decay are always welcome by their communities. The city of Detroit, for example, has increasingly challenged views of its urban landscape as decaying, abandoned, and forlorn. The desire to restore, demolish, or rehabilitate urban ruins continue long-standing efforts to make urban spaces economically and socially productive by defining them in readily understandable ways. Archaeologists of the contemporary world have often found themselves in the vanguard with those interested in documenting abandoned and decaying places before they are destroyed. For example, as we saw in chapter 4, Krysta Ryzewski has worked with a diverse contingent of scholars and community members to document and save buildings associated with Detroit's famous music scene (Ryzewski 2017, 2022). In another less sensational, but no less significant, context, Larry Zimmerman unsuccessfully encouraged the Minnesota State Historical Society to preserve and display graffiti found in the abandoned Washburn flour mill prior to its reconstruction as the Mill City Museum in Minneapolis as evidence for the site's post-abandonment use (Zimmerman 2013: 347–348). Challenges associated with the tensions between the permanence of modern sites and their obsolescence, the scale of industrial and urban ruins as well as their ephemerality, and the practical and aesthetic potential for adaptation and decay have created new attitudes toward our recent past and heritage management (Bangstad 2014; Buchli 2006).

In these contexts, industrial ruins and urban decay reflect a kind of tension within the American experience. On the one hand, they seem to represent the failed promises of development, prosperity, and community. On the other, our fascination with failure has often led us to overlook evidence for human experiences that exist and even thrive at the outside or at the margins of capitalist models of economic development. As we saw in chapter 5, the archaeology of contemporary homelessness does not always reflect the absence of community or meaningful social relationships. This chapter follows a delicate thread that links concepts of industrial ruins to decay, to urban protests, and to views of the city that extend beyond the urban core. In this context, the chronological and spatial limits of contemporary urbanism give way to life among ruins, transgressive protests, cities defined by transnational encounters, and, finally, the decidedly nonurban spaces of the Bakken.

Ruins, Ruin Porn, and Industrial Archaeology

Much of the contemporary fascination with ruins has emphasized industrial sites. Their monumentality, complexity, and close relationship to narratives of modernization attracted the attention of casual observers drawn to their aesthetic qualities, as well as avocational and professional archaeologists intent on understanding the history of these often imposing structures. At its origins in the 1950s and 1960s in the UK, industrial archaeology stood outside the academic, or even professional, branch of the discipline. Amateur archaeologists collected information, objects, and photographs about sites in their area. They were often motivated by nostalgia or connections to companies who had occupied various sites or facilities (Casella and Symonds 2005). The emphasis on sites associated with the recent industrial heritage of a region or standing buildings distanced industrial archaeology from mainstream archaeology's focus on excavation (Palmer 2005; Orange 2008; Palmer and Orange 2016). Moreover, industrial archaeology's tendency to focus on the details of technological development rather than their larger social significance likewise distinguished it from trends emerging in the field of post-medieval archaeology in the UK and historical archaeology in the United States.

In many ways, the traditions of amateur practice in industrial archaeology, particularly photography, has continued into the twenty-first century even as the field has found more of a home in the academic and professional discipline. The tendency to associate the photography of industrial ruins with issues of industrial heritage and archaeology informed a recent forum on ruin photography in the inaugural issue of the *Journal of the Contemporary Archaeology* (2014). The romantic elements of ruin photography, for example, often privileges the aesthetics of buildings and their situation over aspects of formal interest to archaeologists. Classic works of contemporary photography, such as Robert Smithson's "A tour to the monuments of Passaic, New Jersey" (1996[1967]) and approaches that owe more to the flaneur of Walter Benjamin's *Arcades Project* (2002) than the systematic rigor of archaeological methodology, rub shoulders with more technical engagements of the industrial and urban landscapes. Pétursdóttir and Olsen (2014), however, have argued that ruin photography, far from standing outside archaeological practices, provides an opportunity for critical reflection on photography and ruins as the contexts for archaeological performance, affective engagements with the past, and long-standing archaeological documentation practices. The ability to observe the decay of ruins, which continues even in the absence of human intervention, stands as a reminder of the agency of things. The photographer's lens accentuates the affective character of ruins and emphasizes the bodily position of the photographer as flaneur, moving through decaying and obsolete industrial landscapes (Dawdy 2010). The affective power of ruins and the interplay between photography and place finds parallels in the use of ruins as the backdrop to theatrical performances from the Theater of Dionysus in Athens to abandoned factories around the post-industrial world (Murray 2020; see also Pearson and Shanks 2001). The striking images of the Albert Kahn's Packard Plant and the looming visage of the abandoned and deteriorating Michigan Central Station emerge as tragic icons for the failures of capitalism and uneven consequences to the celebrated rise of the post-industrial economy.

Krysta Ryzewski, however, notes that the desire to use the photographs of ruins for certain aesthetic and political effects has real implications for communities where these ruins are located (Ryzewski 2014, 2019). Such photos have shaped the public perception of cities like Detroit. By treating "ruin porn" as a form of industrial archaeology or archaeology of the contemporary world, it substitutes affective power for methodological rigor and complicates the epistemological and ideological commitments at the disciplinary core of archaeological practice. For example, Ryzewski critiques the lack of context for so much ruin photography, which makes it difficult to understand ruins across chronological and geographic scales. As a telling example, she noted that some of the most popular images of the abandoned Michigan Central Station prefer the backside of buildings to the thriving neighborhood across the street, thus projecting the hulking ruins of the railroad station at the expense of a resilient community (Ryzewski 2014: figure 4; see figure 7.2). The absence of individuals in ruin photography often simultaneously conveys a kind of impartial documentary rigor. This practice leverages conventions developed in more methodologically defined archaeological or architectural photography to represent post-industrialized cities like Detroit as depopulated wastelands rather that communities experiencing vibrancy and facing real social and economic challenges.

Ryzewski's multifaceted community archaeology work in Detroit seeks

Figure 7.2. Two views of Michigan Central Station. Photo courtesy of Krysta Ryzewski.

to replace the image of the city often defined by ruin porn with a more complex dynamic, human, and multi-scalar understand of the material culture of the contemporary community there (2017, 2019, 2022). As we saw in chapter 4, she collaborates with her students at Wayne State University in Detroit as well as community members to document structures and places significant to the music industry in the city. The parallel between the distinctive sound of Motown and the global reach of the Detroit's automobile manufacturing not only defined the mid-century landscape of

Detroit but extended its influence far beyond its urban limits. The use of petroleum products as the basis for both record pressing and automobiles is simply a happy coincidence and reflects the complex global economies necessary for both industries to thrive (Devine 2019). In the second decade of the twenty-first century, however, many of the places at the heart of the auto and record industry were abandoned, surrounded by blighted neighborhoods, or slated for demolition by various groups looking to develop new post-industrial identities and to distance themselves from the city's industrial past. Ryzewski's work used digital tools and conventional heritage practices to document the wide range of music practices in Detroit from early twentieth-century ballrooms to jazz and blues joints and the clubs of Motown, rock, techno, and house music. The use of many of these venues for multiple genres of music and musicians of very different styles, races, and ages effectively repopulated long-neglected spaces and challenged the forlorn and depopulated landscapes of ruin porn. These kinds of documentation projects often serve to draw attention to endangered sites or to shift public perceptions related to "blighted" or ruined landscapes.

Attention to the social aspects of urban change (Ryzewski 2014; Paul Mullins 2012, 2014) informs critiques of ruin porn photography and industrial archaeology, which sometimes obfuscates the tremendous human toll that industrial ruins represent. Not only do industrial ruins reveal the loss of jobs and economic activity for communities, but the absence of humans from the images allow viewers to overlook the racial and ethnic aspects of industrial decline and the impact ruins have on economically disadvantaged communities. These criticisms find parallels with recent work in industrial archaeology. As LouAnn Wurst and Stephen A. Mrozowski (2016) and Paul Shackel (2009) have noted, the emphasis on the materiality of technological advancement in industrial archaeology has tended to marginalize the role of labor. By drawing industrial archaeology more fully into the field of historical archaeology, scholars have turned their attention to the role of industrial labor in shaping communities, class, and individual identity. Ventures such as Randall Maguire's Colorado Coalfield War project sought to place labor relationships at the center both of the archaeology of the early twentieth-century Ludlow massacre site and in its modern effort to engage with organized labor in the region (McGuire and Reckner 2002, 2003). Michael Roller's (2018) research in and around the coal mining toward of Pardeesville, Pennsylvania, considered the long reach of structural violence at the intersection of race, labor, and class in Pennsylvania's anthracite region, which continues to influence the lives of contemporary residents. Various short-term efforts to revive the economy in the region involved shifting the economy to increasing casual labor. Situated amid the decaying industrial structures of the coal industry, light industrial and warehouse work offered short-term and irregular employment opportunities for these communities, as capital from outside the region recognizes pools of low-cost labor in these post-industrial communities.

Industrial ruins tell human stories and preserve the past for the present. Thus, plans to remove the ruins often represent efforts to erase the history of struggles preserved in these places and the lessons that they offer for contemporary communities. Roller, for example, demonstrates how federally funded urban renewal in the late 1960s and early 1970s promised to transform abandoned commercial districts of "coal patch" towns by demolishing buildings identified as "blighted" and to encourage the redevelopment of urban spaces and the creation of post-industrial suburbs. Part of these efforts involved determining the place of the region's industrial past in its future directions. The material landscape of the mining industry provided essential context to understanding the strategies employed by residents to negotiate a livelihood in the volatile extractive economy. The industrial ruins of the mining industry preserve the history of organized labor in those industries and management's efforts to undermine those efforts in favor of contingent and precious labor practices that continue to shape the region's post-industrial present. The continuing history of contingent and precarious employment in Pennsylvania's coal mining region has attracted a new wave of immigrants from Central America and the Caribbean. Drawn by the area's low cost of living and availability of low-skilled and light industrial work, these new immigrants soon met with local resistance and racial animosity. Ironically, many of the attacks against the new arrivals came from descendants of the Eastern and Southern European immigrants, who flocked to the region to work for the coal industry some 150 years earlier. Roller's work recognizes the complex relations among capital, race, and nationalism inscribed on the industrial and post-industrial landscape.

The economic challenges facing coal mining regions of central Pennsylvania and the decline of the manufacturing sector in Detroit produced ruins associated with the slow-moving disaster of industrial capitalism. These ruins continue to influence the present and future of contemporary communities. Shannon Lee Dawdy applies a similar lens to the ruins produced in the aftermath of Katrina in New Orleans. She argues that the production of ruins in this context sheds valuable light on how the responses to catastrophe exert shapes the archaeological record. The failure of levies and the intensity of the hurricane presented an obvious and temporally constrained catastrophe for residents of the Crescent City (Dawdy 2006, 2010). Her emphasis on the decisions made during the recovery effort, particularly those associated with the taphonomy of the remains of the structures destroyed by the hurricane, reveal the social priorities, political positions, and environmental realities of communities. As an example, she notes that the assemblages preserved around homesites in the predominantly African American Lower Ninth Ward will invariably be richer than those from more affluent neighborhoods where the recovery and reconstruction process were more thorough and took place much more quickly after the storm. The decision to remove all debris prior to rebuilding was a response to the instability of the soils in New Orleans and their tendency to shift and subside. Sites that saw more rapid reconstruction would have seen less material enter into archaeological levels through natural taphonomic processes than those sites in the less affluent Lower Ninth Ward, where demolition and reconstruction was delayed. Thus natural taphonomic processes, the character of the soils themselves, and the social and racial context for recovery all contribute to the character of the archaeological record and the future record of the city's urban past.

The kind of industrial ruins present in Detroit or other post-industrial cities offer a similar window into the taphonomic processes associated with slower-moving economic changes. While the decline of the urban, industrial economy was not as abrupt as the Hurricane Katrina landfall, the taphonomy of the ruined and abandoned structures nevertheless continues to define the contemporary experience of life in these communities. For example, John Schofield's study (2009) of the abandoned English Heritage offices observes the irregular traces of the building's former function after its longtime residents had left and before it was redeveloped into new office space. Christine Finn's journalistic account of a year in Silicon Valley likewise narrates the constant rhythm of abandonment in the post-industrial landscape where office parks, retail space, and corporate campus constantly undergo redevelopment and intervals of abandonment as they adapt to the rapid pace of the digital economy (Finn 2002). Josh Lepawsky's *Reassembling Rubbish* (2018) reminds us, however, that while the reuse of post-industrial spaces often reduces abandonment process to mere months, many post-industrial sites in Silicon Valley produced the same kind of long-term toxicity as abandoned manufacturing sites associated with the industrial economy. As Haeden Stewart (2017) has noted, the impact of toxic chemicals around abandoned sites persists long after the visible signs of abandonment have vanished. Moreover, the leaching of chemicals into waterways, vegetation, and the wider ecosystem communicates the impact of industrial (and post-industrial) practices well beyond the temporal and spatial constraints of the structures. The varying causes and forms of abandonment and ruins contribute to their status as ontologically ambiguous places (Edensor 2005). From an archaeological perspective, ruins continue to have an impact on individuals and communities long after the events associated with their abandonment, and the impact invariably reflects racial, economic, and political contexts.

Protest, Graffiti, and Urbanism

An interest in ruins and abandonment as well as race and capital in post-industrial contexts contributes to well-established trends in historical archaeology (e.g., Shackel 2009; Wurst and Mrozowski 2014). In the archaeology of the contemporary world, these approaches have informed the archaeology of protest against the way in which the contemporary world defines race, class, gender, and other forms of identity. As discussed in chapter 6, archaeological investigations at the protest camps associated with the Nevada Test Site showed how protesters responded to the testing and development of nuclear weapons as well as the appropriation of traditional range lands from the Western Shoshone. Thus, these protests critiqued both American colonialism and militarized, global, postwar American nationalism (Schofield et al. 2008; Beck et al. 2009). The contemporary Greenham Common Airbase protests in the UK similarly combined a critique of tensions associated with Cold War nationalism with a statement on the gendered natural of military aggression. Women and children occupied the protest camps surrounding the airbase (Schofield and Anderton 2000). As Schofield and Anderton observe, the uniquely gendered aspect of these protests saw women challenging the hyper-masculine militarism of the base by sexually taunting the soldiers on the other side of the fence. In other cases, women used the fence to display knitting, children's clothes, and other items associated with women's role of caring for the next generation. Such gestures used examples of conventionally gendered work to mock the futility of the masculine airbase in mending the present and prepare for the future. Schofield and Anderton recognized that gendered tactics of the protesters at the Greenham Common resembled strategies developed by women in the UK in other situations such as the 1984 coal workers strike and the Prostitution Collective movement that began in the mid-1970s. The archaeological remains of the protests camps at the Greenham Common Airbase and the Nevada Test Site remain modest, but when combined with oral histories and other forms of evidence they help demonstrate the global reach of Cold War protests that parallel the global experience of this conflict, as noted in chapter 5.

The cultural and political significance of materially ephemeral sites offers an important counterpoint to archaeological efforts to document persistent industrial ruins. Carolyn White's archaeology of the Burning Man arts and culture festival in the Nevada Desert presents a sophisticated template for how the archaeology of the contemporary world can approach dynamic, temporary places such as a week-long Burning Man festival in the desert (White 2020). Despite key differences between the well-organized site of Black Rock City, where the Burning Man festival takes place, and more spontaneous protest sites, such as those associated with the Occupy movement, both kinds of site embrace the spirit of self-sufficiency, improvisation, and a commitment to a cause. White's book used photography, scale drawings and sketches, and interviews to document the camping sites associated with Burning Man. She then incorporated surface survey into understanding how the Burning Man organizers removed all traces of the festival site to the satisfaction of the Bureau of Land Management. She carefully considered the way in which active site archaeology navigated the private and public spaces of the festival and respected the wishes of participants whose goals were quite different from those of the research archaeologists. Moreover, White offers another example of how an adaptive archaeology of the contemporary world can capture the complexities of the ephemeral experiences that constitute key moments in twenty-first-century life.

These approaches played a vital role in the archaeology of protests that sought to capture the ephemeral but complex responses to the economic and racial difficulties facing American cities in the late twentieth and early twenty-first centuries. Crystal R. Simms and Julien Riel-Salvatore (2016), for example, examined the sanitary conditions of Occupy Denver (OD), which was part of the larger Occupy Wall Street movement, in response to claims by Colorado Governor John Hickenlooper that the OD protesters were a public health and safety risk. Simms and Riel-Salvatore encountered the challenges facing any archaeological project seeking to document an active and occupied space of habitation, including its constantly changing character and concerns for privacy and ethical documentation practices (cf. White 2020 on similar challenges at Burning Man). Still, an awareness of the dynamic character of the OD encampment revealed that many of the generalizations regarding the OD protest camp reflected the camp's transition from a site largely used by short-term protesters to an encampment comprised of the long-term homeless. Despite the seemingly continuous occupation of the Occupy Denver site, their research project recognized that they collected most of the data on sanitation and safety from when chronically homeless individuals occupied the site rather than when it was occupied by political protesters. The prevalence of drug paraphernalia, for example, and an outbreak of scabies are likely related to challenges associated with long-term homelessness, not with the protesters' encampment. An effort to document the material culture of the Occupy movement in New York's Zuccotti Park produced photographs and descriptions that appeared on a website, were displayed and curated at Columbia University's Archaeology Lab, and were featured in conference papers (http://ows -archaeology.blogspot.com). While this work appears to have produced no formal publications, the assemblages and photographs capture the wide range of behaviors connected to the Occupy movement's temporary camps, as well as patterns of distribution associated with their disruption by police. Authorities sought to challenge the message of the protesters by representing their actions as unsanitary and irresponsible, as well as to undermine the impact of their work by breaking up the camps and obscuring their mark on the urban landscape.

The ephemeral nature of protest events, the opposition of authorities, and the complexity of protesters' goals and organization often make systematic archaeological documentation of even large protests difficult. The recent call of Beisaw and Olin (2020) to document the site of the Dakota Access Pipeline (DAPL) Protest in North Dakota rests on both the disciplinary responsibility toward recognizing the diverse range of Native American claims to land and their history of protests. They frame their call to document the DAPL protest camp by presenting a critical study of the efforts to preserve the Native American occupation of Alcatraz Island from 1969 to 1971. The occupation of the island, the abandoned prison, and its grounds were among the most visible efforts of Native Americans to reassert claims to traditional lands, both in California and across the United States. In recognition of the significance and visibility of this protest, the National Park Service, who now manages the island as a national monument, has preserved painted signs on the walls of the prison and, with the aid of Native American activists and scholars, developed an exhibit room in the penitentiary museum. For Beisaw and Olin, however, the removal or failure to preserve many traces of the Native American occupation of the island and the absence of consistent interpretative signage renders this history of the protest difficult to understand for the casual visitor. Unlike the relatively short-term protests of the Occupy movement or the DAPL protest camp, the more literal occupation of Alcatraz Island would have left more persistent traces that could be preserved and presented to visitors. The intensity of the DAPL protests may well have left a similarly visible material trace to present a vital counter-narrative to the prevailing media view, which characterizes the protest camp as occupied by professional agitators seeking to escalate a conflict with oil companies and the local authorities. At the same time, the protesters themselves often emphasized the 150 years of conflict between white colonial concepts of land use and exploitation and Native American rights and attitudes toward the land (Estes 2019). For Native American protesters, the Dakota Access Pipeline protests were about more than simply the route of the pipeline and the risk it held for the Standing Rock reservation; they also evoked long-held attitudes toward protecting water, land, ancestors, and their communities from damage. A more humane, diverse, and nuanced presentation of this at both Alcatraz and the DAPL site would complicate perceptions rooted in political jurisdiction and authority and call into question the close alliance of capital and militarized law enforcement as representative of public order.

A similar interest in the archaeology of twenty-first-century protests has emerged surrounding the protests that occurred in the wake of George Floyd's murder in 2020 and the related efforts to remove or destroy monuments associated with racist figures in urban areas. Recent work on Confederate statues, for example, places these monuments in the context of early twentieth-century racial politics. Wealthy Southern Whites invoked Confederate leaders as a way to intimidate southern Black political activists. They also sought to divide workers along racial lines to prevent them from forging new political alliances to combat economic exploitation in the industrializing South (Savage 2018; Shackel 2003; Thompson 2022). The destruction and defacing of these statues nearly a century later reflected demographic changes in southern cities and nearly a half-century of Black political leadership in communities that continued to suffer from economic inequality, inadequate social services, blight, and violence. The outpouring of iconoclasm that occurred in cities across the United States (and the world) reflected efforts of Black and minority communities to seize control of their urban spaces in the present by erasing racially motivated efforts to commemorate the past.

As Simms and Riel-Salvatore (2016) noted in their efforts to document the material signature of the Occupy Denver movement, the speed at which many of these protests occurred, their diverse and widespread nature, and the ephemeral character of some of the transformations have required innovative approaches to documenting the protests and their changing manifestations in the urban fabric. The Philadelphia-based Monument Lab project, for example, is performing a National Monument Audit in an effort to document and understand the changing monumental landscape of American cities (Farber et al. 2020). The Smithsonian's National Museum of African American History and Culture is collecting artifacts associated with the 2020 protests against police brutality in Washington, DC's Lafayette Square (Smithsonian National Museum of African American History and Culture 2020). Artists Terry Kilby used drone photography in July 2020 to produce a 3D model of the statue of Robert E. Lee in Richmond, Virginia, and posted it to the 3D viewing site Sketchfab (Kilby 2020). Kilby's model preserved the spray-painted sentiments expressed by protesters, which ranged from expressions of anger, love, unity, and racial solidarity to calls to "tear it down," revolution, and anarchism. The sheer volume and variety of messages jostling with each for attention on the monument embodied the diversity of the protesters, their motivations, and goals (figure 7.3). Absent, of course, were the equally dramatic messages projected on the statue at night, which left no material trace. The techniques employed by Kilby and other historians, journalists, archaeologists, and community members to document the protest were similar to those used during archaeological fieldwork (e.g., Sapirstein and Murray 2017) and also reflect the need and opportunities for ad hoc approaches to recording the often ephemeral remains of protests. There is no doubt that the protests against racism and police brutality and the removal of racist monuments marked a significant moment in the history of both race and urbanism in the United States. The traces of these protests continue a tradition of practices—including graffiti, tagging, and street art—that is fundamental to modern, global urban experience.

Archaeological interest in contemporary graffiti emerged in concert with economic and racial turmoil in the United States in the 1970s, most notably in major urban areas like New York City, Philadelphia, and Chicago (Oliver and Neal 2010). At the time, graffiti represented a challenge to the urban order and was regarded by civic leaders as vandalism and an assault on private and public property. Since that time, archaeologists and anthropologists, as well as a wide range of urban explorers and photogra-

Figure 7.3. Statue of Robert E. Lee on Monument Avenue, Richmond, Virginia.

phers, have documented graffiti and street art as windows into the communities, identities, rituals, and tensions that define urban life. Schiffer and Gould's seminal 1981 book, *Modern Material Culture,* includes C. Fred Blake's chapter analyzing graffiti in bathrooms in and around the University of Hawai'i (Blake 1981). He notes that the use of racial and ethnic insults directed toward white, Japanese, and native Hawaiians confirms the role of liminal places for the public expression of transgressive language that, ironically, reinforces social norms. In other contexts, however, archaeologists have argued that graffiti plays a role in placemaking activities that challenge hegemonic views of what constitutes liminal or marginal places. Gabriel Soto, for example, argued that the presence of graffiti in box culverts along roads in the Sonoran Desert is a form of placemaking along an otherwise sterile and indistinct landscape (Soto 2017). Susan Phillips's landmark efforts to document graffiti in Southern California and Chicago traced its function over nearly a century from marking the route of hobos during the Great Depression to marking out spaces for transgressive sexual liaisons and tracing gang territory. She blends practices associated with urban exploration with ethnography to document graffiti as a subversive practice that represents distinct urban landscapes that often elude the official boundaries and jurisdictions (Phillips 2019). In effect, the shared experiences communicated through the graffiti transformed a marginal space into a place made familiar. This graffiti could offer comfort to individuals encountering a wide range of displacements in an unsympathetic and often hostile urban landscape. The use of graffiti to create a sense of place in the city echoes its place in the classic work of Teun Voeten's *Tunnel People* (2010), which explores the life of residents of New York City's abandoned railroad tunnels. The use of graffiti as part of twenty-first-century protests, then, represented a varied and well-established strategy to stake a claim to urban spaces. By challenging the social and political order's control over public spaces, graffiti represents a significant form of resistance to hegemonic forces that use violence and other forms of social, economic, and institutional power to marginalize groups, suppress dissent, and appropriate public space. Thus the archaeology of industrial ruins, protests, graffiti, and contemporary urbanism share a common interest in understanding the impact of late twentieth- and twenty-first-century capitalism on lived experience.

Cities, Race, and Nature

The role of activists and archaeologists in documenting the experience of contemporary urban protests in the United States paralleled a growing historical and archaeological interest in twentieth- and twenty-first-century urbanism. As Laura McAtackney and Krysta Ryzewski's 2017 edited volume demonstrated, the archaeology of the contemporary city often supported projects that involved commitments to political activism in urban settings. Chris Matthews's recent (2020b) work in East Orange, Orange, and Newark, New Jersey, for example, traced how the construction of Interstate 280, urban renewal, and urban divestment transformed these cities into a carceral landscape for their Black residents. The destruction of parts of the city important for the Black community and limited public transportation from the urban core to the suburbs via the new interstate created a space where Black residents suffered from structural disadvantages created by poverty, high population densities, inadequate social services, unemployment, and policing. The conditions in the urban core contrasted with those in the more suburban townships, which were politically separate from these urban areas and overwhelmingly white. Affluent white civic leaders reinforced the divisions between these two separate communities by maintaining far different forms of investment and policing. Paul Mullins's (2017) recent study of postwar Black suburbs in Indianapolis proved that when Black citizens had an opportunity to move into suburbs where Black homeowners could buy homes, they continued to remain active in anti-racist causes. Their material surroundings, however, appeared consistent with suburban life irrespective of race. Mullins argued that this revealed not only the limits of archaeological investigations into issues of race in American suburbs but also how stylistic conformity could reflect residents' aspiration for racial equality with their white neighbors.

Mullins's work elsewhere in Indianapolis provides greater context to the emergence of Black suburbs in this city. The establishment of the Indiana University–Purdue University, Indianapolis (IUPUI) in the city in 1969 led to the destruction of neighborhoods occupied by African American families. Efforts at urban renewal led city leaders to designate many of these neighborhoods slums in the postwar decades and to authorize their demolition as part of the university's expansion. Archaeological and archival work by Mullins and his students demonstrated that this blanket designation overwrote the complex history of these neighborhoods and supported narratives that reinforced a negative view of Black urban residents. At the turn of the twentieth century, the ethnically and racially diverse community succumbed to more racially segregated housing practices that resulted in these neighborhoods becoming home to a growing population of Black migrants to Indianapolis. The reluctance of white city leaders to extend utilities and services to these neighborhoods and the neglect of absentee white landlords resulted in the continued use of outhouses to serve a population swollen by wartime migrants to the area. Mullins's archaeological excavations of boarding houses, residences, and privies beneath the IUPUI campus complemented archival and oral histories to show that despite the material poverty of these neighborhoods, there continued to be vibrant social life, creative economic strategies, and ongoing aesthetic investment in these communities (Mullins 2006; Mullins and Glenn 2010; Mullins and Lewis 2011). By revealing the dynamics of life within these communities in the mid–twentieth century, Mullins challenged the characterization of Black neighborhoods as blighted slums. Moreover, he revealed how a legacy of racism obscured both the processes that led to poverty in these communities and the resilience of the groups who made these neighborhoods home.

Krysta Ryzewski's work on Detroit perhaps provides the most fully realized example of the potential for the archaeology of American cities to trace the range of experiences encountered by their residents (Ryzewski 2022). In chapter 4, we discussed how her work to document the iconic Detroit music scene revealed the economic, social, spatial, and performative dimensions of the Blue Bird Inn jazz club and the Grande Ballroom. Her urban excavations and survey projects throughout Detroit followed many of the same processes that Mullins documented across Indianapolis. Her excavations at the Gilded Age mansion, the Ransom Gillis House, for example, revealed more about the home's later history as a boarding house and a grocery serving a diverse range of white immigrants than its more glamorous past. Its renovation in the early twenty-first century was part of a larger gentrification project in the neighborhood, which restored the mansion in ways that evoked its early twentieth-century history at the expense of its later life. Ryzewski's work at Gordon Park, which stands at the epicenter of the 1967 Detroit uprising, further revealed the ways in which the city and its communities negotiated the sometimes painful history of racial animosity. The city constructed the park as part of its larger effort to remove the damaged, ruined, and vacant buildings in the aftermath of the riots. Ryzewski's fieldwork unpacked a history of local ambivalence and neglect at the park itself, which reflected the complex attitudes associated with understanding the racial history of the city and its uprising. These attitudes gave way only some fifty years after the event, when Gordon Park received a thoughtful renovation in efforts to acknowledge the painful legacy of racial tension in the city and provide a space for the local community to gather, reflect, and socialize.

The works of Roller, Mullins, Matthews, and Ryzewski highlight the complex legacies of urban renewal, racial tension, and violence in the

America's recent past and the ways in which archaeologists can produce more complex and inclusive narratives from sites characterized as blighted, slums, or ruins. This work also clarifies that a chronologically defined concept of contemporaneity often falls short of recognizing the impact of the past on lives of the local communities. Recent work to expand our understanding of the Greenwood neighborhood in Tulsa destroyed by the U.S. government in 1921, for example, has emphasized its economic vitality and impact of its loss on the social lives of Tulsa's Black community (Messer 2021; Odewale and Slocum 2020; Franklin et al. 2020: 758–759). Excavations and efforts to repatriate the remains of Black residents discovered in an unmarked mass grave has emphasized the human scale of the massacre. The one-hundredth anniversary of this massacre coincided with growing protests against racially motivated police violence and stressed the contemporaneity of past and present state-sanctioned violence against Black Americans in U.S. cities. Edward González-Tennant's study of the site of the Black town of Rosewood, Florida, which was destroyed by white rioters in 1923 showed how the Tulsa riots were not an isolated pattern of violence toward prosperous Black communities but part of a larger pattern of racial violence in the first quarter of the twentieth century. While these events fall earlier than the main periods of study in this book, there is no doubt that the destroyed lives, wealth, and community reverberated throughout the twentieth and into the twenty-first century. The pain of these massacres persists, and each episode of police violence against Black communities in the twenty-first century serves as a reminder of this shameful history. This reality challenges a narrow view of the contemporary world framed by arbitrary chronological limits, global conflicts like World War II or the Cold War, or economic changes associated with the 1980s. As noted in the introduction, the very concept of contemporaneity is racially, economically, politically, and socially experienced.

As cities often represent different notions of the contemporary, they also reflect different concepts of what it means to experience American life. Historical archaeologists, anthropologists, and historians have come to recognize that the intersection of race and urbanism in the United States often involves the transnational character of many of these communities. Recent work by Edward González-Tennant, Barbara Voss, and Laura Ng have maintained that understanding the place of Chinese immigrants in contemporary urbanism requires the same kind of transnational attention as understanding borders and migrants, the archaeology of the Cold War, and the character of contemporary consumer culture (González-Tennant 2011; Voss and Allen 2008, Ng 2021; see Rose and Kennedy 2020 for a survey of Chinese diaspora archaeology in the United States). Laura Ng's study of the archaeology of early twentieth-century Chinatowns in Riverside and San Bernardino, California, for example, reveals a material culture and social strategies that developed as much in mainland Chinese communities with long traditions of transnational migration as in American contexts (Ng 2021). Ng conducted surveys in two Chinese home village associated with Southern California Chinatowns. These relationships facilitated the trans-Pacific circulation of ceramic vessels, for example, as well as the construction of religious shrines that supported both communities' hope for agricultural prosperity. Barbara Voss and Edward González-Tennant likewise noted that multisite methods supported more nuanced and sophisticated understandings of Chinese urban communities, which found economic and often extralegal ways to maintain ties with their home villages. These ties continued to shape Chinese material culture and architecture in American cities even as American efforts sought to homogenize Chinese immigrants according to race and to make movement between China and the United States more difficult. While this kind of transnational work remains relatively new in historical archaeology, the work of historian A. K. Sandoval-Strausz on neighborhoods in Chicago and Dallas with a high number of Mexican immigrants demonstrates the significance of these approaches for understanding the changing nature of American urbanism. He argues that these neighborhoods, with their small businesses, high rates of home ownership, and tight-knit communities, have adopted economic and social patterns consistent with communities in Mexico (Sandoval-Strausz 2019). Thus, new urbanist fantasies anchored in nostalgic views of life in American cities have given way to the often more informal realities of transnational forms of urbanism. As we have seen in the study of trash, consumer goods, and the Cold War, archaeologists are coming to recognize American experience in transnational and global contexts that stretches far beyond national borders.

The complex spatial and temporary geographies of cities provide an emerging context for American efforts to reconcile its industrial past with the post-industrial world. The emergence of global supply chains and distributed and just-in-time production practices have transformed the urban landscape in the United States and Europe. The rise of suburbs, white flight, and the decline in tax revenue available to increasingly impoverished cities have contributed to economic, regional, and racial tensions. As we have seen, cities such as Detroit and the South Bronx in New York have become iconic as much for their industrial ruins and poverty as for their storied pasts as manufacturing and cultural centers (e.g., L'Official 2020; Apel 2015). The decaying industrial landscapes of these cities form a backdrop not only for economic and racial protests but also environmental concerns. A growing interest prevails among historical and contemporary archaeologists to understand the environmental impact of industrial practices and urbanization (e.g., Benjamin 2017; Dawdy 2010). As Jeff Benjamin observed, contemporary industrial ruins do more than simply commemorate the limits of capitalism—they also provide opportunities to consider the environmental legacy of our industrial past. Dawdy's understanding of the ruins of post-Katrina New Orleans offers new ways of viewing both the city and disasters. When Hurricane Katrina destroyed the levies holding back the waters of the Mississippi, the literal boundary between the city and river collapsed. The devastation left behind preserved the blurred line between the ordered space of the city, the devastation of Katrina, and the natural and political forces that constituted destruction and recovery.

For Dawdy, the ruins revealed inequalities in economic, social, and political power within the city that dictated which sites were rebuilt, when they saw attention, and how they were rebuilt. Ruins also cultivate the emergence of alternate forms of social and material relations. Anna Tsing studied the social and economic networks that bring matsutake mushrooms to the market (Tsing 2015). These valuable mushrooms thrive in landscapes produced by industrial logging and abandoned intensive agriculture and rely on global networks that stretch from southeast Asian immigrants who harvest mushrooms from the heavily logged forests of Northern California to distribution networks that extend to their markets in Japan. Tsing contends that much as the matsutake mushroom develops rhizomic networks in degraded landscapes, so do new networks emerge that create social and economic meaning in these marginal spaces. As Edensor (2005) and DeSilvey (2005) have observed for industrial ruins, the generative capacity of these places draw on their blurring of social and ontological divisions that define our world, much as cities already call on us to question what we regard as contemporary or even American. The natural and the cultural, the industrial and the rural, the past and the present, the neatly ordered and the chaotic—all coincide in the space of ruins.

By blurring the division between the natural and the human, these views of ruins open onto a larger critique of the relationship between humans and their environment (Millington 2013). This has immense potential for an archaeology of the contemporary cities that goes beyond the level of the site and operates at the scale of city itself. Just as the archaeology of things requires an understanding of object's place within complex global networks of production and contemporary industrial ruins represent the changing flows of capital, so cities embody a wide range of infrastructural, ecological, economic, political, and social networks that converge to create contemporary urban places (Mrozowski 2012). As a result, it seems inevitable that the thriving field of urban environmental history will exert a significant influence (see Culver 2014 for a survey). The work of William Cronon, including his epic study of Chicago, *Nature's Metropolis* (1991), recognizes the relationship between cities and their often expansive hinterlands. Recent scholars following Cronon's lead have eschewed envisioning connections between places as spokes on a wheel or a series of connections and nodes. Instead, some scholars suggest that the ontological blurriness that describes the fuzzy relationship between ruins and nature might likewise apply to the reciprocal relationships that co-create cities and their hinterland. For example, A. Beisaw's article (2017) on the archaeology of New York City's massive water supply parallels David Soll's recent history (2013) of the network of watersheds, reservoirs, aqueducts, communities, agencies, and policies that bring New York its fresh water. The requirements and habits of the New York residents have shaped the landscape and ecology though dams, reservoirs, and watershed conservation designed to ensure the security of New York's water. These efforts, however, have limited the opportunities among upstate communities to develop economically despite their access to lakes and natural space. Amahia Mallea's work (2018) on the relationship between Kansas City and the Missouri River locates the political life of the city at the messy intersection of social, economic, and regional attitudes along the longest river in North America. The river's political reach extends to the protests associated with the Dakota Access Pipeline's route beneath its waters. As the protesters made clear, their protests were not simply a response to local concerns for the pipeline's route but also a response to the massive reach of the Missouri's course and the diverse communities impacted should the pipeline become compromised. The dense web of infrastructure that allows contemporary society to function continuously redefines the character of urban space and transgresses the limits of traditional demographic and administrative divisions. For example, Andrew Needham's environmental history of Phoenix, Arizona (2014), goes beyond the blurry "Crabgrass Frontier" (*sensu* Jackson 1985) of the southwestern city's suburbs and follows the high-current power lines to the coal mines and power plants on the Navajo Reservation that made Phoenix's postwar expansion possible. Matthew Klingle's environmental history of Seattle begins and ends with the journey of Pacific salmon, whose annual efforts to return to their spawning grounds invariably take them past the industrial ruins celebrated in Richard Haag's Gas Works Park (Klingle 2007). The preservation of industrial ruins forms a backdrop to more recent efforts to restore the ruins of city's waterways.

Conclusion

This sprawling chapter extends from the gritty representations of ruin porn to the rhizomatic networks of flows that pool and eddy around protest sites and coalesce in the material form of the contemporary city. The complexities of the contemporary city and industrial ruins provide a backdrop for protests against racial, economic, and environmental injustice precisely because these places resist easy categorization and remain open for transgressive and transformational forms of expression. The emphasis on flows that are constitutive of urban landscapes parallels our recognition that things—whether media objects, discarded consumer goods, or newly acquired devices—represent the momentary coalescing of global networks with their wide range of social, political, and economic contexts. The ability of archaeology to unpack these diverse contexts allows us to understand the implications of ruins as spaces that cultivate transgressive acts, understand the limits of our ontological categories of human and nature, and reflect on foreclosed future and the contingency of capital. These challenges, in turn, force us to interrogate how concepts like the contemporary, or even the American, experience produce meaning in our discipline.

In the final chapter of this book, we will finally reach the Bakken oil patch, where in the second decade of the twenty-first century many key flows constituent of American society came together in a dynamic and precarious archaeological landscape. Forms of settlement and even urbanism developed evocative of favelas in the Global South. The contracted contemporaneity of a twenty-first-century oil boom contrasts with the rusted ruins of past booms and the deep geological time of the Bakken oil patch. Our encounters with industrial, institutional, and even nationalist sites and references in Bakken compelled us to expand our research to discursive dives into the archaeology of modern nations, military bases, institutions, and industrial ruins, as well as sites of protest, accommodation, and production. The final chapter, which also serves as a kind of conclusion for the book, brings our second case study into focus, and then to a close.

8

Extractive Industries and Global Change

This book began in 2014 with me joining colleagues at the edge of a New Mexico landfill to document the excavation of a deposit of Atari games. This final chapter begins in 2012 with me and some of the same colleagues standing in an RV park housing workers who arrived in western North Dakota during the Bakken oil boom. That year, the North Dakota Man Camp Project started its inaugural season of fieldwork in a dusty camp on the outskirt of Tioga, North Dakota. The town of Tioga, situated atop the Nesson Anticline, calls itself the Oil Capital of North Dakota. The region around the town has produced oil at a commercial scale on and off since 1951, when the Iverson Well No. 1 came in (for general background see Conway 2020). Booms in the 1950s and the 1980s brought thousands of workers not only to Tioga but to the sparsely populated counties of western North Dakota as well. With each boom, local housing stock proved inadequate to accommodate the influx of workers, and the new arrivals resorted to a wide range of temporary, mobile, and ad hoc solutions to the housing crunch. The North Dakota Man Camp Project team sought to document the various forms of boom-time workforce housing and visited the Bakken regularly over five years to take photographs, record workforce housing sites amid the changing landscape, and conduct interviews (Caraher et al. 2017). To accomplish this, our team—comprised of archaeologists, an architectural historian, a historian and social worker with a specialization in housing, as well as artists, students, and colleagues—committed to the documentation and study of the twenty-first-century Bakken oil boom.

The early twenty-first-century Bakken oil boom grabbed international media headlines and introduced the term "man camp" to American vocabulary (Caraher et al. 2017). Alec Soth's famous photograph on the cover of the *New York Times Magazine* depicted an oil-smeared worker sitting atop an overturned oil drum on the North Dakota prairie. The photo combined the desolation of the setting and the rugged, masculine labor associated with extractive industries (see Dunham 2016: 297–298; Brown 2013). Similar media coverage appeared around the same time in *The Atlantic, Harpers, National Geographic,* and the *Washington Post* (Becker 2016). Journalists and writers drawn to the Bakken produced a series of thoughtful books. Many situated the region's oil boom in the aftermath of the subprime mortgage crisis and the Great Recession. They present the complicated promise of the improvements in hydraulic fracturing—or fracking—technologies issuing a new age of national energy independence and reigniting the long-standing hope of using "black gold" to get rich quick (e.g., Gold 2014; Rao 2018; Briody 2017). Artists, poets, and novelists also looked to the Bakken for inspiration and critique (e.g., Dunham 2016; Brorby et al. 2016; Czerwiec 2016; Brorby 2017; Anderson 2017; Sayles 2020), including writers of commercial paperbacks (e.g., Martin 2017). Television series played on the reputation of the oil patch as a kind of new "Wild West," where the potential of the frontier and freedom at the margins of Eastern civilization "intersect to produce the ideal backdrop for transgressive tales of violence, capitalism, and wealth" (see Caraher 2016 for a critique).

As a resident of North Dakota, I felt the Bakken boom as a contemporary event. Even 200 miles (~320 km) east of the epicenter of the oil boom, our daily lives were impacted. Our students worked in the oil fields, skilled laborers in our community decamped to the Bakken for higher-paying opportunities, while unemployment dropped and wages rose across the state and region. North Dakota also began a conversation about the cost of extractive industries to the state's communities, the environmental risks, and impact of oil on the state's political culture. These conversations made proximate and contemporary the relationship between the oil industry and pressing global concerns from environmental degradation and climate change, social and economic disruptions, and the impact of fossil fuels on global democracies. The use of military-type vehicles, air power, and violence against the Dakota Access Pipeline protesters highlighted the complicated connections among the state, the oil industry, and the communities impacted by the boom (see chapter 7; Estes 2019; Beisaw and Olin 2020). In these tragic events, Indigenous land claims, environmentalism, and concerns for public health led to a direct confrontation with the power of the state.

Needless to say, we encountered little militarized violence or conflict in our work in the Bakken. That said, we did witness the impact of slow violence on the tired, hardworking, and sincere faces of the individuals we met during our work. They recognized their place within an increasingly precarious economy, and they demonstrated both creativity and experience in adapting their often temporary housing conditions to the North Dakota weather. As this chapter will show, even the most temporary workforce housing in the Bakken carried with it certain aspirational elements of the suburban landscapes. This suggested that despite an awareness of the changing character of the American economy, suburban aspirations persist. The temporary character of housing set it apart from the existing small towns in western North Dakota, and the tension between the highly local and ephemeral character of the boom itself and the global and long-term impact of carbon-based energy made manifest the speed of contemporary capital and the supermodern, even geological, impact of extractive industries on the modern world.

Extractive Industries and the West

Historical archaeologists of the American West have long been interested in extractive industries (Dixon 2020, 2014). This is as much because these industries defined the West both in the popular imagination and in terms of its economic and environmental history as an extension of most populous settlements on the coast and in older centers in the Midwest. As we saw in the last chapter, the story of American urbanism often extends from the changing fabric, economy, and demography of the city itself into its vast hinterland of extractive industries, agriculture, and industry. Rail, highway, aqueduct, and high-tension wire connect the extractive hinterlands to their urban cores and make contemporary urbanism possible. As Andrew Needham (2014) noted, high-voltage wires connected the new cities of the American West to extractive landscapes, which often benefited last from rural electrification initiatives. Coal mining and coal-fired power plants both relied on and produced the poverty of the Navajo Nation in the Four Corner's region. The relationship between the reservation and the postwar cities of Arizona represents one of the more egregious examples of the role of extractive industries in producing the colonial hinterland required for the sprawling urban sites of the New West. In fact, the materiality of the power lines themselves manifested a slow violence. Timothy LeCain has shown that the copper in the high-tension wires that transported power across the New West required the mining of copper on a massive scale (LeCain 2009). This led to the growth of communities such as Butte, Montana, where the massive Berkeley Pit mine produced millions of tons of copper, extracted from millions more tons of rock, leaving today a massive and highly toxic scar on the landscape and a community beset by economic and health woes.

The key roles that mining and extractive industries played in the American West gave rise to the field of mining archaeology, which sought to trace the technological, social, economic, and eventually environmental impact of mining in the region. Donald Hardesty, in particular, defined the field of mining archaeology through his study of sites in Nevada (Hardesty 2010). Starting in the 1980s, he produced a series of studies that examined not only the economic and technological character of these sites, but he also argued that these sites offered ways to understand the social and political aspects of western expansion (e.g., Hardesty 1991). Hardesty provided the concluding commentary to a special issue of *Historical Archaeology* in 2002 that considered the place of workforce housing in the organization of labor and society in the West. The contributions to this issue traced a continued shift from studies concerned with documenting sites connected with extractive industries themselves toward an interest in the lives of the workers and the kinds of communities they formed (Van Buren 2002a). The study of turn-of-the-century camps in California oil fields (Baxter 2002), the site of the Ludlow massacre (McGuire and Rechner 2002), and the camps that followed the construction of the Los Angeles aquifer (Van Buren 2002b) reveal how the work undertaken in the American West shaped the domestic lives of workers in these contexts. Kelly Dixon's work on Virginia City, Nevada, extends this research to boom towns associated with extractive industries and forms of recreation, diet, and social life (Dixon 2006). Much of this work in the American West remains informed by historical archaeology in the East. For example, scholars found inspiration in Stephen Mrozowski's excavations around working-class neighborhoods in nineteenth-century Boott Mills in Lowell, Massachusetts (Mrozowski et al. 1996); in several studies synthesized in Paul Shackel's work on the archaeology of labor and working-class life (Shackel 2009); and in LouAnn Wurst's work on the archaeology of capitalism (Wurst and Mrozowski 2016; Wurst 2002; Dézsi and Wurst 2023). This work has emphasized the wide range of agency and resistance among worker communities. Archaeology has shown how worker housing becomes a space where workers negotiate ethnic, class, and political identity.

This emphasis on agency and resistance has also informed global views of workers and extractive industries. While the scholarship in the historical archaeology of colonialism is vast (see Silliman 2020 for a useful survey), recent scholarship has stressed the link between the ecological destruction of colonial regimes (e.g., Mrozowski 2014; Costa 2018; Garcia 2018) and the various kinds of violence brought to bear on colonized populations in the name of capitalism (e.g., Smit and Proctor 2020). The violence associated with nineteenth- and twentieth-century extractive regimes transformed colonial settlement, for example, toward more intensive, efficient, and industrial forms of organization (Richard 2015; Van Bueren and Weaver 2012: 90–97). González-Ruibal (2015) traced the emergence of a more predatory form of colonialism in the abandoned homes and buildings of Equatorial Guinea's eighteenth- and early nineteenth-century bourgeoise. Excluding colonized populations from the wealth produced by research extraction continued the twentieth-century collapse of the Guinean bourgeoise. In Equatorial Guinea, the twenty-first-century discovery of oil has intensified the predatory colonial practices that originated in the late nineteenth century when a more intensive colonial regime effectively cut out local middle men. Today, wealth from oil collects in the hands of only a few local actors, and the rest goes offshore (González-Ruibal 2015: 438–439). In this context, the abandoned homes of the nineteenth-century Guinean bourgeoise are evidence of an increasingly deterritorialized and global form of capitalism that undermines the modern organization of space that shapes so many of our contemporary expectations. Colonialized and peripheral regions, such as North Dakota's Bakken or the Navajo Nation, continue to become "industrial landscapes" complete with housing designed to ensure the efficient extraction of oil. Profits, rather than returning to an urbanized, metropolitan, and politically dominant core, however, depart for the coffers of deterritorialized global corporations that exist amid eddying networks of capital (Caraher 2016; Caraher and Weber 2017; see chapter 5). The willingness of the state to intervene in these processes, as the violent suppression of the Dakota Access Pipeline demonstrated, serves as a reminder that the networks of deterritorialized capital may still remain partially embedded amid territorial claims to authority and power.

The deterritorialization of capital informed the growing interest in efforts to control the movement of individuals across borders, as well as increasing investments in various forms of workforce housing inspired by military bases, campuses, and schools and producing new forms of urbanism designed to concentrate the labor necessary to respond to capitalism's ever-more-rapid demands. As discussed in chapters 5, 6, and 7, the study of new and abandoned landscapes of work and control shaped our engagement with workforce housing in the twenty-first-century Bakken. At the same time, the challenge of housing workers in the twenty-first-century American West continued a trajectory revealed in the archaeology of late nineteenth and early twentieth-century practices. In 2009, the absence of existing housing in the sparsely populated counties of western North Dakota resulted in a series of ad hoc solutions among workers flooding the region. At around the same time, major companies associated with the oil boom developed housing to accommodate their workforce and to ensure their efficient deployment to drilling and fracking sites throughout the region. Thus, as the national media breathlessly reported, workers arriving in the Bakken without connections to major oil companies or related concerns found themselves without housing. As a result, they camped out in the Williston Walmart parking lot, public parks, and hastily arranged RV hook-ups in and around the cities of Tioga, Williston, and Watford City. By 2011, the chaotic early years of the twenty-first-century oil boom gave way to local legislation that attempted to limit the number of RVs and other forms of temporary housing in the city limits. The private sector, in turn, stepped up their efforts to profit by providing temporary housing for the increasing influx of workers. Outside investors developed a wide range of formal housing facilities and graded RV parks with water, sewage, and electricity on the outskirts of the major towns in the region. Beyond and sometimes amid this workforce housing emerged the growing grid of drilling rigs, well pads, wastewater injection sites, pipeline scars, and tank farms. The reconfigured geography of western North Dakota may not represent the same kind of racialized landscape characteristic of nineteenth-century colonial violence, but it did superimpose on the long-standing settlement and land-use pattern a new, externally imposed spatial logic defined by the intensified needs of extractive production (see Caraher and Weber 2017).

The North Dakota Man Camp Project began at the height of the oil boom. Like previous archaeologists interested in workers in the American West, our project focused on the relationship between domestic spaces and social relations in the region's man camps. Our methods for documenting workforce housing sites were consistent with many recent "active site" archaeological projects (e.g., White 2020; see chapter 7). As part of our project's goal was to produce a descriptive archive of the twenty-first-century Bakken boom, we developed a multimodal practice of recording workforce housing sites. This involved not only traditional archaeological practices involving the descriptions and illustration of particular units but also the intensive use of photography and video, which allowed us to capture sites systematically. We also worked with ethnographers, who collected hundreds of hours of unstructured interviews with residents in the camps. While the analysis and archiving of this material is ongoing, and we continue to make periodic trips to the Bakken to update our documentation of our research sites, we have collected sufficient data to support a basic interpretation of workforce housing during a contemporary, extractive industries boom.

To facilitate our analysis, we developed a working typology of camps (see Caraher et al. 2017). Type 1 camps were prefabricated camps with communal dining, recreation, and housing areas typically operated by large logistic companies. Type 2 camps were RV parks, where residents typically owned their RVs and rented a space and access to water, sewage, and electricity. Type 3 camps were essentially squats established by small groups without access to water or sewage and ad hoc access to electricity. These were often illegal, informal, and sufficiently ephemeral that we heard about their existence more than we encountered them in the field. Type 2 camps, in contrast, were a common, visible, easy-to-access, and particularly diverse class. These camps thus attracted most of our attention and allowed us to explore the diverse ways in which temporary workforce housing sites developed the material aspects of settlement and community in a precarious, extractive landscape.

Domesticity and Precarity in the Bakken

The twenty-first-century Bakken oil boom gained momentum at the same time as the United States began to emerge from the "Great Recession" at the end of the first decade of the twenty-first century (Gold 2014). Beginning with the work in the Parshall oil field in Mountrail County in 2006, the technologies of horizontal drilling and hydraulic fracturing (fracking) renewed interest in the potential of the Bakken oil. The deployment of these technologies across the Bakken and Three Forks formations in North Dakota and Montana opened the region to large-scale oil development in subsequent years. The demands of drilling and fracking as well as related infrastructural development drew thousands of workers to the region at the very time when the U.S. economy was struggling to emerge from a period of economic stagnation. In many cases, the role of the subprime mortgage crisis in the Great Recession and the steep increase in foreclosures across the United States emphasized the financial aspects of housing and its role in the national and global economy. Thus the potential for even temporary employment in the Bakken represented an opportunity

Investors, of course, recognized that a resource boom offered only a short window to recoup losses. This and the intense competition for housing in the Bakken counties meant that rent and hook-ups (utilities) were often priced more than $1,000 per month, making them comparable to apartment rents in many mid-sized American cities. Despite the costs, the quality and character of the facilities offered by a Type 2 camp were uneven. Some offered amenities such as wireless internet, on-site managers, and common spaces for laundry, mailboxes, and socializing. One of the most spectacular facilities in the region was the "indoor RV park" that provided heated garages for RVs. Far more frequently, however, these camps suffered from uneven management and poor quality of construction. In one of the largest Type 2 camps in the region, contractors violated building codes when installing the sewage pipes. As a result, the pipes froze during a January cold snap, leaving most of the camp without waste disposal. Frozen water pipes, inconsistent electrical hook-ups, poor drainage, rutted roads, and unreliable maintenance plagued Type 2 camps throughout the Bakken. These reflect not only the hasty and irregular construction of many of these camps (for a particularly egregious example see Rothaus et al. 2021) but also the pressures on investors to recover their initial investment quickly. The ownership of camps often changed hands and led to new policies and approaches to maintenance.

Despite the inconsistencies associated with Type 2 camps, the residents of these facilities often took advantage of the less restrictive environment to individualize their living spaces. In contrast to the austere functionalism of Type 1 camps, the individual units in Type 2 camps could feature a wide range of practical, recreational, and decorative embellishments. The most prominent addition to a unit in a Type 2 camp was a mudroom (figure 8.2), which consisted of a lean-to with three walls and a single pitched roof set against the side of the RV around the door. Residents most often used scrap wood available around the camp to build their mudrooms, which contributed to the rough appearance of these structures. Most simply, the mudroom served the same function that it does in a modern home: it provided a space for a resident to remove muddy or dirty work clothes before entering the living space. In Type 2 camps, however, particularly early in the boom before municipalities passed more restrictive guidelines, mudrooms allowed residents to exercise their creativity in expanding their living space. Large mudrooms were sometimes nearly half the size of the RV and offered storage and living space as well as their traditional function as

Figure 8.2. An RV with an attached mudroom typical of Type 2 camps in the Bakken. Author photo.

a social and physical barrier between the outside and interior of the RV (Caraher et al. 2017).

The mudrooms also fit into a number of strategies that allowed residents of Type 2 camps to develop a more complex sense of domestic space. For example, the mudrooms transformed the RV into an L-shaped building that created boundaries on two sides of the lot. Residents often used the space defined by the RV, the mudroom, and frequently the neighboring unit for outdoor activities, gardens, and storage. Neatly arranged furniture, improved gardens, exercise equipment, and sometimes unsecured storage demonstrated that residents recognized this space as private. The most elaborate examples included fences, dog runs, and in one case a tree planted in the arid soil of the North Dakota prairie. The appearance of well-appointed outdoor spaces in Type 2 camps belied the nearly constant turnover of residents in these camps. It suggests, however, that unlike Type 1 camps, which offer austere but functional accommodation for a temporary workforce, in Type 2 camps, some workers continue to conform to models of domesticity grounded in suburban practices and attitudes.

The architectural elaboration associated with Type 2 camps demon-strates a tension between the increasingly precarious state of workers and their effort to preserve some aspects of suburban life with its exaggerated commitment to permanence. The workforce needs of extractive industries and their penchant for booms and busts highlights larger changes in the global economy that privileges just-in-time manufacturing and gig labor where the availability of a mobile labor pool on short notice remains a key to economic flexibility and low costs. The use of dormitory labor in Asia (Ngai and Smith 2007), for example, and guest workers for construc-tion positions in the Persian Gulf (Bruslé 2012) offer just two examples of the key role that workforce housing plays in supporting short-term and precarious employment on a global scale (Caraher 2016). Extractive in-dustries with their dependence on the vagaries of the international mar-kets and finite access to resources have frequently relied on dormitories or camps to house temporary workers on a global scale. Archaeologists have only begun to explore these sites in a late twentieth-century or twenty-first-century context. For example, Andreassen and colleagues (Andreas-sen et al. 2010) studied workforce housing in extractive industries in the late twentieth century in their work to document the Soviet mining town of Pyramiden in the Svalbard archipelago of Norway. The Russian mining company Arktikugol abandoned this site in the mid-1990s, and its remote location has left it more or less intact. While the conditions at this remote settlement differed significantly from those in the Bakken, the tension be-tween the institutional needs of the mining operation, which also provided entertainment, recreation, and even schooling to the 1,000 inhabitants of the community, and the individual needs of the workers who adapted their spaces to their needs and personalities remained prominent throughout the abandonment site.

The ad hoc and innovative practices associated with Type 2 housing like-wise reflect the development of forms of global urbanism. The improvised construction practices associated with mudrooms reflect the flexible and adaptive design that characterize domestic structures in favelas that sur-round cities in the Global South, refugee settlements in North Africa and the Middle East, and *colonias* that have appeared along the U.S.-Mexico border (Simone 2004; Perlman 2010; Ward 2014). Mobile populations used available materials to create domestic spaces and a sense of home even in difficult environments and uncertain circumstances. The peripheral lo-cation of the Bakken as the destination for capital and as the source of raw materials often led to a relationship with the centers of political and economic power characterized by what Andre Gunder Frank called "the development of underdevelopment" (Caraher 2016: 187–190; Frank 1966). In these situations, the center—or perhaps more simply, those providing capital—favored limited regulations and discouraged policies that developed political and social infrastructure that could inhibit the extraction of material from the region. As a result, regulations on housing, for example, lagged behind the significant increase in new workers to the region, and this helped ensure that temporary housing could meet demand. It also created the opportunity for the range of ad hoc adaptations present in Type 2 camps.

Labor, the Environment, and Climate Change

The details of workforce housing in the Bakken represent regional variations on a number of emerging trends in archaeology that have served as undercurrents for many of the issues and projects presented in this book. The final section of this chapter brings together how the archaeological study of labor, consumption, and capitalism, which has been so central to work in historical archaeology and this book, informs attitudes toward the environment and climate change. Here we introduce three vignettes that explore the connection between the labor regime that made the Bakken boom possible and issues of environmental justice that exist at the intersection between our historical dependence on fossil fuels, geological time, and climate change on a global scale. In general, historical archaeologists, and especially archaeologists of the contemporary world, have recognized how the study of recent material culture plays a key role in understanding humanity's role in the transformation of the Earth. They have traced global supply chains, unpacked colonial economic and political practices, and recognized how consumption and discard endanger vital ecologies. As we saw in chapter 2, Bill Rathje's Garbage Project developed in parallel with the larger program of historical archaeology amid the environmental concerns in the 1960s and 1970s that gained momentum in the long shadow of Rachel Carson's *Silent Spring* (1962), the organization of Earth Day in 1970, and an increasingly energized environmentalist movement. Chapters 3 and 4 explored how consumer culture even in the digital age has scarred the surface of the planet with the detritus of industrialization and extractive industries. The traces of our supermodern age that permeate our planet, our bodies, and the atmosphere dovetail with concerns present in the wide-ranging debate among historical and contemporary archaeologists on the "Anthropocene" in the *Norwegian Archaeological Review* in 2011 (Soli et al. 2011). The centrality of the Anthropocene for archaeology of the contemporary world accounts for it being the central theme of the inaugural issue of the *Journal of Contemporary Archaeology* in 2014 (Edgeworth et al. 2014). Our attention to the contemporary environmental and climate crises suggests a growing awareness that the violence associated with the traditional haunts of historical archaeology—colonialism, Eurocentrism, capitalism, and modernity—manifest as much in past and present human suffering as in our common, compromised future. This damage arrives with the slow violence of climate change, which promises to exacerbate the social, political, and economic instability inherent in a system that relies upon and promotes global inequality. The three vignettes below present a multi-scalar perspective on the American experience anchored in our work in the Bakken. These awkward and provisional sketches also point back to the introduction of the book by asking what the contemporary means in an age of planetary crisis (*sensu* Chakrabarty 2021).

The parking lot of the Williston Walmart forms the first vignette. This might seem an unlikely place to unpack relations among the haunts of historical archaeology, environmental degradation, and climate change. At the same time, it offers a window into the changing landscape of labor in the United States. As early as 2010, new arrivals in the Bakken congregated in the Williston Walmart parking lot. Nationally, Walmart had a long-standing policy of allowing the overnight parking of RVs in their lots, and new arrivals looking for work in the booming Bakken oil patch took advantage of this policy with longer-term housing both scarce and expensive. By 2011, evening transformed the Walmart parking lot into a bustling settlement. The store provided groceries and other amenities, but as the media coverage made clear, life in the parking lot was not comfortable. While it is likely that some of the reports on crime in the parking lot represented local anxieties about change as much as the reality on the ground, there is no reason to think that living in an RV in a parking lot in the North Dakota winter was pleasant. That said, many of those who ended up staying in the parking lot had left communities hard hit by the Great Recession and saw the hardships of living in an RV as the price of opportunity (Donovan 2012).

The Walmart parking lot represented a degraded parody of the mid-century suburb. Planned suburbs such as Lakewood, California, and Levittown, New York, combined housing and shopping with abundant parking (Jackson 1985). This not only made clear the link between mid-century middle-class domesticity and consumer culture but also emphasized the crucial role of the automobile in postwar life. In contrast, the Williston Walmart parking lot appeared in the national consciousness as an uncanny image. In the aftermath of the subprime mortgage crisis, the Williston Walmart located the faltering middle-class dream of home ownership amid our persistent attachment to the convenience of consumer culture. Workers seeking jobs flowed to the Bakken following routes already established by the global supply chains that deliver consumer goods on the Walmart shelves. Upon arrival, workers clustered around the familiar convenience of the Walmart in a poignant and depressing reproduction of the design of modern suburbia, but in a significantly degraded form. They did this to work in the oil industry that would continue to power the cars and trucks that transported their housing to the Bakken, that made Walmart a suburban icon, and that undoubtedly contributed to the global displacement of populations made vulnerable by petroleum's contribution to climate change.

The second vignette zooms in to focus on the RV in the Type 2 camp in the Bakken. The arrival of job seekers in the Bakken, by car and RV, reinforces our dependence on fossil fuels and our increasingly mobile society. The RV, a recreational vehicle, provided the middle class with a means to escape the fixity of suburban life (Hart et al. 2002). Its streamlined design marked its modernity and compatibility with car culture. The use of RVs as long-term, albeit temporary, housing in the Bakken demonstrated how the ever-more-rapid and dynamic flow of capital complicates notions of settled suburban life (Caraher et al. 2017). The same vehicles used to house middle-class families as they visited National Parks of the American West now serve to house workers extracting oil from the region. At the same time, efforts by workers to embellish their RVs and their lots suggests that notions of suburban fixity and private space persist even in housing manufactured with mobility in mind. The blurring of distinctions between settled suburban life and the mobility of capital and the middle class echoes the increasingly fuzzy distinctions that define the core and the periphery even in the historically peripheral space of the American West (Caraher 2016). The speed and mobility of modern capital and labor has complicated the spatial and conceptual boundaries that have defined not only regions but also our relationship to the landscape and resources.

As noted elsewhere in this book, natural resources including oil, minerals, natural beauty, and "open spaces" (produced partly through the displacement or exploitation of Native American populations) defined the

American West. In many ways, this definition has followed the modern division between the natural world and the human world that archaeology has recently sought to problematize (see Olsen 2010 for discussion). National parks, for example, represented efforts to preserve natural beauty from human interference while the resources of the West exist for the advancement of American society. In effect, the American West became a model for the distinction between the cultural and the natural as well as between the human and the nonhuman, which reinforced its location at the periphery of the settled urban center of the Midwest and East. Fossil fuels first powered rail, and later cars, trucks, and air travel. These forms of transportation formed the connective tissue that bound the center to the natural regions that they dominated politically and economically. Scholars critical of the nature/culture dyad have come to regard this as a fundamental feature of modern and colonialist thinking that justified extractive industry and industrialization and their attendant disregard for the environment. In effect, fossil fuels facilitated closing the gap between the distant periphery, which was the domain of nature and held resources destined for human consumption or preservation, and a core defined by human culture. Concerns over climate change, accelerated largely by our rampant consumption of fossil fuels, requires that we recognize the irreducible tangle of ties that connect culture with nature, the human with the nonhuman, and the fate of our species with dynamic transformation taking place on a global scale. When workers in the Bakken oil field turn their RVs into semi-permanent homes, they make visible the porous boundaries between the fixity of home and the mobility of the RV, the remoteness of the Bakken and the ubiquity of capital, and speed at which peripheries can become new centers visible not only on the ground but from outer space.

The third and final vignette is the widely circulating NASA photograph of the Northern Plains from space (figure 8.3). This photograph showed various clusters of light across North America. Surprisingly, a cluster of lights in the Bakken region glowed almost as brightly as Minneapolis. The light was often incorrectly attributed to flares burning off natural gas from oil wells in the region, which reinforced perceptions of the Bakken as an ecologically irresponsible zone of exploitation. A more likely explanation for the light was the artificial lighting use to illuminate around-the-clock activity at drill sites, pipeline terminals, new rail yards, workforce housing sites, and other facilities developed to support extractive industries (Orange 2018). Whatever the cause of its brilliant glow, the photograph evoked the famous 1972 image of the Earth from space colloquially known as the

Figure 8.3. The Bakken as viewed from space. NASA image modified by William Caraher. The base image is NASA Earth Observatory image by Robert Simmon, using Suomi NPP VIIRS data provided courtesy of Chris Elvidge (NOAA National Geophysical Data Center). Suomi NPP is the result of a partnership among NASA, NOAA, and the Department of Defense.

Blue Marble, which served as an inspiration for James Lovelock's and Lyn Margulis's Gaia Hypothesis (Lovelock 1979; Latour 2017). This theory conceived of the Earth as a self-regulating system comprised of all organic and inorganic entities, which constantly adapt to one another (de Souza and Costa 2018: 6). The image of Earth as a Blue Marble reduced humans to yet another species barely distinguishable from space and existing within a global system of agents.

While archaeologists have been slow to embrace the Gaia Hypothesis, it has informed similar views of the world that seek to unsettle and complicate the human/nature dichotomy. Matthew Edgeworth's notion of the "archaeosphere," for example, reinforces the impossibility of separating human actions from wider material and the natural world by emphasizing the full range of human modifications to the physical environment (Edgeworth 2018, based on a concept developed by Capelotti 2009 and Capelotti 2010). The commingling of the organic and inorganic and the human and the nonhuman has become a key assumption in the effort to define the current geological age as the "Anthropocene." This term, coined by Paul Crutzen and Eugene Stroemer in 2000 (2000; Crutzen 2002), proposes that humans have transformed the planet in geological ways. The radiation from nuclear weapons testing, the redistribution of material through mining and drilling, the use of plastics and other manufactured inorganic compounds at a massive scale, and the increase in the amount of atmospheric greenhouse gases, among other indicators, will leave indelible traces in the geological strata (Steffen et al. 2007, 2011). In some cases, these impacts are very localized, but many of them, such as the accumulation of plastics on seabeds and the traces of radioactivity from detonations of nuclear weapons, will occur on a planetary scale. While it has not been officially accepted as a geological epoch, it has nevertheless been a touchpoint for more expansive understandings of the impact of humanity on the physical environment. This has, in turn, fueled a growing interest among archaeologists in environmental change in the past and has added urgency to archaeological critiques aimed at understanding long-term trends (Lane 2015). All of this has contributed to the realization among historical archaeologists that concepts such as the Gaia Hypothesis, the archaeosphere, and the Anthropocene offer important concepts for interrogating the complex interplay between human and nonhuman actors in ongoing environmental change. These perspectives situate the contemporary American experience as part of an emerging and open-ended geological epoch that is global in scope.

The leap from the Walmart parking lot to the Blue Marble may appear vast in terms of time and scale. The travails of Bakken workers doing dangerous work and enduring substandard housing conditions, however, connect the human costs of extractive industries to the global changes in both the economy and the environment. It also marks the potential for both historical archaeology and the archaeology of the contemporary American experience to bridge between local concerns—in this case, workforce housing—and global concerns, such as climate change. Like so much archaeological work of the last two decades, this ability to move between scales, agents, and situations relies on our ability to complicate long-standing ontologies that have supported how archaeologists describe and interpret the world. Archaeology has the unique capacity to recognize that categories of core and periphery, human and nonhuman, and natural and cultural are not only dependent on one another for meaning but also collapsing under the weight of the ever-increasingly speed of capital, the contingency of human labor and living conditions, and new ways of seeing the Earth.

Conclusion

This chapter serves as a kind of conclusion for the book as it attempts to consider the American experience at a planetary level and taking place at an emerging geological contemporary. Our work in the Bakken engaged with issues of production and consumption, colonialism, capitalism, and domesticity that have so long constituted the haunts of American historical archaeology. This chapter also sketched a course for an archaeology of the contemporary world that connects the archaeology of labor, extractive industries, and the American West with longer-term global archaeology of the environment, the Anthropocene, and climate change. Just as the rise of consumer culture coincided with a growing concern for contemporary discard practices and the development of garbology, so the global scale of the emerging climate crisis pushed us to reframe our sense of the contemporary and local.

When I first proposed this book in 2017, this seemed like the most pressing and urgent direction that the archaeology of the contemporary world could address, and it bridged the gap between the immediacy of our everyday lives and their long-term consequences. The events of 2020, however, overtook this book manuscript, as they did for so many parts of our lives. As a result, this chapter remains a kind of conclusion, but a much more tentative one that failed to recognize the contemporary consequences of the generational anger fueled by racial inequality, the impact of the ongoing COVID-19 pandemic, the violent political backlash from President Trump's failure to win re-election, and the shockwaves of the Russian invasion of Ukraine. The urgency of these issues may speak more immediately to our sense of the contemporary than does the related uncertainty surrounding the future of human society forced to content with climate change. Maybe in the end, this realization establishes more clearly the complicated limits of what constitutes a shared sense of the contemporary and what experiences Americans feel most intensely as they navigate the contemporary world.

Afterword

Acknowledging our contemporaneity with the planetary changes that constitute the Anthropocene transforms the scale and scope of the archaeology of the contemporary American experience. In this context, it is tempting to lose sight of what constitutes our experiences as "American" in a globalizing and globalized world. It is also challenging to consider how we should imagine the contemporary as a meaningful chronological periods. This book has offered one perspective on what an archaeology of the contemporary American experience might look like. I have endeavored to employ approaches and priorities manifest at the intersection of American historical archaeology and the archaeology of the contemporary past as practiced outside the United States and to trace American experiences within a growing sense of being part of a densely interconnected world. At the same time, the book has attempted to embrace a sense of the contemporary that recognized it as a challenging and sometimes contested lens through which to focus archaeological inquiry. The book's chapters have proposed concepts of the contemporary that vary situationally. The concept of the contemporary among Native American communities struggling with the pain of residential school–era burials or among African American communities who continue to endure the loss of life and generational wealth in the Tulsa massacre cannot be the same as the contemporary conceived in the ephemeral immediacy of the Burning Man Festival or in the multiple temporalities manifest in the Bakken oil boom.

That said, it remains difficult to ignore the most insistent aspects of the contemporary American experience that loomed over the writing of this book. I completed the first drafts of this manuscript against the backdrop of the COVID-19 pandemic and protests following the murder of George Floyd. I was checking citations while keeping one eye on the stunning events of January 6, 2021, and working on edits as the Russians invaded Ukraine. This afterword has come into focus as the U.S. Supreme Court has compromised women's reproductive freedom and severe drought continues to wrack the American West. These events, and our disciplinary responses to them, continuously provoke and expand my view of the archaeology of the contemporary world and the American experience. Awareness of contemporary crises infuses the discipline with a sense of persistent urgency as these flashpoints often reveal deeper fractures and structures in our society. The urgent and essential work by Maria Franklin and her colleagues (2020), while situated amid BLM protests, nevertheless speaks to a century-long struggle for racial equality both in the discipline of archaeology and in American society more broadly. Similar sentiments emerged in a recent article in *American Antiquity*, composed jointly by the editors, which situated the contemporary COVID pandemic in the long history of pandemics, marginal communities, and race (Gamble et al. 2020). By considering the uneven social impact of pandemics in the past, the authors push us to consider how our ongoing response to the COVID-19 outbreak can avoid further marginalizing groups who have historically suffered from inadequate medical care and economic opportunities. Like so many issues confronting contemporary American society, the COVID pandemic requires us to think beyond traditional disciplinary, national, and geographic boundaries (Angelo et al. 2021). The contributors to a special issue of the *African Archaeological Review* have similarly sought to situate our contemporary response to COVID to past practices and to understand how an understanding of long-term change, Indigenous knowledge, social resilience, and colonialism can shape how communities reacted to such traumatic events. Shadreck Chirikure (2020) calls for archaeologists to not just content themselves with the study of past pandemics but to use this knowledge to collaborate with other disciplines and to shape policy in the present. Kristina Douglass (2020) considers how the disciplinary knowledge that archaeology produces about the past might form the basis for a more resilient present both for the communities where we live and study and for our discipline. As these examples show, the archaeology of the headlines contributes to how we understand and address the slow violence of situations that date to the start of the twentieth century, to the beginning of modernity, or even emerge from deep time itself. In this context, the archaeology of the Anthropocene marks yet another example of how the proximate crises of climate change, whether manifest in unpredictably violent storms or severe drought, nonetheless depend on ecological, geological, and structural limits expressed at a planetary scale and over deep time.

An archaeology of our contemporary experiences, then, reflects a range of temporal and geographic concepts at play. This book's first case study emphasized discard, consumer culture, and the digital world that embodied the anxieties, expectations, and dreams of the turn-of-the-twenty-first-century middle class. These experiences were distinctly American in their particular concern for garbage barges, Hummers, jazz and rock music, and, of course, Atari games, but these encounters, objects, and expressions relied upon global networks and produced global consequences. The second case study explored the role of domestic spaces, institutions, urbanism, protest, and extractive industries in shaping the late twentieth- and twenty-first-century experience. To understand something as regional, if not parochial, as the short-lived Bakken oil boom, I considered the archaeology of national borders and homeless camps, college campuses and military bases, protest sites and urban landscapes. This suggested to me that while the displacements, deployments, occupations, and migrations that characterize a range of contemporary experiences may leave ephemeral or obscure traces in the material record, they nevertheless reflect the often tense negotiations among the modern, national, and institution spaces, on one hand, and the supermodern, global, and even (inter)planetary spaces on the other. In the end, the archaeology of contemporary America represents an effort to locate our experiences, possessions, trash, habits, and ultimately our sense of the present in their local and planetary contexts.

APPENDIX

Archaeology has long enjoyed a tradition of reflexive critique. Historically, this has involved attention to field methods, interpretative practices, and forms of argumentation. Reflexivity has also focused attention on the identities of individuals involved in knowledge making. Joan Gero's pathbreaking work in the 1980s demonstrated what was long known: women historically had fewer opportunities for fieldwork than men and received less research funding as a result (Gero 1983, 1994). Gero went on to show that in Mesoamerican archaeology, women's contribution to archaeology tended to focus on the analysis of finds, and this reciprocally reinforced the character of this work, both professionally and in the eyes of the public, as less significant than original excavations. This bias invariably shaped the publication record in the field as well, with men publishing far more consistently than women in the leading journal of American archaeology, *American Antiquity*.

A decade later, in the early 1990s, Mary Beaudry and Jacquelyn White traced a similar trend in the field of historical archaeology (Beaudry and White 1994). They noted that by the mid-1980s women were publishing approximately half of the articles in the leading American journal in this field, *Historical Archaeology*, increasing from just a third of the articles in the late 1970s. They noted that while the topics of publications are often hard to categorize, it appeared that women tended to publish more regularly in areas of artifact analysis, zooarchaeology, and paleobotany. This suggests that some of the trends in Mesoamerican archaeology observed by Gero reflected the discipline in in an American context as well. Beaudry and White also documented the gender division in works cited by the articles in *Historical Archaeology*, noting that by the early 1990s when their study appeared, articles by women made up about a third of the references. Scott Hutson's 2002 study of citation practices across a number of archaeological journals offered a more nuanced view that sought to take into account the rate at which women cite the work of women and at which men cite the work of women (Hutson 2002). Complex and robust, Hutson's analysis suggests that while citational practices among men and women do not differ in statistically significant ways other than in a few specific journals, women's scholarship appears to be cited less frequently than the number of publications produced by women would predict. Hutson thus argued that archaeologists generally under-utilize, or at least under-credit, women's contributions to the field. As Dana Bardolph observed in her important 2014 study of gendered publishing trends in archaeology, who publishes about the past shapes the way in which we understand the past (Bardolph 2014).

As a modest contribution to this discussion, I have archived in table form the citations in my book and attempted to indicate the gender of the authors: https://core.tdar.org/dataset/475430/citation-table-for-the-archaeology-of-contemporary-america

This presents only a rather rudimentary metric to assess the citational politics of the work. Recent efforts to understand practices of citation and authorship in academia and in archaeology have focused increased attention on intersectional variables of race, sexual orientation, class, and ethnicity that exert a fundamental influence over the kinds of pasts (and presents) that archaeology seeks to reproduce (Heath-Stout 2020).

It is my hope that this reflexive study of citational practices offers at the very least another data set for the ongoing conversations. I was disappointed with the overall distribution of citations in my work: 73 percent of my citations include at least one male author, and 36 percent contain at least one woman. The gender balance improves when I consider all citations more recent than 2000: men still appear in 70 percent of the citations, but women now appear in 41 percent. For citations since 2015, women appear as authors in 46 percent of the citations and men in 66 percent. Men appear in 65 percent of the most recent citations (since 2020) and women in 45 percent.

Citations, of course, tell only part of the story, and I hope that the text of this volume at least partially compensates for the metrical shortcomings of my citation practice.

WORKS CITED

Abourahme, Nasser.
2015. "Assembling and Spilling-Over: Towards an 'Ethnography of Cement' in a Palestinian Refugee Camp." *International Journal of Urban and Regional Research* 39(2): 200–217.

Agamben, G.
1995. "We Refugees." *Symposium* 49(2): 114–119. https://doi.org/10.1080/00397709.1995 .10733798

Agier, Michel, Richard Nice, and Loïc Wacquant.
2002. "Between War and City: Towards an Urban Anthropology of Refugee Camps." *Ethnography* 3(3): 317–41.

Agier, Michel, Yasmine Bouagga, Maël Galisson, Cyrille Hanappe, Mathilde Pette, Philippe Wannesson, Céline Barré, Nicolas Lambert, Sara Prestianni, Madeleine Trépanier, and Julien Saison.
2018. *La jungle de Calais: Les migrants, la frontière et le camp.* Paris: PUF.

Alexander, Catherine, and Joshua Reno.
2012. *Economies of Recycling: The Global Transformations of Materials, Values and Social Relations.* London: Zed Books.

Anderson, Erik.
2017. *Flutter Point: Essays.* Clarksville, TN: Zone 3 Press.

Andreassen, Elin.
2014. "Silent Power." In *Materiality, Aesthetics and the Archaeology of the Recent Past,* eds. Bjørnar Olsen and Þóra Pétursdóttir, 251–267. London: Routledge.

Andreassen, Elin, Hein B. Bjerck, and Bjørnar Olsen.
2010. *Persistent Memories: Pyramiden, a Soviet Mining Town in the High Arctic.* Trondheim, Norway: Tapir Academic Press.

Angelo, D., Kelly M. Britt, Margaret Lou Brown, and Stacy L. Camp.
2021. "Private Struggles in Public Spaces: Documenting COVID-19 Material Culture and Landscapes." *Journal of Contemporary Archaeology* 8(1): 154–184.

Antczak, Konrad A., and Mary C. Beaudry.
2019. "Assemblages of Practice. A Conceptual Framework for Exploring Human–Thing Relations in Archaeology." *Archaeological Dialogues* 26(2): 87–110.

Apel, Dora.
2015. *Beautiful Terrible Ruins: Detroit and the Anxiety of Decline.* New Brunswick, NJ: Rutgers University Press.

Appadurai, Arjun., ed.

1986. *The Social Life of Things: Commodities in Cultural Perspective.* Cambridge: Cambridge University Press.

Archaeology of OWS.

2012. "The Archaeology of OWS." Blog. http://ows-archaeology.blogspot.com

Arnshav, M.

2014. "The Freedom of the Seas: Untapping the Archaeological Potential of Marine Debris." *Journal of Marine Archaeology* 9: 1–25. https://doi.org/10.1007/s11457-014-9129-5

Augé, Marc.

1995. *Non-Places: An Introduction to Supermodernity.* Trans. John Howe. London: Verso.

Aycock, John.

2016. *Retrogame Archeology: Exploring Old Computer Games.* Cham: Springer.

Bangstad, Torgeir Rinke.

2014. "Industrial Heritage and the Ideal of Presence." In *Ruin Memories: Materialities, Aesthetics, and the Archaeology of the Recent Past,* eds. B. Olsen and Þ. Pétursdóttir, 92–105. Abingdon: Routledge.

Baker, Brenda J., and Takeyuki Tsuda, eds.

2015. *Migration and Disruptions: Toward a Unifying Theory of Ancient and Contemporary Migrations.* Gainesville: University Press of Florida.

Baker, Nicholson.

1988. *The Mezzanine.* New York: Weidenfeld & Nicolson.

Bardolph, Dana N.

2014. "A Critical Evaluation of Recent Gendered Publishing Trends in American Archaeology." *American Antiquity* 79:522–540.

Bartolini, Nadia, and Caitlin DeSilvey.

2021. "Recording Loss: Film as Method and the Spirit of Orford Ness." *International Journal of Heritage Studies* 26(1): 19–36. doi:10.1080/13527258.2019.1570311

Barton, Christopher.

2021. "Introduction." In *Trowels in the Trenches: Archaeology as Social Activism,* ed. Christopher Barton, 1–19. Gainesville: University Press of Florida.

Basu, Paul, and Simon Coleman.

2008. "Introduction: Migrant Worlds, Material Cultures." *Mobilities* 3(3): 313–30.

Bath, Joyce E.

1981. "The Raw and the Cooked: The Material Culture of a Modern Supermarket." In *Modern Material Culture: The Archaeology of Us,* eds. Richard Gould and Michael Schiffer, 183–196. New York: Academic Press.

Baugher, Sherene.

2001. "Visible Charity: The Archaeology, Material Culture, and Landscape Design of New York City's Municipal Almshouse Complex, 1736–1797." *International Journal of Historical Archaeology* 5(2): 175–202.

Baxter, R. Scott.

2002. "Industrial and Domestic Landscapes of a California Oil Field." *Historical Archaeology* 36(3): 18–27.

Beaudry, Mary C.

2007. "Preface: Historical Archaeology with Canon on the Side, Please: The ABC of CHAT." Contemporary Historical Archaeology in Theory. In *Contemporary and Historical Archaeology in Theory: Papers from the 2003 and 2004 CHAT Conferences,* eds. Laura McAtackney, Matthew Palus, and Angela Piccini, 1–3. Oxford: Archaeopress.

Beaudry, Mary C., and Jacquelyn White.

1994. "Cowgirls with the Blues? A Study of Women's Publication and the Citation of Women's Work in Historical Archaeology." In *Women in Archaeology,* ed. Cheryl Claassen, 138–158. Philadelphia: University of Pennsylvania Press.

Beck, Colleen M.

2002. "The Archaeology of Scientific Experiments at a Nuclear Testing Ground." In *Materiel Culture: The Archaeology of Twentieth-Century Conflict,* eds. A. John Schofield, William Gray Johnson, and Colleen M. Beck, 65–79. London: Routledge.

Beck, Colleen M., Harold Drollinger, and John Schofield.

2007. "Archaeology of Dissent: Landscape and Symbolism at the Nevada Peace Camp." In *A Fearsome Heritage: Diverse Legacies of the Cold War,* eds. J. Schofield and W. D. Cocroft, 297–320. Walnut Creek, CA: Left Coast Press.

Beck, Colleen M., John Schofield, and Harold Drollinger.

2011. "Archaeologists, Activists, and a Contemporary Peace Camp." In *Contemporary Archaeologies: Excavating Now!* 2nd edition, eds. Cornelius Holtorf and Angela Piccini, 95–111. Frankfurt: Peter Lang.

Beck, Jess, Ian Ostericher, Gregory Sollish, and Jason De León.

2015. "Animal Scavenging and Scattering and the Implications for Documenting the Deaths of Undocumented Border Crossers in the Sonoran Desert." *Journal of Forensic Sciences* 60: S11–S20.

Becker, Karin.

2016. "The Paradox of Plenty: Blessings and Curses in the Oil Patch." In *The Bakken Goes Boom: Oil and the Changing Geographies of Western North Dakota,* eds. William Caraher and Kyle Conway, 369–376. Grand Forks: The Digital Press at the University of North Dakota.

Beisaw, April M.

2017. "Ruined by the Thirst for Urban Prosperity." In *Contemporary Archaeology and the City,* eds. Laura McAtackney and Krysta Ryzewski, 132–148. Oxford: Oxford University Press.

Beisaw, April M., and Glynnis E. Olin.

2020. "From Alcatraz to Standing Rock: Archaeology and Contemporary Native American Protests (1969–Today)." *Historical Archaeology* 54(3): 537–555.

Benjamin, Jeff.

2017   "Ariadne's Gift." *The Journal of the Society for Industrial Archeology* 43(1/2): 5–12.

Benjamin, Walter.

2002. *The Arcades Project,* ed. Rolf Tiedemann, trans. Howard Eiland and Kevin McLaughlin. New York: Belknap Press.

Blake, C. Fred.

1981. "Graffiti and Racial Insults: The Archaeology of Ethnic Relations in Hawaii." In *Modern Material Culture: The Archaeology of Us,* eds. Richard Gould and Michael Schiffer, 87–99. New York: Academic Press.

Bloom, Micah.

2017. *Codex.* Grand Forks: The Digital Press at the University of North Dakota.

Bogost, Ian.

2015. *How to Talk about Videogames.* Minneapolis: University of Minnesota Press.

Bollmer, Grant.

2015. "Fragile Storage, Digital Futures." *Journal of Contemporary Archaeology* 2(1): 66–72.

Bourgois, Philippe, and John Schonberg.

2009. *Righteous Dopefiend.* Berkeley: University of California Press.

Bourdieu, Pierre.

1977. *Outline of a Theory of Practice.* Trans. Richard Nice. Cambridge: Cambridge University Press.

Breithoff, Esther.

2021. "Oil Matters." In *Heritage Ecologies,* eds. Torgeir Rinke Bangstad and Þóra Pétursdóttir, 92–103. London: Routledge.

Briody, Blaire.

2017. *The New Wild West: Black Gold, Fracking, and Life in a North Dakota Boomtown.* New York: St. Martin's Press.

Brorby, Taylor.

2017. *Crude: Poems.* North Liberty, IA: Ice Cube Press.

Brorby, Taylor, and Stephanie Brook Trout, eds.

2016. *Fracture: Essays, Poems, and Stories on Fracking in America.* North Liberty, IA: Ice Cube Press.

Brown, Chip.

2013   "North Dakota Went Boom." *New York Times Magazine,* January 13. www .nytimes.com/2013/02/03/magazine/north-dakota-went-boom.html

Brown, Wendy.

2010. *Walled States, Waning Sovereignty.* New York: Zone.

Bruslé, T.

2012. "What Kind of Place Is This? Daily Life, Privacy and the Inmate Metaphor in a Nepalese Workers' Labour Camp (Qatar)." *South Asia Multidisciplinary Academic Journal* 6. samaj.revues.org/3446

Bryant, Rebecca, and Daniel M. Knight.

2019. *The Anthropology of the Future.* Cambridge: Cambridge University Press.

Brylowe, Thora.

2017. "The Flood, the Mill, and the Body of the Book." In *Codex,* ed. Micah Bloom, 25–30. Grand Forks: The Digital Press at the University of North Dakota.

Buchli, Victor.

2006. "Architecture and Modernism." In *Handbook of Material Culture,* eds. C. Tilley, W. Keane, S. Küchler, M. Rowlands, and P. Spyer, 254–266. London: Sage.

2007. "Afterword: Towards an Archaeology of the Contemporary Past." In *Contemporary and Historical Archaeology in Theory: Papers from the 2003 and 2004 CHAT Conferences*, eds. Laura McAtackney, Matthew Palus, and Angela Piccini, 115–117. Oxford: Archaeopress.

Buchli, Victor, and Gavin Lucas, eds.

2001. *Archaeologies of the Contemporary Past*. London: Routledge.

Bullard, Robert D.

1990. *Dumping in Dixie: Race, Class, and Environmental Quality*. Boulder, CO: Westview Press.

Burström, Mats, Tomás Diez Acosta, Estrella González Noriega, Anders Gustafsson, Ismael Hernández, Håkan Karlsson, Jesús M. Pajón, Jesús Rafael Robaina Jaramillo, and Bengt Westergaard.

2009. "Memories of a World Crisis: The Archaeology of a Former Soviet Nuclear Missile Site in Cuba." *Journal of Social Archaeology* 9(3): 295–318.

Burström, Mats, Anders Gustafsson, and Karlsson Karlsson.

2011. *World Crisis in Ruin: The Archaeology of the Former Soviet Nuclear Missile Sites in Cuba*. Lindome: Bricoleur Press.

Burton, Jeffery F., and Mary M. Farrell.

2001. *This Is Minidoka: An Archeological Survey of Minidoka Internment National Monument, Idaho*. No. 80. Western Archeological and Conservation Center, National Park Service, US Department of the Interior, 2001.

2019. "From Forgotten to National Monument: Community Archaeology at a World War II Internment Camp in Hawai'i." In *Transforming Heritage Practice in the 21st Century: Contributions from Community Archaeology*, eds. John H. Jameson and Sergiu Musteață, 283–301. Cham: Springer.

Calafate-Faria, F.

2013. "Countercycling: An Ethnographic Study of Waste, Recycling, and Waste-Pickers in Curitiba, Brazil." Doctoral thesis, Goldsmiths, University of London.

2016. "Marginal Attachment and Countercycling in the Age of Recycling." In *Rethinking Life at the Margins: The Assemblage of Contexts, Subjects, and Politics*, ed. Michele Lancione, 153–168. London: Routledge.

Camp, Stacey L.

2010. "Teaching with trash: Archaeological Insights on University Waste Management." *World Archaeology* 42(3): 430–442.

2013. *The Archaeology of American Citizenship*. Gainesville: University Press of Florida.

2016. "Landscapes of Japanese American Internment." *Historical Archaeology* 50(1): 169–186.

2020. "The Future of Japanese Diaspora Archaeology in the United States." *International Journal of Historical Archaeology* 25(1): 1–18.

Campbell, Collin.

1987. *The Romantic Ethic and the Spirit of Modern Consumerism*. Oxford: Blackwell.

Capelotti, P.J.

2009. "Surveying Fermi's Paradox, Mapping Dyson's Sphere: Approaches to Archaeological Field Research in Space." In *Handbook of Space Engineering, Archaeology, and Heritage,* eds. A. G. Darrin and B. L. O'Leary, 855–867, Boca Raton: CRC Press.

2010. *The Human Archaeology of Space: Lunar, Planetary and Interstellar Relics of Exploration.* Jefferson, NC: McFarland.

Caraher, William.

2016. "The Archaeology of Man Camps: Contingency, Periphery, and Late Capitalism." In *The Bakken Goes Boom: Oil and the Changing Geographies of Western North Dakota,* eds. William Caraher and Kyle Conway, 181–198. Grand Forks: The Digital Press at the University of North Dakota.

2019. "Slow Archaeology, Punk Archaeology, and the 'Archaeology of Care.'" *European Journal of Archaeology* 22(3): 372–385.

Caraher, William R., Bret A. Weber, Kostis Kourelis, and Richard Rothaus.

2017. "The North Dakota Man Camp Project: The Archaeology of Home in the Bakken Oil Fields." *Historical Archaeology* 51: 267–287. https://doi.org/10.1007/s41636-017-0020-8

Caraher, William R., and Bret A. Weber.

2017. *The Bakken: An Archaeology of an Industrial Landscape.* Fargo: North Dakota State University Press.

Carpenter, Evan, and Steve Wolverton.

2017. "Plastic Litter in Streams: The Behavioral Archaeology of a Pervasive Environmental Problem." *Applied Geography* 84: 93–101.

Carson, Rachel.

1962. *Silent Spring.* Boston: Houghton Mifflin.

Carver, Raymond.

1981. *What We Talk about When We Talk about Love.* New York: Alfred Knopf.

Casella, Eleanor C.

2007. *The Archaeology of Institutional Confinement.* Gainesville: University Press of Florida.

Casella, Eleanor C., and James Symonds.

2005. *Industrial Archaeology: Future Directions.* New York: Springer.

Cass, Stephen.

2007. "How Much Does the Internet Weigh?" *Discover Magazine.* www.discovermagazine.com/technology/how-much-does-the-internet-weigh

Cassidy, Kyle.

2016. "Photographing the Bakken." In *The Bakken Goes Boom: Oil and the Changing Geographies of Western North Dakota,* eds. William Caraher and Kyle Conway, 369–376. Grand Forks: The Digital Press at the University of North Dakota.

Chakrabarty, Dipesh.

2021. *The Climate of History in a Planetary Age.* Chicago: University of Chicago Press.

Chambers, Chad.

2020. "Beneath the Surface: Capital-Labor Relations, Housing and the Making of the Bakken Boom." *The Extractive Industries and Society* 7(3): 908–917. https://doi.org/10.1016/j.exis.2020.04.012

Champion, Eric.

2015. "Roleplaying and Rituals For Cultural Heritage-Orientated Games." In *DiGRA'15- Proceedings of the 2015 DiGRA International Conference, Digital Games Research Association* 12, 1–16.

2021. *Virtual Heritage: A Guide.* London: Ubiquity Press.

Cherry, John, Krysta Ryzewski, and Luke J. Pecoraro.

2013. "'A Kind of Sacred Place': The Rock-and-Roll Ruins of AIR Studios, Montserrat." In *Archaeologies of Mobility and Movement,* eds. Mary C. Beaudry and Travis G. Parno, 181–198. New York: Springer.

Chirikure, Shadreck.

2020. "Issues Emerging: Thoughts on the Reflective Articles on Coronavirus (COVID-19) and African Archaeology." *African Archaeological Review* 37: 503–507. https://doi .org/10.1007/s10437-020-09402-w

City of Alamogordo.

2011. City Commission Regular Meeting Minutes, December 6.

2013a. City Commission Regular Meeting Minutes, May 14.

2013b. City Commission Regular Meeting Minutes, June 11.

Clarke, Andy, and Grethe Mitchell.

2013   *Videogames and Art.* 2nd edition. Bristol: Intellect.

Cline, Ernest.

2011. *Ready Player One.* New York: Crown Publishers.

Collins, Robert M.

2006. *Transforming America: Politics and Culture in the Reagan Years.* New York: Columbia University Press.

Conway, Kyle.

2020. "Introduction: Sixty Years of Boom and Bust." In *Sixty Years of Boom and Bust: The Impact of Oil in North Dakota, 1958–2018,* ed. Kyle Conway, 19–33. Grand Forks: The Digital Press at the University of North Dakota.

Costa, Diogo M.

2018. "Eco-historical Archaeology in the Brazilian Amazon: Material, Natural and Cultural Western Transformations." In *Historical Archaeology and Environment,* eds. M. de Souza and D. M. Costa, 65–86. Cham: Springer. https://doi.org/10.1007/978-3-319 -90857-1_4

Cowie, Sarah E., Diane L. Teeman, and Christopher C. LeBlanc.

2019. *Collaborative Archaeology at Stewart Indian School.* Reno: University of Nevada Press.

Cowen, D.

2014. *The Deadly Life of Logistics: Mapping the Violence in Global Trade.* Minneapolis: University of Minnesota Press.

Cremin, Colin.

2016. *Exploring Videogames with Deleuze and Guattari: Towards an Affective Theory of Form.* London: Routledge.

Crogan, Patrick.
2011. *Gameplay Mode: War, Simulation, and Technoculture.* Minneapolis: University of Minnesota Press.

Cronon, William.
1991. *Nature's Metropolis Chicago and the Great West.* New York: Norton.

Crutzen, Paul J., and Eugene F. Stoermer.
2000. "The Anthropocene." *Global Change Newsletter* 41: 17–18.

Crutzen, Paul J.
2002. "The Anthropocene." *Journal de Physique IV (Proceedings)* 12(10): 1–5.

Cubbit, Sean.
2014. "Global Media and the Archaeologies of Network Technologies." In *The Oxford Handbook of the Archaeology of the Contemporary World,* eds. Paul Graves-Brown, Rodney Harrison, and Angela Piccini, 135–148. Oxford: Oxford University Press.

Culver, Lawrence.
2014. "Confluences of Nature and Culture: Cities in Environmental History." In *The Oxford Handbook of Environmental History,* ed. Andrew C. Isenberg, 533–572. Oxford: Oxford University Press.

Czerwiec, Heidi.
2016. *Sweet/Crude: A Bakken Boom Cycle.* Fairfax, VA: Gazing Grain Press.

Daggett, Cara.
2018. "Petro-Masculinity: Fossil Fuels and Authoritarian Desire." *Millennium* 47(1): 25–44. doi:10.1177/0305829818775817

Danis, Ann Elena Stinchfield.
2020. "Landscapes of Inequality: Creative Approaches to Engaged Research," PhD Dissertation, University of California, Berkeley.

Dawdy, Shannon Lee.
2006. "The Taphonomy of Disaster and the (Re)Formation of New Orleans." *American Anthropologist* 108(4): 719–730.
2010. "Clockpunk Anthropology and the Ruins of Modernity." *Current Anthropology* 51(6): 761–93.
2016. *Patina: A Profane Archaeology.* Chicago: University of Chicago Press.

Dawdy, Shannon Lee, and Daniel Zox.
2021. *American Afterlives: Reinventing Death in the Twenty-First Century.* Princeton, NJ: Princeton University Press.

Dear, M.
2013. *Why Walls Won't Work: Repairing the US Mexico Divide.* New York: Oxford University Press.

Deetz, James.
1977. *In Small Things Forgotten: The Archaeology of Early American Life.* Garden City, NY: Anchor Press/Doubleday.

DeLanda, Manuel.
1991. *War in the Age of Intelligent Machines.* New York: Zone Books.
2016. *Assemblage Theory.* Edinburgh: Edinburgh University Press.

De León, Jason.

2013. "Undocumented Use-Wear and the Materiality of Habitual Suffering in the Sonoran Desert." *Journal of Material Culture* 18(4): 1–32.

2015. *The Land of Open Graves: Living and Dying on the Migrant Trail.* Oakland: University of California Press.

De León, Jason, and Cameron Gokee.

2019. "Lasting Value? Engaging with the Material Traces of America's Undocumented
Migration 'Problem.'" In *Cultural Heritage, Ethics and Contemporary Migrations,* eds.
C. Holtorf, A. Pantazatos, and G. Scarre, 70–86. London: Routledge.

Deleuze, Gilles, and Felix Guattari.

1987. *A Thousand Plateaus: Capitalism and Schizophrenia.* Trans. Brian Massumi. Minneapolis: University of Minnesota Press.

Dennis, L.M.

2016. "Archaeogaming, Ethics, and Participatory Standards." *SAA Archaeological Record*
16(5): 29–33.

DeSilvey, Caitlin.

2006. Observed Decay: Telling Stories with Mutable Things. *Journal of Material Culture*
11(3): 318–338.

2014. Palliative Curation: Art and Entropy on Orford Ness. In *Ruin Memories: Materialities, Aesthetics, and the Archaeology of the Recent Past,* eds. B. Olsen and Þ. Pétursdóttir, 79–91. Abingdon: Routledge.

2017. *Curated Decay: Heritage Beyond Saving.* Minneapolis: University of Minnesota
Press.

Desmond, Matthew.

2016. *Evicted: Poverty and Profit in the American City.* New York: Crown Publishers.

de Souza, Marcos A.T., and Diogo M. Costa.

2018. "Introduction: Historical Archaeology and Environment." In *Historical Archaeology and Environment,* eds. M. de Souza and D. M. Costa, 1–15. Cham: Springer.

Devine, Kyle.

2019. *Decomposed: The Political Ecology of Music.* Cambridge, MA: MIT Press.

Dézsi, A., and L. Wurst.

2023. "Theorizing Capitalism's Cracks." *International Journal of Historical Archaeology.*
doi.org/10.1007/s10761-022-00690-3

Dinzey-Flores, Zaire Z.

2013. *Locked In, Locked Out: Gated Communities in a Puerto Rican City.* Philadelphia:
University of Pennsylvania Press.

2020. "Race Walls: (In)Visible Codes of Neighborhood Inequality in Puerto Rico." In
Walling In and Walling Out: Why Are We Building New Barriers to Divide Us?, eds.
Laura McAtackney and Randall H. McGuire, 47–62. Albuquerque: University of
New Mexico Press.

Dixon, Kelly J.

2006. *Boomtown Saloons: Archaeology and History in Virginia City.* Reno: University of
Nevada Press.

2014. "Historical Archaeologies in the American West." *Journal of Archaeological Research* 22(3): 177–228.

2020. "Repercussions of Rapid Colonization: Archaeological Insights from the North American West." In *Handbook of Global Historical Archaeology,* eds. Charles E. Orser Jr., Andrés Zarankin, Pedro Paulo, A. Funari, Susan Lawrence, and James Symonds, 851–893. London: Routledge.

Dolff-Bonekämper, Gabi.

2002. "The Berlin Wall: An Archaeological Site in Progress." In *Materiel Culture: The Archaeology of Twentieth-Century Conflict,* eds. A. John Schofield, William Gray Johnson, and Colleen M. Beck, 236–248. London: Routledge.

Dondero, Jeff.

2019   *Throwaway Nation: The Ugly Truth about American Garbage.* Lanham, MD: Rowman & Littlefield.

Díaz-Barriga, Miguel, and Margaret E. Dorsey.

2020   *Fencing in Democracy: Border Walls, Necrocitizenship, and the Security State.* Durham, NC: Duke University Press.

Douglas, Mary, and Baron Isherwood.

1990   *The World of Goods: Towards an Anthropology of Consumption.* London: Routledge.

Douglass, Kristina.

2020. *Amy ty lilin-draza'ay:* Building Archaeological Practice on Principles of Community. *African Archaeological Review* 37: 481–485. https://doi.org/10.1007/s10437-020-09404-8

Dufton, J. Andrew, Linda R. Gosner, Alex R. Knodell, and Catherine Steidl.

2019. Archaeology Underfoot: On-Campus Approaches to Education, Outreach, and Historical Archaeology at Brown University. *Journal of Field Archaeology* 44(5): 304–318. doi:10.1080/00934690.2019.1605123

Dunham, Rebecca.

2016. "Bakken Boom! Artists Respond to the North Dakota Oil Rush." In *The Bakken Goes Boom: Oil and the Changing Geographies of Western North Dakota,* eds. William Caraher and Kyle Conway, 293–356. Grand Forks: The Digital Press at the University of North Dakota.

Dyer-Witheford, Nick, and Peuter G. De.

2009. *Games of Empire: Global Capitalism and Video Games.* Minneapolis: University of Minnesota Press.

Edgeworth, Matthew.

2018. "More than Just a Record: Active Ecological Effects of Archaeological Strata." In *Historical Archaeology and Environment,* eds. M. de Souza and D. M. Costa, 19–40, Cham: Springer.

Edgeworth, Matthew, Jeffery Benjamin, Bruce Clarke, Zoe Crossland, Ewa Domanska, Alice C. Gorman, Paul Graves-Brown, Edward C. Harris, Mark J. Hudson, Jason M. Kelly, Victor J. Paz, Melissa M. Salerno, Christopher Witmore, and Andrés Zarankin.

2014. "Archaeology of the Anthropocene." *Journal of Contemporary Archaeology* 1(1): 73–132. https://doi.org/10.1558/jca.v1.i1.73

Edensor, Tim.

2005. *Industrial Ruins: Spaces, Aesthetics, and Materiality.* Oxford: Berg.

Edwards, Susan.

1997. "Atomic Age Training Camp: The Historical Archaeology of Camp Desert Rock." Unpublished MA Thesis, University of Nevada, Las Vegas.

Eighmy, Jeffrey L.

1981. "The Use of Material Culture in Modern Anthropology." In *Modern Material Culture: The Archaeology of Us,* eds. Richard Gould and Michael Schiffer, 31–49. New York: Academic Press.

Ellis, Bret Easton.

1991. *American Psycho.* New York: Vintage Books.

Estes, Nick.

2019. *Our History Is the Future.* London: Verso.

Ernst, Wolfgang.

2016. *Chronopoetics: The Temporal Being and Operativity of Technological Media.* Trans. Anthony Enns. London: Rowman & Littlefield.

Evans, Sterling.

2007. *Bound in Twine: The History and Ecology of the Henequen-Wheat Complex for Mexico and the American and Canadian Plains, 1880–1950.* College Station: Texas A&M University Press.

Fabian, Johannes.

1983. *Time and the Other: How Anthropology Makes its Object.* New York: Columbia University Press.

Farber, Paul, Laurie Allen, and Sue Mobley.

2020   National Monument Audit. Monument Lab. www.monumentlab.com/projects/national-monument-audit

Farrell, Mary M., and Jeffrey F. Burton.

2004. "Civil Rights and Moral Wrongs: World War II Japanese American Relocation Sites." *SAA Archaeological Record* 4(5):22–25.

2019. "From Forgotten to National Monument: Community Archaeology at a World War II Internment Camp in Hawai'i." In *Transforming Heritage Practice in the 21st Century: Contributions from Community Archaeology.* Eds. John H. Jameson, Sergiu Musteață. 283–301. Cham: Springer.

Ferrell, Jeff.

2006. *Empire of Scrounge: Inside the Urban Underground of Dumpster Diving, Trash Picking, and Street Scavenging.* New York: New York University Press.

Feversham, Polly, and Leo Schmidt.

2007. "The Berlin Wall: Border, Fragment, World Heritage." In *A Fearsome Heritage: Diverse Legacies of the Cold War,* eds. J. Schofield, and W. D. Cocroft, 193–209. Walnut Creek, CA: Left Coast Press.

Finn, Christine A.

2002. *Artifacts: An Archaeologist's Year in Silicon Valley.* Cambridge, MA: MIT Press.

Flick, Catherine, with L. Megan Denis and Andrew Reinhard.

2018. "*A No Man's Sky* Archaeological Survey Code of Ethics." In *Archaeogaming: An*

Introduction to Archaeology in and of Video Games, ed. Andrew Reinhard, 203–209. New York: Berghahn Books.

Flannery, Kent V.

1982. "The Golden Marshalltown: A Parable for the Archeology of the 1980s." *American Anthropologist* 84(2): 265–278.

Foucault, M.

1970. *The Order of Things: An Archaeology of the Human Sciences.* Trans. Alan Sheridan. London: Routledge.

1972. *The Archaeology of Knowledge.* Trans. Alan Sheridan. New York: Pantheon Books.

Frank, A. G.

1966. *The Development of Underdevelopment.* Boston: New England Free Press.

Franklin, Maria.

2020. "Gender, Clothing Fasteners, and Dress Practices in Houston's Freedmen's Town, ca. 1880–1904." *Historical Archaeology* 54(3): 556–580.

Franklin, Maria, Justin P. Dunnavant, Ayana Omilade Flewellen, and Alicia Odewale.

2020. "The Future is Now: Archaeology and the Eradication of Anti-Blackness." *International Journal of Historical Archaeology* 24: 753–766. https://doi.org/10.1007/s10761-020-00577-1

Friedman, Andrew.

2013. *Covert Capital: Landscapes of Denial and the Making of U.S. Empire in the Suburbs of Northern Virginia.* Berkeley: University of California Press.

Gabrys, Jennifer.

2011. *Digital Rubbish: A Natural History of Electronics.* Ann Arbor: University of Michigan Press.

Gamble, Lynn H., Cheryl Claassen, Jelmer W. Eerkens, Douglas J. Kennett, Patricia M. Lambert, Matthew J. Liebmann, Natasha Lyons, Barbara J. Mills, Christopher B. Rodning, Tsim D. Schneider, Stephen W. Silliman, Susan M. Alt, Douglas Bamforth, Kelley Hays-Gilpin, Anna Marie Prentiss, and Torben C. Rick.

2021. "Finding Archaeological Relevance during a Pandemic and What Comes After." *American Antiquity* 86(1): 2–22. https://doi.org/10.1017/aaq.2020.94

Garcia, Patricia Fournier.

2018. "Indigenous Charcoal Production and Spanish Metal Mining Enterprises: Historical Archaeology of Extractive Activities and Ecological Degradation in Central and Northern Mexico." In *Historical Archaeology and Environment,* eds. M. de Souza and D. M. Costa, 87–109, Cham: Springer.

Garrow, Duncan, and Thomas Yarrow.

2010. *Archaeology and Anthropology: Understanding Similarity, Exploring Difference.* Oxford: Oxbow Books.

Garstki, Kevin.

2017. "Virtual Representation: The Production of 3D Digital Artifacts." *Journal of Archaeological Method and Theory* 24(3): 726–750.

2020. *Digital Innovations in European Archaeology.* Cambridge: Cambridge University Press.

Gero, Joan M.

1985. "Socio-Politics and the Woman-at-Home Ideology." *American Antiquity* 50: 342–350.

1991. "Gender Divisions of Labor in the Construction of Archaeological Knowledge." In *The Archaeology of Gender: Proceedings of the 22nd Annual Chacmool Conference*, eds. D. Walde and N. D. Willows, 96–102. Archaeological Association of the University of Calgary, Calgary.

Gibb, James G.

1996. *The Archaeology of Wealth: Consumer Behavior in English America*. New York: Plenum.

Gibson, William.

1984. *Neuromancer*. New York: Berkley.

Gibson, William, and Bruce Sterling.

1990. *The Difference Engine*. London: Vista.

Gifford-Gonzalez, D.

2011. "Just Methodology? A Review of Archaeology's Debts to Michael Schiffer." *Journal of Archaeological Method Theory* 18: 299–308. https://doi.org/10.1007/s10816-011-9113-4

Gille, Zsuzsa.

2007. *From the Cult of Waste to the Trash Heap of History: The Politics of Waste in Socialist and Postsocialist Hungary*. Bloomington: Indiana University Press.

Gillem, Mark L.

2007. *America Town: Building the Outputs of Empire*. Minneapolis: University of Minnesota Press.

Gnecco, C.

2013. "Digging Alternative Archaeologies." In *Reclaiming Archaeology: Beyond the Tropes of Modernity*, ed. A. González-Ruibal. 67–78. New York: Routledge.

Gokee, Cameron, and Jason De León.

2014. "Sites of Contention." *Journal of Contemporary Archaeology* 1: 133–163.

Gokee, Cameron, Haeden Stewart and Jason De León.

2020. "Scales of Suffering in the US-Mexico Borderlands." *International Journal of Historical Archaeology* 24: 823–851. https://doi.org/10.1007/s10761-019-00535-6

Gold, Russell.

2014. *The Boom: How Fracking Ignited the American Energy Revolution and Changed the World*. New York: Simon and Schuster.

Goldberg, Marty, and Curt Vendell.

2012. *Atari Inc.: Business Is Fun*. Carmel, NY: Syzygy Company.

González-Ruibal, Alfredo.

2008. "Time to Destroy. An Archaeology of Supermodernity." *Current Anthropology* 49(2): 247–279.

2014. *An Archaeology of Resistance: Materiality and Time in an African Borderland*. Lanham, MD: Rowman & Littlefield Publishers.

2015. "An Archaeology of Predation: Capitalism and the Coloniality of Power in Equatorial Guinea (Central Africa)." In *Historical Archaeologies of Capitalism,* eds. M. Leone and J. Knauf, 421–444. New York: Springer.

2019. *An Archaeology of the Contemporary Era.* London: Routledge.

González-Tennant, Edward.

2011. "Creating a Diasporic Archaeology of Chinese Migration: Tentative Steps across Four Continents." *International Journal of Historical Archaeology* 15: 509–532.

2018. *The Rosewood Massacre: An Archaeology and History of Intersectional Violence.* Gainesville: University Press of Florida.

Goodwin, Lorinda B. R.

1999. *An Archaeology of Manners: The Polite World of the Merchant Elite of Colonial Massachusetts.* New York: Plenum.

Gorman, Alice.

2019. *Dr Space Junk vs the Universe: Archaeology and the Future.* Cambridge: MIT Press.

Gould, Richard.

1978. "The Anthropology of Human Residues." *American Anthropologist* 80(4): 815–835.

1980. *Living Archaeology.* Cambridge: Cambridge University Press.

1981. "Early and Late Americana." In *Modern Material Culture: The Archaeology of Us,* eds. Richard Gould and Michael Schiffer, 57–66. New York: Academic Press.

2007. *Disaster Archaeology.* Salt Lake City: University of Utah Press.

Graham, Shawn.

2020. "An Approach to the Ethics of Archaeogaming." *Internet Archaeology* 55. https://doi.org/10.11141/ia.55.2

Graves-Brown, Paul.

2007. "Concrete Islands." In *Contemporary and Historical Archaeology in Theory: Papers from the 2003 and 2004 CHAT Conferences,* eds. Laura McAtackney, Matthew Palus, and Angela Piccini, 75–82. Oxford: Archaeopress.

2014. "Plugging In: A Brief History of Some Audio Connectors." *World Archaeology* 46(3): 448–461.

Graves-Brown, Paul. ed.

2000 *Matter, Materiality, and Modern Culture.* London: Routledge.

Graves-Brown P, Harrison R, Piccini A, eds.

2013. *The Oxford Handbook of the Archaeology of the Contemporary World.* Oxford & New York: Oxford University Press.

Guins, Raiford.

2009. *Edited Clean Version: Technology and the Culture of Control.* Minneapolis: University of Minnesota Press.

2014. *Game After: A Cultural Study of Video Game Afterlife.* Cambridge, MA: MIT Press.

Haeselin, David.

2017. "Bookish." In *Codex,* ed. Micah Bloom, 37–44. Grand Forks: The Digital Press at the University of North Dakota.

Hailey, Charlie.

2009. *Camps: A Guide to 21st-Century Space.* Cambridge, MA: MIT Press.

Hailey, Charlie, and Donovan Wylie.

2018. *Slab City: Dispatches from the Last Free Place.* Cambridge, MA: MIT Press.

Hageneuer, Sebastian.

2021. "Archaeogaming: How Heaven's Vault Changes the 'Game.'" In *Pearls, Politics and Pistachios: Essays in Anthropology and Memories on the Occasion of Susan Pollock's 65th Birthday,* eds. Aydin Abar, Maria Bianca D'Anna, Georg Cyrus, Vera Egbers, Barbara Huber, Christine Kainert, Johannes Köhler, Birgül Ögüt, Nolwen Rol, Giulia Russo, Julia Schönicke, and Francelin Tourtet, 631–642. Heidelberg: Propylaeum.

Hall, Martin.

2000. *Archaeology and the Modern World: Colonial Transcripts in South Africa and the Chesapeake.* Oxford: Routledge.

Hamilakis, Yannis.

2016. "Archaeologies of Forced and Undocumented Migration." *Journal of Contemporary Archaeology* 3(2): 121–139.

Hamilakis, Yannis, and Fotis Ifantidis.

2015. "The Photographic and the Archaeological: The 'Other' Acropolis." In *Camera Graeca: Photographs, Narratives, Materialities,* eds. P. Carabott, Y. Hamilakis, and E. Papargyriou, 133–157. London: Ashgate.

2016. *Camera Kalaureia: An Archaeological Photo-Ethnography.* Oxford: Archaeopress.

Hamilakis, Yannis, and Andrew Meirion Jones.

2017. "Archaeology and Assemblage." *Cambridge Archaeological Journal* 27(1): 77–84.

Hanson, Christopher.

2018. *Game Time: Understanding Temporality in Video Games.* Bloomington: Indiana University Press.

Hanson, Todd A.

2010. "Uncovering the Arsenals of Armageddon The Historical Archaeology of North American Cold War Ballistic Missile Launch Sites." *Archaeological Review from Cambridge* 25(1): 157–172.

2015. *The Archaeology of the Cold War.* Gainesville: University Press of Florida.

Haraway, Donna J.

1991. *Simians, Cyborgs, and Women: The Reinvention of Nature.* New York: Routledge.

Hardesty, Donald L.

1991. "Toward an Historical Archaeology of the Intermountain West." *Historical Archaeology* 25(3): 29–35.

2010. *Mining Archaeology in the American West: A View from the Silver State.* Lincoln: University of Nebraska Press.

Hardt, Michael, and Antonio Negri.

2000. *Empire.* Cambridge, MA: Harvard University Press.

Harrison, Rodney.

2011. "Surface Assemblages: Towards an Archaeology in and of the Present." *Archaeological Dialogues* 18(2): 141–196.

Harrison, Rodney, and Esther Breithoff.

2017. "Archaeologies of the Contemporary World." *Annual Review of Anthropology* 46(1): 203–221.

Harrison, Rodney, and John Schofield.

2010. *After Modernity: Archaeological Approaches to the Contemporary Past.* Oxford & New York: Oxford University Press.

2011. "Archaeo-Ethnography, Auto-Archaeology: Introducing Archaeologies of the Contemporary Past." *Archaeologies* 5: 185–209.

Hart, John Fraser, Michelle J. Rhodes, and John Morgan.

2002. *The Unknown World of the Mobile Home.* Baltimore, MD: Johns Hopkins University Press.

Hartog, François.

2016. *Regimes of Historicity: Presentism and Experiences of Time.* Trans. Saskia Brown. New York: Columbia University Press.

Harvey, David.

2005. *A Brief History of Neoliberalism.* Oxford: Oxford University Press.

Hasian, Jr. M. A, and Nicholas S. Paliewicz.

2020. *Memory and Monument Wars in American Cities. New York, Charlottesville and Montgomery.* Cham: Springer International Publishing.

Hattam, Victoria.

2016. "Imperial Designs: Remembering Vietnam at the US–Mexico Border Wall." *Memory Studies* 9(1): 27–47. doi:10.1177/1750698015613971

Heath, Barbara J.

2017. "An Historical Archaeology of Consumerism: Re-centering objects, Re-engaging with Data." In *Material Worlds: Archaeology, Consumption, and the Road to Modernity,* eds. Barbara J. Heath, Eleanor E. Breen, and Lori A. Lee, 9–34. New York: Routledge.

Heath, Barbara J., Eleanor E. Breen, Lori A. Lee, eds.

2017. *Material Worlds: Archaeology, Consumption, and the Road to Modernity.* New York: Routledge.

Heath-Stout, L.E.

2020. "Who Writes about Archaeology? An Intersectional Study of Authorship in Archaeological Journals." *American Antiquity* 85(3): 407–26.

Herz, M.

2013. *From Camp to City: Refugee Camps of the Western Sahara.* Zürich: L. Müller.

Hicks, Dan.

2010. "The Material-Cultural Turn: Event and Effect." In *The Oxford Handbook of Material Culture Studies,* eds. Dan Hicks and Mary C. Beaudry, 25–98. Oxford & New York: Oxford University Press.

2016. "Reply to Comments: Meshwork Fatigue." *Norwegian Archaeological Review* 49(1): 33–39.

Hicks, Dan, and Mary C. Beaudry.

2006. "Introduction: The Place of Historical Archaeology." In *The Cambridge Companion to Historical Archaeology,* eds. Dan Hicks and Mary C. Beaudry, 1–11. Cambridge: Cambridge University Press.

Hicks, Dan, and Sarah Mallet.

2019. *Lande: The Calais "Jungle" and Beyond.* Bristol: Bristol University Press.

Hodder, Ian.

1982. *Symbols in Action: Ethnoarchaeological Studies of Material Culture.* Cambridge: Cambridge University Press.

2007. *Symbolic and Structural Archaeology.* Cambridge: Cambridge University Press.

2012. *Entangled: An Archaeology of the Relationships between Humans and Things.* Malden, MA: Wiley-Blackwell.

Hodder, Ian, Mark P. Leone, Reinhard Bernbeck, Michael Shanks, Silvia Tomášková, Patricia A. McAnany, Stephen Shennan, and Colin Renfrew.

2007. "Revolution Fulfilled? Symbolic and Structural Archaeology, a Generation On." *Cambridge Archaeological Journal* 17(2): 199–228.

Hodder, Ian and Gavin Lucas.

2017. "The Symmetries and Asymmetries of Human-Thing Relations. A Dialogue." *Archaeological Dialogues* 24(2): 119–137.

Holmgren, John.

2016. "Man Camp #1, #2, #3, #5, #8, #9, #10, #12, #16, and #17." In *The Bakken Goes Boom: Oil and the Changing Geographies of Western North Dakota,* eds. William Caraher and Kyle Conway, 357–368. Grand Forks: The Digital Press at the University of North Dakota.

Holtorf, Cornelius.

2005. *From Stonehenge to Las Vegas: Archaeology As Popular Culture.* Walnut Creek, CA: Altamira Press.

2013. "On Pastness: A Reconsideration of Materiality in Archaeological Object Authenticity." *Anthropological Quarterly* 86(2): 427–443.

Hubbs, Mark E.

1992. *The Stanley R. Mickelson Safeguard Complex, Nekoma, Cavalier County, ND.* HAER ND-9. Historic American Engineering Record. U.S. Department of the Interior, National Park Service, Washington, DC.

Hughes, Wilson W.

1984. "The Method to Our Madness: The Garbage Project Methodology." *American Behavioral Scientist* 28(1): 41–50. https://doi.org/10.1177/000276484028001005

Humes, Edward.

2012   *Garbology: Our Dirty Love Affair with Trash.* New York: Avery.

Huhtamo, Erkki, and Jussi Parikka.

2011. *Media Archaeology: Approaches, Applications, and Implications.* Berkeley: University of California Press.

Hutson, S.R.

2002. "Gendered Citation Practices in American Antiquity and Other Archaeology Journals." *American Antiquity* 67(2): 331–342.

Ingold, Tim.

2011. "Networks of Objects, Meshworks of Things." In *Redrawing Anthropology: Materials, Movements, Lines,* ed. Tim Ingold, 45–64. Burlington, VT: Ashgate.

Ifantidis, Fotis.

2011. *Archaeographies: Excavating Neolithic Dispilio.* Oxford: Archaeopress.

Jackson, Antoinette T.

2016. "Exhuming the Dead and Talking to the Living: The 1914 Fire at the Florida Industrial School for Boys—Invoking the Uncanny as a Site of Analysis." *Anthropology and Humanism* 41(2): 158–177.

Jackson, Kenneth T.

1985. *Crabgrass Frontier: The Suburbanization of America.* New York: Oxford University Press.

Jameson, Frederick.

1982. "Progress versus Utopia; Or, Can We Imagine the Future? (Progrès contre Utopie, ou: Pouvons-nous imaginer l'avenir)." *Science Fiction Studies* 9(2): 147–158. www .jstor.org/stable/4239476

2005. *Archaeologies of the Future: The Desire Called Utopia and Other Science Fictions.* London: Verso.

Jayemanne, Darshana.

2018. *Performativity in Art, Literature and Videogames.* Cham: Springer.

Jelfs, Tim.

2017. "Matter Unmoored: Trash, Archaeological Consciousness and American Culture and Fiction in the 1980s." *Journal of American Studies* 51(2): 553–571. doi:10.1017/ S0021875816000578

2018. *The Argument about Things in the 1980s: Goods and Garbage in the Age of Neoliberalism.* Morgantown, WV: West Virginia University Press.

Johnson, Matthew.

1996. *An Archaeology of Capitalism.* Oxford: Blackwell.

Johnson, William, Robert Jones, and Barbara Holz.

2000. *A Cold War Battlefield: Frenchman Flat Historic District, Nevada Test Site, Nye County, Nevada.* Washington, DC: United States National Nuclear Security Administration.

Jones, Reece.

2012. *Border Walls: Security and the War on Terror in the United States, India, and Israel.* London: Zed Books.

2016. *Violent Borders: Refugees and the Right to Move.* London: Verso.

Joyce, Rosemary.

2020. *The Future of Nuclear Waste: What Art and Archaeology Can Tell us about Securing the World's Most Hazardous Material.* New York: Oxford.

Robinson, Kaniqua L.

2018. "The Performance of Memorialization: Politics of Memory and Memory-Making at the Arthur G. Dozier School for Boys." PhD dissertation, University of South Florida.

Kansa, Eric, Sarah Whitcher Kansa, and Ethan Watrall.

2011. *Archaeology 2.0: New Approaches to Communication and Collaboration.* Los Angeles: Cotsen Institute of Archaeology.

Kerner, Aaron, and Julian Hoxter, eds.

2019. *Theorizing Stupid Media: De-naturalizing Story Structures in the Cinematic, Televisual, and Videogames.* Cham: Springer.

Kibler, Robert E.

2017. "'Ribbit,' Said the Frog." In *Codex,* ed. Micah Bloom, 53–56. Grand Forks: The Digital Press at the University of North Dakota.

Kiddey, Rachael.

2017. *Homeless Heritage: Collaborative Social Archaeology as Therapeutic Practice.* Oxford: Oxford University Press.

2018. "From the Ground Up: Cultural Heritage Practices as Tools for Empowerment in the Homeless Heritage Project." *International Journal of Heritage Studies* 24(7): 694–708.

Kiddey, Rachael, and John Schofield.

2010. "Digging for (Invisible) People." *British Archaeology* (113): 18–24.

2011. "Embrace the Margins: Adventures in Archaeology and Homelessness." *Public Archaeology* 10(1): 4–22.

Kilby, Terry.

2020. Robert E. Lee Monument: 6.15.2020. 3D Model. Sketchfab. https://skfb.ly/6TtSV

Kimmerle, Erin H., E. Christian Wells, and Antoinette Jackson.

2016. "Summary of Findings on the Investigation into the Deaths and Burials at the Former Arthur G. Dozier School for Boys in Marianna, Florida." University of South Florida, Tampa, Florida.

Kittler, Friedrich A.

1999. *Gramophone, Film, Typewriter.* Trans. Geoffrey Winthrop-Young. Stanford, CA: Stanford University Press.

Klingle, Matthew W.

2007. *Emerald City: An Environmental History of Seattle.* New Haven, CT: Yale University Press.

Kopytoff, Igor.

1986. "The Cultural Biography of Things: Commoditization as Process." In *The Social Life of Things: Commodities in Cultural Perspective,* ed. Arjun Appadurai, 64–92. Cambridge: Cambridge University Press.

Kourelis, Kostis, ed.

2008. *The Archaeology of Xenitia: Greek Immigration and Material Culture.* New Griffon 10. American School of Classical Studies at Athens, Princeton, New Jersey.

2020. "Three Elenis: Archaeologies of the Greek American Village Home." *Journal of Modern Greek Studies* 38(1): 85–108.

Klein, T. H., L. Goldstein, D. Gangloff, W. B. Lees, K. Ryzewski, B. W. Styles, and A. P. Wright.

2018. "The Future of American Archaeology: Engage the Voting Public or Kiss Your Research Goodbye!" *Advances in Archaeological Practice* 6(1): 1–18. doi:10.1017/aap.2017.34

Krell, David.

2002. *The Devil's Rope: A Cultural History of Barbed Wire.* London: Reaktion Books.

Kuletz, Valerie L.

2016. *The Tainted Desert: Environmental and Social Ruin in the American West.* London: Routledge.

Lane, Matthew R.

2011. "A Conversation with William Rathje." *Anthropology Now* 3(1): 78–83. doi:10.1080/ 19428200.2011.11869126

Lane, Paul J.

2015. "Archaeology in the Age of the Anthropocene: A Critical Assessment of Its Scope and Societal Contributions." *Journal of Field Archaeology* 40(5): 485–498.

Latour, Bruno.

2017. *Facing Gaia: Eight Lectures on the New Climatic Regime.* Trans. Catherine Porter. Cambridge: Polity.

Latour, Bruno, and Steve Woolgarl.

1979. *Laboratory Life: The Social Construction of Scientific Facts.* Beverly Hills, CA: Sage.

2005. *Reassembling the Social: An Introduction to Actor-Network-Theory.* Oxford: Oxford University Press.

LeCain, Timothy J.

2009. *Mass Destruction: The Men and Giant Mines That Wired America and Scarred the Planet.* New Brunswick, NJ: Rutgers University Press.

2014. "The Ontology of Absence: Uniting Materialist and Ecological Interpretations at an Abandoned Open-Pit Copper Mine." In *Ruin Memories: Materiality, Aesthetics and the Archaeology of the Recent Past,* eds. Bjørnar Olsen and Þóra Pétursdóttir, 62–78. London: Routledge.

2017. *The Matter of History: How Things Create the Past.* Cambridge: Cambridge University Press.

Lehmann, La V.

2015. "The Garbage Project Revisited: From a 20th Century Archaeology of Food Waste to a Contemporary Study of Food Packaging Waste." *Sustainability* 7(6): 6994–7010. https://doi.org/10.3390/su7066994

Leighton, M.

2015. "Excavation Methodologies and Labour as Epistemic Concerns in the Practice of Archaeology: Comparing Examples from British and Andean Archaeology." *Archaeological Dialogues* 22(1): 65–88.

Leone, Mark.

1981. "Archaeology's Relationship to the Present and the Past." In *Modern Material Culture: The Archaeology of Us,* eds. Richard Gould and Michael Schiffer, 5–14. New York: Academic Press.

1984. "Interpreting Ideology in Historical Archaeology: The William Paca Garden in Annapolis, Maryland." In *Ideology, Power and Prehistory,* eds. Daniel Miller and Christopher Tilley, 25–36. Cambridge: Cambridge University Press.

2010. *Critical Historical Archaeology.* Walnut Creek, CA: Left Coast Press.

Lepawsky, Josh.

2018. *Reassembling Rubbish: Worlding Electronic Waste.* Cambridge, MA: MIT Press.

Lewis, Kenneth E.

2010. "Introduction: The Archaeology of Academia." In *Beneath the Ivory Tower: The Archaeology of Academia,* eds. Russell K. Skowronek and K. E. Lewis, 1–7. Gainesville: University Press of Florida.

Lindauer, Owen.

2009. "Individual Struggles and Institutional Goals." In *The Archaeology of Institutional Life,* eds. April M. Beisaw and James G. Gibbs, 86–104. Tuscaloosa: University of Alabama Press.

Little, Adrian.

2015. "The Complex Temporality of Borders: Contingency and Normativity." *European Journal of Political Theory* 14(4): 429–447.

Liming, Sheila.

2017. "(De)Composition: or, How Matter Matters." In *Codex,* ed. Micah Bloom, 31–36. Grand Forks: The Digital Press at the University of North Dakota.

L'Official, Peter.

2020. *Urban Legends. The South Bronx in Representation and Ruin.* Cambridge, MA: Harvard University Press.

Lovelock, James.

1979. *Gaia: A New Look at Life on Earth.* Oxford: Oxford University Press.

Low, Setha.

2003. *Behind the Gates: Life, Security and the Pursuit of Happiness in Fortress America.* New York & London: Routledge.

Lucas, Gavin.

2002. "Disposability and Dispossession in the Twentieth Century." *Journal of Material Culture* 7(1): 5–22.

2015. "Archaeology and Contemporaneity." *Archaeological Dialogues* 22(1): 1–15. doi:10.1017/S1380203815000021

2021. *Making Time: The Archaeology of Time Revisited.* London: Routledge.

Ludlow Collective, The.

2001. "Archaeology of the Colorado Coal Field War 1913–1914." In *Archaeologies of the Contemporary Past,* eds. Victor Buchli and Gavin Lucas, 94–107. London: Routledge.

Lyons, Siobhan, ed.

2018. *Ruin Porn and the Obsession with Decay.* Cham: Palgrave Macmillan.

McGuire, R. H.

2013   "Steel Walls and Picket Fences: Rematerializing the U.S.–Mexican Border in Ambos Nogales." *American Anthropologist* 115: 466–480. https://doi.org/10.1111/aman.12029

2020. "The Materiality and Heritage of Contemporary Forced Migration." *Annual Review of Anthropology* 49(1): 175–191.

McGuire, R. H., and Paul Reckner.

2002. "The Unromantic West: Labor, Capital, and Struggle." *Historical Archaeology* 36(3): 44–58. https://doi.org/10.1007/BF03374359

2003. "Building a Working-Class Archaeology: The Colorado Coal Field War Project." *Industrial Archaeology Review* 25(2): 83–95.

Madden, David J, and Peter Marcuse.

2016. *In Defense of Housing: The Politics of Crisis.* New York: Verso.

Magnani, Matthew, Natalia Magnani, Anatolijs Venovcevs, and Stein Farstadvoll.
2022. "A Contemporary Archaeology of Pandemic." *Journal of Social Archaeology* 22(1): 48–81.

Majewski, Teresita, and Michael B. Schiffer,
2001. "Beyond Consumption: Toward an Archaeology of Consumerism." In *Archaeologies of the Contemporary Past,* eds. Victor Buchli and Gavin Lucas, 26–50. London: Routledge.

Mallea, Amahia.
2018. *A River in the City of Fountains: An Environmental History of Kansas City and the Missouri River.* Lawrence: University of Kansas Press.

Matthews, Christopher.
2019. "Assemblages, Routines, and Social Justice Research in Community Archaeology." *Journal of Community Archaeology & Heritage* 6(3): 220–226.
2020a. *A Struggle for Heritage: Archaeology and Civil Rights in a Long Island Community.* Gainesville: University Press of Florida.
2020b. "Binocular Vision: Making the Carceral Metropolis in Northern New Jersey." In *Archaeologies of Violence and Privilege,* eds. Christopher Matthews and Bradley D. Phillippi, 169–200. Gainesville: University Press of Florida.

Maloney, Liam, and John Schofield.
2022. "Records as Records: Excavating the DJ's Sonic Archive." *Archives and Records* (2022): 1–23.

Martin, Ann Smart.
2017. "'Open the Mind and Close the Sale': Consumerism and the Archaeological Record." In In *Material Worlds: Archaeology, Consumption, and the Road to Modernity,* eds. Barbara J. Heath, Eleanor E. Breen, and Lori A. Lee, 282–290. New York: Routledge.

Martin, Larry J.
2014. *The Bakken.* Clinton, MT: Wolfpack Publishing.

Maxwell, Richard, and Toby Miller.
2014. "The Material Cellphone." In *The Oxford Handbook of the Archaeology of the Contemporary World,* eds. Paul Graves-Brown, Rodney Harrison, and Angela Piccini, 669–712. Oxford: Oxford University Press.

Mayer-Oakes, William J.
1955. *Prehistory of the Upper Ohio Valley: An Introductory Archeological Study.* Pittsburgh, PA: Carnegie Museum.

McAtackney, Laura.
2011. "Peace Maintenance and Political Messages: The Significance of Walls during and after the Northern Irish 'Troubles.'" *Journal of Social Archaeology* 11(1): 77–98. https://doi.org/10.1177/1469605310392321
2020. "Contemporary Archaeology." In the *The Routledge Handbook of Global Historical Archaeology,* eds. Charles E. Orser Jr., Andrés Zarankin, Pedro Paulo A. Funari, Susan Lawrence, and James Symonds, 215–230. London: Routledge.

McAtackney, Laura, and Krysta Ryzewski, eds.

2017. *Contemporary Archaeology and the City.* Oxford & New York: Oxford University Press.

McAtackney, Laura, and Randall H. Maguire, eds.

2020. *Walling In and Walling Out: Why Are We Building New Barriers to Divide Us?* Albuquerque: University of New Mexico Press.

McAtackney, Laura, Matthew M. Palus, and Angela Piccini.

2007. "Contemporary and Historical Archaeology in Theory." Papers from the 2003 and 2004 CHAT Conferences. Oxford: Archaeopress.

McAtackney, Laura, and Matthew M. Palus.

2007. "Introduction." In *Contemporary and Historical Archaeology in Theory: Papers from the 2003 and 2004 CHAT Conferences,* eds. Laura McAtackney, Matthew Palus, and Angela Piccini. Oxford: Archaeopress.

McFadyen, Lesley, and Dan Hicks.

2020. "Introduction: From Archaeography to Photology." In *Archaeology and Photography: Time, Objectivity and Archive,* eds. Lesley McFadyen and Dan Hicks, 1–20. London: Bloomsbury.

McGehee, E. D., S. McCarthy, K. Towery, J. Ronquillo, K. L. Garcia, and J. Isaacson.

2003. "Sentinels of the Atomic Dawn: A Multiple-Property Evaluation of the Remaining Manhattan Project Properties." Historic Building Survey Report No. 215. Los Alamos National Laboratory, Los Alamos, New Mexico. https://permalink.lanl.gov/object/tr?what=info:lanl-repo/lareport/LA-UR-03-0726

McWilliams, A.

2013. *An Archaeology of the Iron Curtain: Material and Metaphor.* Huddinge: Södertörns högskola.

2014. "Borders in Ruins." In *Ruin Memories: Materiality, Aesthetics and the Archaeology of the Recent Past,* eds. Bjørnar Olsen and Þóra Pétursdóttir, 390–410, London: Routledge.

Melosi, Martin V.

1981. *Garbage in the Cities: Refuse, Reform, and the Environment: 1880–1980.* College Station: Texas A&M University Press.

Meierotto, L.

2015. "Human Rights in the Context of Environmental Conservation on the US-Mexico Border." *Journal of Human Rights* 14(3): 401–418.

Messer, Chris.

2021. *The 1921 Tulsa Race Massacre: Crafting a Legacy.* Cham: Springer.

Meyers Emery, K., and Andrew Reinhard.

2015. "Trading Shovels for Controllers: A Brief Exploration of the Portrayal of Archaeology in Video Games." *Public Archaeology* 14(2): 137–149.

Mickel, A.

2015. "Reasons for Redundancy in Reflexivity: The Role of Diaries in Archaeological Epistemology." *Journal of Field Archaeology* 40(3): 300–309.

Miller, G. Logan.

2017. "No Smoking Please? Campus Cigarette Butt Collection as an Archaeological Field Exercise." *Journal of Archaeology and Education* 1(2): 1–17.

Miller, Daniel.

1987. *Material Culture and Mass Consumption.* New York: Basil Blackwell.

1995. "Consumption as the Vanguard of History." In *Acknowledging Consumption,* ed. Daniel Miller. London: Routledge.

Miller, Tim.

2010. "The Birth of the Patio Daddy-O: Outdoor Grilling in Postwar America." *Journal of American Culture* 33(1): 5–11.

Millington, Nate.

2013. "Post-Industrial Imaginaries: Nature, Representation and Ruin in Detroit, Michigan." *International Journal of Urban and Regional Research* 37(1): 279–296.

Moshenska, Gabriel.

2013. *The Archaeology of the Second World War: Uncovering Britain's Wartime Heritage.* Barnsley: Pen & Sword Archaeology.

Mol, A., C. Ariese-Vandemeulebroucke, K. Boom, A. Politopoulos, and V. Vandemeulebroucke.

2016. "Video Games in Archaeology: Enjoyable but Trivial?" *SAA Archaeological Record* 16(5): 11–15.

Montfort, Nick, and Ian Bogost.

2009. *Racing the Beam: The Atari Video Computer System.* Cambridge, MA: MIT Press.

Morgan, Colleen L.

2009. "(Re)building Çatalhöyük: Changing Virtual Reality in Archaeology." *Archaeologies* 5(3): 468–487.

2016. "Analog to Digital: Transitions in Theory and Practice in Archaeological Photography at Çatalhöyük." *Internet Archaeology* 42. https://doi.org/10.11141/ia.42.7

2019. "Avatars, Monsters, and Machines: A Cyborg Archaeology." *European Journal of Archaeology* 22(3): 324–337.

2022. "Current Digital Archaeology." *Annual Review of Anthropology* 51: 213–231.

Morgan, Colleen, and H. Wright.

2018. "Pencils and Pixels: Drawing and Digital Media in Archaeological Field Recording." *Journal of Field Archaeology* 43(2): 136–151.

Morgan, Jennifer.

2016. "Periodizing Problems: Race and Gender in the History of the Early Republic." *Journal of the Early Republic* 32: 351–357.

Morrissey, James.

2015. "Rethinking 'Causation' and 'Disruption': The Environment-Migration Nexus in Northern Ethiopia." In *Migration and Disruptions: Toward a Unifying Theory of Ancient and Contemporary Migrations,* eds. Brenda J. Baker and Takeyuki Tsuda, 196–222. Gainesville: University Press of Florida.

Mullins, Paul R.

1999. *Race and Affluence: An Archaeology of African America and Consumer Culture.* New York: Plenum.

2006. "Racializing the Commonplace Landscape: An Archaeology of Urban Renewal along the Color Line." *World Archaeology* 38(1): 60–71.

2011. *The Archaeology of Consumer Culture*. Gainesville: University Press of Florida.

2012. "The Politics and Archaeology of 'Ruin Porn.'" Archaeology and Material Culture. Blog. September 2, 2012. https://paulmullins.wordpress.com/2012/09/02/archaeologies-of-prosaic-materiality-and-traumatic-heritage

2014. "Imagining Ruin Images: The Aesthetics of Ruination." *Journal of Contemporary Archaeology* 1(1): 27–29.

2017. "The Optimism of Absence: An Archaeology of Displacement, Effacement, and Modernity." In *Contemporary Archaeology and the City*, eds. Laura McAtackney and Krysta Ryzewski, 244–261. Oxford: Oxford University Press.

Mullins, Paul R., and Glenn White.

2010. *The Price of Progress: IUPUI, the Color Line, & Urban Displacement*. Indianapolis: Office of External Affairs, Indiana University–Purdue University, Indianapolis.

Mullins, Paul R., and Lewis C. Jones.

2011. "Archaeologies of Race and Urban Poverty: The Politics of Slumming, Engagement, and the Color Line." *Historical Archaeology* 45(1): 33–50.

Mullins, Paul R., and Jordan Ryan.

2020. "Imagining Musical Place: Race, Heritage, and African American Musical Landscapes." *Journal for the Anthropology of North America* 23: 32–46. https://doi.org/10.1002/nad.12122

Muriel, Daniel, and Garry Crawford.

2018. *Video Games as Culture: Considering the Role and Importance of Video Games in Contemporary Society*. London: Routledge.

Murray, Simon.

2020. *Performing Ruins*. Cham: Palgrave Macmillan.

Mrozowski, Stephen A.

2012. "Ethnobiology for a Diverse World: Spaces and Natures. Archaeology and the Political Ecology of Modern Cities." *Journal of Ethnobiology* 32(2): 129–133.

2014. "Imagining an Archaeology of the Future: Capitalism and Colonialism Past and Present." *International Journal of Historical Archaeology* 18(2): 340–360.

Mrozowski, Stephen A., Grace H. Ziesing, and Mary Carolyn Beaudry.

1996. "Living on the Boott: Historical Archaeology at the Boott Mills Boardinghouses, Lowell, Massachusetts." Amherst: University of Massachusetts Press.

Myers, Adrian.

2010. "Camp Delta, Google Earth and the Ethics of Remote Sensing in Archaeology." *World Archaeology* 42(3): 455–467.

Needham, Andrew.

2014. *Power Lines: Phoenix and the Making of the Modern Southwest*. Princeton, NJ: Princeton University Press.

Netz, Reviel.

2004. *Barbed Wire: The Ecology of Modernity*. Middletown, CT: Wesleyan University Press.

Newman, Michael Z.
2017. *Atari Age: The Emergence of Video Games in America.* Cambridge: MIT Press.
Newland, Cassie.
2004. "A Historical Archaeology of Mobile Phones in the UK." Master's Thesis, University of Bristol.
Ng, Laura Wai.
2021. "An Archaeology of Chinese Transnationalism," PhD dissertation, Stanford University, Stanford, California.
Ngai, Pun, and Chris Smith.
2007. "Putting Transnational Labour Process in Its Place: The Dormitory Labour Regime in Post-Socialist China." *Work Employment Society* 21(1): 27–45.
Nichols, Katherine Lyndsay.
2015. "Investigation of Unmarked Graves and Burial Grounds at the Brandon Indian Residential School." Master's Thesis, University of Manitoba.
2020. "The Brandon Indian Residential School Cemetery Project: Working Towards Reconciliation Using Forensic Anthropology and Archaeology." In *Working with and for Ancestors: Collaboration in the Care and Study of Ancestral Remains,* eds. Chelsea H. Meloche, Laure Spake, and Katherine L. Nichols, 43–55. London: Routledge.
Nixon, Rob.
2011. *Slow Violence and the Environmentalism of the Poor.* London: Harvard University Press.
O'Brien, Tim.
1990. *The Things They Carried.* New York: Houghton Mifflin Harcourt.
Odewale, A., and Slocum, K.
2020. "The Rise, Destruction, and Rebuilding of Tulsa's Greenwood District: A Source List." https://tulsasyllabus.web.unc.edu
Offenhuber, Dietmar, and Carlo Ratti.
2017. *Waste Is Information: Infrastructure Legibility and Governance.* Cambridge, MA: MIT Press.
Olivier, Laurent.
2015. *The Dark Abyss of Time: Archaeology and Memory.* Trans. Arthur Greenspan. Lanham, MD: Rowman & Littlefield, 2015.
2019. "The Future of Archaeology in the Age of Presentism." *Journal of Contemporary Archaeology* 6(1): 16–31.
Oliver, Jeff, and Tim Neal.
2010. "Wild Signs: An introduction." *Wild Signs: Graffiti in Archaeology and History,* eds. Jeff Oliver and Tim Neal, 1–4. Oxford: Archaeopress.
Olsen, Bjørnar.
2010. *In Defense of Things: Archaeology and the Ontology of Objects.* Lanham, MD: Altamira.
Olsen, Bjørnar, Michael Shanks, Timothy Webmoor, and Christopher Witmore.
2012. *Archaeology: The Discipline of Things.* Berkeley: University of California Press.

Orange, Hilary.

2008. "Industrial Archaeology: Its Place within the Academic Discipline, the Public Realm and the Heritage Industry." *Industrial Archaeology Review* 30(2): 83–95.

2018. "Artificial light, Night-Work, and Daycentrism in Post-Medieval and Contemporary Archaeology." *Post-Medieval Archaeology* 52(3): 409–414.

Orser, Charles E., Jr.

1996. *A Historical Archaeology of the Modern World*. New York: Plenum Press.

2020. *The Routledge Handbook of Global Historical Archaeology*. London: Routledge.

Packard, Vance.

1960. *The Waste Makers*. Harmondsworth: Penguin.

Palmer, Marilyn.

2005. "Industrial Archaeology: Constructing a Framework of Inference." In *Industrial Archaeology. Contributions to Global Historical Archaeology*, eds. Elenor C. Casella and James Symonds. Boston: Springer.

Palmer, Marilyn, and Hilary Orange.

2016. "The Archaeology of Industry: People and Places." *Post-Medieval Archaeology* 50(1): 73–91.

Papadopoulos, Dimitri.

2020. "Ruins of the Borderland: Ruin Affect, Aesthetics, and Otherness in the Prespa Lakes Region." *Journal of Modern Greek Studies* 38(2): 399–423. doi:10.1353/mgs.2020.0026

Parkman, E. Break.

2014. "A Hippie Discography: Vinyl Records from a Sixties Commune." *World Archaeology* 46(3): 431–447.

Parikka, Jussi.

2012. *What Is Media Archaeology?* Cambridge: Polity Press.

2016. *The Geology of Media*. Minneapolis: University of Minnesota Press.

Paul, Christopher A.

2018. *The Toxic Meritocracy of Video Games: Why Gaming Culture Is the Worst*. Minneapolis: University of Minnesota Press.

Pearson, Marlys, and Paul R. Mullins.

1999. "Domesticating Barbie: An Archaeology of Barbie Material Culture and Domestic Ideology." *International Journal of Historical Archaeology* 3(4): 225–259.

Pearson, Mike, and Michael Shanks.

2001. *Theatre/Archaeology: Disciplinary Dialogues*. London: Routledge.

Perlman, Janice.

2010. *Favela: Four Decades of Living on the Edge in Rio de Janeiro*. Oxford: Oxford University Press,

Perry, Sara.

2009. Fractured Media: Challenging the Dimensions of Archaeology's Typical Visual Modes of Engagement. *Archaeologies* 5(3): 389–415.

2014. "Crafting knowledge with (digital) visual media in archaeology." In *Material Evidence: Learning from Archaeological Practice*, eds. R. Chapman and A. Wylie, 189–210. London: Routledge.

Perry, Sara, and Colleen Morgan,
2015. "Materializing Media Archaeologies: The MAD-P Hard Drive Excavation." *Journal of Contemporary Archaeology* 2(1): 94–105.
Petrini, C.
2006. *Slow Food Revolution: A New Culture for Dining and Living.* New York: Rizzoli International Publications.
Pétursdóttir, Þóra.
2017. "Climate Change? Archaeology and Anthropocene." *Archaeological Dialogues* 24(2): 175–205. doi:10.1017/S1380203817000216
Pétursdóttir, Þóra, and Bjørnar Olsen.
2014. "An Archaeology of Ruins." In *Ruin Memories: Materiality, Aesthetics and the Archaeology of the Recent Past,* eds. Bjørnar Olsen and Þóra Pétursdóttir, 3–29, London: Routledge.
Petroski, Henry.
1989. *The Pencil: A History of Design and Circumstance.* London: Faber and Faber.
Pezzullo, Phaedra.
2007. *Toxic Tourism: Rhetorics of Pollution, Travel, and Environmental Justice.* Tuscaloosa: University of Alabama Press.
Phillips, Susan A.
2019. *The City Beneath: A Century of Los Angeles Graffiti.* New Haven, CT: Yale University Press.
Portnoy, Alice W.
1981. "A Microarchaeological View of Human Settlement Space and Function." In *Modern Material Culture: The Archaeology of Us,* eds. Richard Gould and Michael Schiffer, 213–224. New York: Academic Press.
Powers N., and L. Sibun.
2013. "Forensic Archaeology." In *The Oxford Handbook of the Archaeology of the Contemporary World,* eds. P Graves-Brown, R. Harrison, and A. Piccini, 40–53. Oxford & New York: Oxford University Press.
Praetzellis, Adrian, and Mary Praetzellis.
2001. "Mangling Symbols of Gentility in the Wild West: Case Studies in Interpretive Archaeology." *American Anthropologist* 103(3): 645–654.
Prugh, Brian.
2017. "Micah Bloom's Books." In *Codex,* ed. Micah Bloom, 65–73. Grand Forks: The Digital Press at the University of North Dakota.
Pynchon, Thomas.
2013. *Bleeding Edge.* London: Jonathan Cape.
Rabinowitz, Adam.
2016. "Response: Mobilizing (Ourselves) for a Critical Digital Archaeology." In *Mobilizing the Past for a Digital Future: The Potential of Digital Archaeology,* eds. Erin Walcek Averett, Jody Michael Gordon, and Derek B. Counts, 493–518. Grand Forks: The Digital Press at the University of North Dakota.
2021. "(Re)imagining the Archaeological Archive for the Twenty-Second Century." In

Critical Archaeology in the Digital Age, ed. K. Garstki. Los Angeles: Costen Institute of Archaeology Press.

Rao, Maya.

2018. *Great American Outpost: Dreamers, Mavericks, and the Making of an Oil Frontier.* New York: PublicAffairs.

Rassalle, Tine.

2021. "Archaeogaming: When Archaeology and Video Games Come Together." *Near Eastern Archaeology* 84(1): 4–11.

Rathje, William.

1981. "A Manifesto for Modern Material Culture Studies." In *Modern Material Culture: The Archaeology of Us,* eds. Richard Gould and Michael Schiffer, 51–56. New York: Academic Press.

1984. The Garbàge Decade. *American Behavioral Scientist* 28(1): 9–29. https://doi.org/10.1177/000276484028001003

1995. "Forever Separate Realities." In *Expanding Archaeology,* eds. J. M. Skibo, W. H. Walker, and A. E. Nielsen, 36–43. Salt Lake City: University of Utah Press.

2001. Integrated Archaeology: A Garbage Paradigm. In *Archaeologies of the Contemporary Past,* eds. Victor Buchli and Gavin Lucas, 63–76. London: Routledge.

Rathje, William, and Michael B. Schiffer.

1982. *Archaeology.* New York: Harcourt Brace Jovanovich.

Rathje, William L., Michael D. Reilly, and Wilson W. Hughes.

1985. "Household Garbage and the Role of Packaging: The United States/Mexico City Household Refuse Comparison." Solid Waste Council of the Paper Industry.

Rathje, William L., and E. E. Ho.

1987. "Meat Fat Madness: Conflicting Patterns of Meat Fat Consumption and their Public Health Implications." *Journal of American Dietetics Association* 87(10): 1357–1362.

Rathje, William, and Cullen Murphy.

1992. *Rubbish! The Archaeology of Garbage.* New York: HarperCollins.

Rathje, W. L, W. W. Hughes, D. C. Wilson, M. K. Tani, G. H. Archer, R. G. Hunt, and T. W. Jones.

1992. "The Archaeology of Contemporary Landfills." *American Antiquity* 57(3): 437–447. doi:10.1017/S0002731600054330

Rathje, William, Michael Shanks, and Christopher Witmore.

2013. *Archaeology in the Making: Conversations through a Discipline.* London: Routledge.

Razac, Olivier.

2003. *Barbed Wire: A Political History.* New York: New Press.

Reid, Jefferson J., Michael B. Schiffer, and Willam L. Rathje.

1975. "Behavioral Archaeology: Four Strategies." *American Anthropologist* 77: 864–869.

Reinhard, Andrew.

2015. "Excavating Atari: Where the Media was the Archaeology." *Journal of Contemporary Archaeology* 2(1): 86–93.

2018. *Archaeogaming: An Introduction to the Archaeology in and of Video Games.* Oxford: Berghahn Books.

2019. "Archaeology of Digital Environments: Tools, Methods, and Approaches." PhD Dissertation, the University of York.

Renfrew, Colin.

1986. "Varna and the Emergence of Wealth in Prehistoric Europe." In *The Social Life of Things: Commodities in Cultural Perspective,* ed. Arjun Appadurai, 141–168. Cambridge: Cambridge University Press.

Reno, Joshua O.

2009. "Your Trash Is Someone's Treasure: The Politics of Value at a Michigan Landfill." *Journal of Material Culture* 14(1): 29–46.

2014. "Toward a New Theory of Waste: From 'Matter out of Place' to Signs of Life." *Theory, Culture & Society* 31(6), 3–27. https://doi.org/10.1177/0263276413500999

Richard, F. G.

2015. "The Ruins of French Imperialism: An Archaeology of Rural Dislocations in Twentieth-Century Senegal." In *Historical Archaeologies of Capitalism*, eds. M. Leone and J. Knaupf, 445–465. New York: Springer.

Rizvi, Uzma.

2013. "Checkpoints as Gendered Spaces: An Autoarchaeology of War, Heritage, and the City." In *The Oxford Handbook of the Archaeology of the Contemporary World*, eds. Paul Graves-Brown, Rodney Harrison, and Angela Piccini, 494–507. Oxford: Oxford University Press.

Rogers, Heather.

2005. *Gone Tomorrow: The Hidden Life of Garbage.* New York: New Press.

Roller, Michael P.

2018. *An Archaeology of Structural Violence: Life in a Twentieth-Century Coal Town.* Gainesville: University Press of Florida.

2019. "The Archaeology of Machinic Consumerism: The Logistics of the Factory Floor in Everyday Life." *Historical Archaeology* 53(1): 3–24.

2023. "'The Song of Love': An Archaeology of Radio History and Surveillance Capitalism." *International Journal of Historical Archaeology.* https://doi.org/10.1007/s10761-022-00684-1

Rose, Chelsea, and J. Ryan Kennedy.

2020. "Charting a New Course for Chinese Diaspora Archaeology in North America." In *Chinese Diaspora Archaeology in North America*, eds. Chelsea Rose and J. Ryan Kennedy, 1–34. Gainesville: University Press of Florida.

Ross, Douglas E.

2011. "Factors Influencing the Dining Habits of Japanese and Chinese Migrants at a British Columbia Salmon Cannery." *Historical Archaeology* 45(2): 68–96.

Rothschild, Nan A.

1981. "Pennies from Denver." In *Modern Material Culture: The Archaeology of Us*, eds. Richard Gould and Michael Schiffer, 161–181. New York: Academic Press.

Rothschild, Nan A., and Diana diZerega Wall, eds.

2014. *The Archaeology of American Cities.* Gainesville: University Press of Florida.

Rothaus, Richard.

2013. "Return on Sustainability: Workforce Housing for People, Planet and Profit." *Engineering and Mining Journal* 214(12): 88–90.

Rothaus, Richard, William R. Caraher, Bret Weber, and Kostis Kourelis.

2021. "Wheelock, North Dakota: 'Ghost-Towns,' Man Camps, and Hyperabundance in an Oil Boom." In *Deserted Villages: Perspectives from the Eastern Mediterranean*, eds. Rebecca M. Seifried and Deborah E. Brown Stewart, 389–428. Grand Forks: The Digital Press at the University of North Dakota.

Rothenberg, Miriam.

2021. "Community and Corrosion: A Contemporary Archaeology of Montserrat's Volcanic Crisis in Long-Term Comparative Perspective." PhD Dissertation, Brown University.

Royte, Elizabeth.

2006. *Garbage Land: On the Secret Trail of Trash*. New York: Back Bay Books.

Ruggill, Judd Ethan, Ken S. McAllister, Carly A. Kocurek, and Raiford Guins.

2015. "Dig? Dug!: Field Notes from the Microsoft-Sponsored Excavation of the Alamogordo, NM Atari Dump Site." *Reconstruction: Studies in Contemporary Culture* 15(3).

Ryzewski, Krista.

2007. "An Epidemic of Medicine." In *Contemporary and Historical Archaeology in Theory: Papers from the 2003 and 2004 CHAT Conferences*, eds. Laura McAtackney, Matthew Palus, and Angela Piccini, 15–22. Oxford: Archaeopress.

2014. "Ruin Photography as Archaeological Method: A Snapshot from Detroit." *Journal of Contemporary Archaeology* 1(1): 36–41.

2017. "Making Music in Detroit: Archaeology, Popular Music, and Post-Industrial Heritage." In *Contemporary Archaeology and the City*, eds. Laura McAtackney and Krysta Ryzewski, 69–90. Oxford & New York: Oxford University Press.

2019. "Detroit 139: Archaeology and the Future-Making of a Post-Industrial City." *Journal of Contemporary Archaeology*, 6(1): 85–100.

2022. *Detroit Remains: Archaeology and Community Histories of Six Legendary Places*. Tuscaloosa: University of Alabama Press.

Salmon, John S.

2011. *Protecting America: Cold War Defensive Sites A National Historic Landmark Theme Study*. National Historic Landmarks Program, National Park Service, U.S. Department of the Interior, Washington, DC.

Salmond, Wendy, Justin Walsh, and Alice Gorman.

2020. "Eternity in Low Earth Orbit: Icons on the International Space Station." *Religions* 11: 611. https://doi.org/10.3390/rel11110611

Sapirstein, Philip, and Sarah Murray.

2017. "Establishing Best Practices for Photogrammetric Recording during Archaeological Fieldwork." *Journal of Field Archaeology* 42(4): 337–350.

Sandoval-Strausz, Andrew K.

2019. *Barrio America: How Latino Immigrants Saved the American City*. New York: Basic Books.

Sassen, Saskia.

2014. *Expulsions: Brutality and Complexity in the Global Economy.* Cambridge, MA: Belknap Press.

Savage, Kirk.

2018. *Standing Soldiers, Kneeling Slaves: Race, War, and Monument in Nineteenth-Century America.* Princeton, NJ: Princeton University Press.

Sayles, John.

2020. *Yellow Earth.* Chicago: Haymarket Books.

Schiffer Michael B.

1972. "Archaeological Context and Systemic Context." *American Antiquity* 37(2): 156–165.

1991. *The Portable Radio in American Life.* Tucson: University of Arizona Press.

1994. *Taking Charge: The Electric Automobile in America.* Washington, DC: Smithsonian.

1995. *Behavioral Archaeology: First Principles.* Salt Lake City: University of Utah Press.

1999. *The Material Life of Human Beings: Artifacts, Behavior, and Communication.* London & New York: Routledge.

2000. "Indigenous Theories, Scientific Theories and Product Histories." In *Matter, Materiality, and Modern Culture,* ed. P Graves-Brown, 172–196. London & New York: Routledge.

2013. *The Archaeology of Science: Studying the Creation of Useful Knowledge.* Heidelberg: Springer.

2015. "William Laurens Rathje: The Garbage Project and Beyond." *Ethnoarchaeology* 7(2): 179–184.

Schiffer, Michael B., Theodore E. Downing, and Michael McCarthy.

1981. "Waste Not, Want Not: An Ethnoarchaeological Study of Reuse in Tucson, Arizona." In *Modern Material Culture: The Archaeology of Us,* eds. Richard Gould and Michael Schiffer, 67–86. New York: Academic Press.

Schofield, A. John.

2002. "Monuments and the Memories of War: Motivations for Preserving Military Sites in England." In *Materiel Culture: The Archaeology of Twentieth-Century Conflict,* eds. A. John Schofield, William Gray Johnson, and Colleen M. Beck, 143–158. London: Routledge.

2005. *Combat Archaeology: Material Culture and Modern Conflict.* London: Duckworth.

2008. *Aftermath: Readings in the Archaeology of Recent Conflict.* New York: Springer.

2009. "Office Cultures and Corporate Memory: Some Archaeological Perspectives." *Archaeologies* 5(2): 293–305.

Schofield, John, Colleen Beck, and Harold Drollinger.

2008. "Alternative Archaeologies of the Cold War: The Preliminary Results of Fieldwork at the Greenham and Nevada Peace Camps." In *Landscapes under Pressure: Theory and Practice of Cultural Heritage Research and Preservation,* ed. Ludomir R. Lozny, 149–162. Boston: Springer.

Schofield, John, and Mike Anderton.

2000. "The Queer Archaeology of Green Gate: Interpreting Contested Space at Greenham Common Airbase." *World Archaeology* 32(2): 236–251.

Schofield, John, William Gray Johnson, and Colleen M. Beck, eds.

2002. *Materiel Culture: The Archaeology of Twentieth-Century Conflict.* London: Routledge.

Schofield, John, Estelle Praet, Kathy A. Townsend, and Joanna Vince.

2021. "'COVID Waste' and Social Media as Method: An Archaeology of Personal Protective Equipment and Its Contribution to Policy." *Antiquity* 95(380): 435–449. doi:10.15184/aqy.2021.18

Schofield, John, Wayne Cocroft, and Marina Dobronovskaya.

2021. "Cold War: A Transnational Approach to a Global Heritage." *Post-Medieval Archaeology* 55(1): 39–58.

Schwartz, Scott W.

2021. *An Archaeology of Temperature: Numerical Materials in the Capitalized Landscape.* London: Routledge.

Skibo, James M., and Michael B. Schiffer.

2008. *People and Things: A Behavioral Approach to Material Culture.* New York: Springer.

Schmidt, Dietmar.

2001. "Refuse Archeology: Virchow—Schliemann—Freud." *Perspectives on Science* 9(2): 210–232.

Shackel, Paul A.

2003. *Memory in Black and White: Race, Commemoration, and the Post-Bellum Landscape.* Walnut Creek, CA: Altamira Press.

2009. *The Archaeology of American Labor and Working-class Life.* Gainesville: University Press of Florida.

Shanks, Michael.

2007. "Digital Media, Agile Design and the Politics of Archaeological Authorship." In *Archaeology and the Media,* eds. Timothy Clack and Marcus Brittain, 273–289. London: Routledge.

Shanks, Michael, and Christopher Tilley.

1987. *Re-constructing Archaeology.* Cambridge & New York: Cambridge University Press.

Shanks, Michael, David Platt, and William L. Rathje.

2004. "The Perfume of Garbage: Modernity and the Archaeological." *Modernism/Modernity* 11(1): 61–83. doi:10.1353/mod.2004.0027

Shanks, Michael, and Christopher Witmore.

2012. "Archaeology 2.0? Review of *Archaeology 2.0: New Approaches to Communication and Collaboration* [Web Book]." *Internet Archaeology* 32. https://doi.org/10.11141/ia.32.7

Silliman, Stephen W.

2020. "Colonialism in Historical Archaeology: A Review of Issues and Perspectives." In *Handbook of Global Historical Archaeology,* eds. Charles E. Orser Jr., Andrés Zarankin, Pedro Paulo, A. Funari, Susan Lawrence, and James Symonds, 41–60. London: Routledge.

Simons, Eric, Andrew Martindale, and Alison Wylie.
2020. "Bearing Witness: What Can Archaeology Contribute in an Indian Residential School Context?" In *Working with and for Ancestors: Collaboration in the Care and Study of Ancestral Remains,* eds. Chelsea H. Meloche, Laure Spake, and Katherine L. Nichols, 21–31. London: Routledge.
Simms, Crystal R., and Julien G. Riel-Salvatore.
2016. "Occupy Archaeology! Towards an Activist Ethnoarcheaology of Occupy Denver." *SAA Archaeological Record* 16(3): 33–42.
Simone, Abdou Maliq.
2004. *For the City yet to Come: Changing African Life in Four Cities.* Durham, NC: Duke University Press.
Simonetti, Cristián.
2018. *Sentient Conceptualisations: Feeling for Time in the Sciences of the Past.* London: Routledge.
Sinclair, Upton.
1926–1927. *Oil!* New York: Albert & Charles Boni.
Singleton, Courtney.
2017. "Encountering Home: A Contemporary Archaeology of Homelessness." In *Contemporary Archaeology and the City,* eds. Laura McAtackney and Krysta Ryzewski, 229–243. Oxford: Oxford University Press.
2021. "Vague Dwelling: An Archaeology of The Pelham Bay Park Homeless Encampment." PhD dissertation, Columbia University, New York.
Skiles, Stephanie A., and Bonnie J. Clark.
2010. "When the Foreign Is Not Exotic: Ceramics at Colorado's WWII Japanese Internment Camp." *Trade and Exchange: Archaeological Studies from History and Prehistory,* eds. Carolyn D. Dillian and Carolyn L. White, 179–192. New York: Springer.
Skowronek, Russell K., and Kenneth E. Lewis, eds.
2010. *Beneath the Ivory Tower: the Archaeology of Academia.* Gainesville: University Press of Florida.
Smit, Douglas K., and Terren K. Proctor,
2020. "'An Incurable Evil': Direct and Structural Violence in the Mercury Mines of Colonial Huancavelica (AD 1564–1824)." In *Archaeologies of Violence and Privilege,* eds. Christopher Matthews and Bradley D. Phillippi, 89–106. Gainesville: University Press of Florida.
Smithson, Robert.
1996[1967]. "A Tour to the Monuments of Passaic, New Jersey." In *Robert Smithson: Collected Writings,* ed. Jack Flam, 68–74. Berkeley: University of California Press.
Smithsonian National Museum of African American History and Culture.
2020. Statement on Efforts to Collect Objects at Lafayette Square. https://nmaahc.si.edu/about/news/statement-efforts-collect-objects-lafayette-square
Soli, Britt, Mats Burström, Ewa Domanska, Matt Edgeworth, Alfredo González-Ruibal, Cornelius Holtorf, Gavin Lucas, Terje Oestigaard, Laurajane Smith, and Christopher Witmore.

2011 "Some Reflections on Heritage and Archaeology in the Anthropocene." *Norwegian Archaeological Review* 44(1): 40–88.

Soll, David.
2013. *Empire of Water: An Environmental and Political History of the New York City Water Supply.* Ithaca, NY: Cornell University Press.

Sorensen, Justin.
2017. "Four Parts Water." In *Codex,* ed. Micah Bloom, 45–52. Grand Forks: The Digital Press at the University of North Dakota.

Soto, Gabriella.
2017. "Place Making in Non-Places: Migrant Graffiti in Rural Highway Box Culverts." *Journal of Contemporary Archaeology* 3(2): 174–195.

Souder, Miller & Associates.
2014a. "Revised Site Excavation Plan: Old Alamogordo Landfill." Unpublished Report.
2014b. Waste Excavation Plan Amendment Letter. April 14.

South, Stanley.
2010. "Campus Archaeology at the University of South Carolina's Horseshoe." In *Beneath the Ivory Tower: The Archaeology of Academia,* eds. Russell K. Skowronek and K. E. Lewis, 52–73. Gainesville: University Press of Florida.

Spencer-Wood, Suzanne M.
1987. *Consumer Choice in Historical Archaeology.* New York: Plenum Press.

Staski, Edward.
2008. "Living in Cities Today." *Historical Archaeology* 42(1): 5–10.

Steffen, Will, Paul J. Crutzen, and John R. McNeill.
2007. "The Anthropocene: Are Humans Now Overwhelming the Great Forces of Nature?" *AMBIO: A Journal of the Human Environment* 36(8): 614–621.
2011. "The Anthropocene: Conceptual and Historical Perspectives." *Philosophical Transactions of the Royal Society A: Mathematical, Physical and Engineering Sciences* 369 (1938): 842–867.

Stengers, I.
2018. *Another Science Is Possible: A Manifesto for Slow Science.* Trans. Stephen Muecke. New York: Wiley.

Stephenson, Neal.
1992. *Snow Crash.* New York: Bantam Books.

Stewart, Haeden.
2017. "Toxic landscape: Excavating a Polluted World." *Archaeological Review from Cambridge* 32(2): 25–37. https://doi.org/10.17863/CAM.23660

Stickle, Benjamin F.
2017. *Metal Scrappers and Thieves: Scavenging for Survival and Profit.* Cham, Switzerland: Palgrave Macmillan.

Standing, Guy.
2011. *The Precariat: The New Dangerous Class.* London: Bloomsbury Academic.

Strasser, Susan.
1999. *Waste and Want: A Social History of Trash.* New York: Metropolitan Books.

Stubbs, John D., Patricia Capone, Christina Hodge, and Diane D. Loren.

2010. "Campus Archaeology/Public Archaeology at Harvard University, Cambridge, Massachusetts." In *Beneath the Ivory Tower: The Archaeology of Academia,* eds. Russell K. Skowronek and K. E. Lewis, 99–120. Gainesville: University Press of Florida.

Surface-Evans, Sarah L.

2016. "A Landscape of Assimilation and Resistance: The Mount Pleasant Indian Industrial Boarding School." *International Journal of Historical Archaeology* 20(3): 574–588.

Tamm, Marek, and Laurent Olivier, eds.

2019   *Rethinking Historical Time, New Approaches to Presentism.* London: Bloomsbury.

Thomas, Judith.

2011. "Archaeological Investigations of Second World War Prisoner of War Camps at Fort Hood, Texas." In *Archaeologies of Internment,* eds. Adrian Myers and Gabriel Moshenska, 147–169. New York: Springer.

Thomas, Julian.

2004. *Archaeology and Modernity.* London: Routledge.

Thompson, Raymond Harris.

2002. "A.V. Kidder and the Andover Town Dump." *KIVA* 68(2): 129–133. https://doi.org/10.1080/00231940.2002.11758472

Thompson, Erin L.

2022. *Smashing Statues: The Rise and Fall of America's Public Monuments.* New York: W.W. Norton.

Thompson, Michael.

1979. *Rubbish Theory: The Creation and Destruction of Value.* Oxford: Oxford University Press.

Tilley, Christopher.

1994. *A Phenomenology of Landscape: Places, Paths, and Monuments.* Oxford: Berg.

Tilley, Christopher, and Michael Shanks.

1987. *Re-constructing Archaeology: Theory and Practice.* Cambridge: Cambridge University Press, 1987.

Tilley, Christopher Y., and Kate Cameron-Daum.

2017. *An Anthropology of Landscape: the Extraordinary in the Ordinary.* London: UCL Press.

Trigger, Bruce G.

1981. "Archaeology and the Ethnographic Present." *Anthropologica* 23(1): 3–17.

Tsing, A.

2015. *The Mushroom at the End of the World: On the Possibility of Life in Capitalist Ruins.* Princeton, NJ: Princeton University Press.

Tsuda, Takeyuki.

2015. "Unequal in the Court of Public Opinion: Mexican and Asian Immigrant Disruptions in the United States." In *Migration and Disruptions: Toward a Unifying Theory of Ancient and Contemporary Migrations,* eds. Brenda J Baker and Takeyuki Tsuda, 243–269. Gainesville: University Press of Florida.

Two Bears, Davina.

2019. "'Shimasani doo shicheii bi'olta'—My Grandmother's and Grandfather's School: The Old Leupp Boarding School, A Historic Archaeological Site on the Navajo Reservation." PhD dissertation, Indiana University, Bloomington, Indiana.

Van Bueren, Thad M.

2002a. "The Changing Face of Work in the West: Some Introductory Comments." *Historical Archaeology* 36(3): 1–7.

2002b. "Struggling with Class Relations at a Los Angeles Aqueduct Construction Camp." *Historical Archaeology* 36(3): 28–43.

Van Bueren, Mary, and J. M. Weaver.

2012. "Contours of Labor and History: A Diachronic Perspective on Andean Mineral Production and the Making of Landscapes in Porco, Bolivia." *Historical Archaeology* 46(3): 79–101.

VanderMeer, Jeff.

2014. *Annihilation.* New York: Farrar, Straus and Giroux.

2014. *Authority.* New York: Farrar, Straus and Giroux.

2014. *Acceptance.* New York: Farrar, Straus and Giroux.

VanValkenburgh, Parker, and J. Andrew Dufton, eds.

2020. "Archaeology in the Age of Big Data." *Journal of Field Archaeology* Supplement 45(1).

Virilio, Paul.

1994. *Bunker Archeology.* Trans. George Collins. New York: Princeton Architectural Press.

Virilio, Paul, and Sylvère Lotringer.

1983. *Pure War.* Trans. Mark Polizzotti and Brian O'Keeffe. New York: Semiotext(e).

Vizenor, Gerald R.

1999. *Manifest Manners: Narratives on Postindian Survivance.* Lincoln: University of Nebraska Press.

Voss, Barbara L.

2010. "Matter Out of Time: The Paradox of the 'Contemporary Past.'" *Archaeologies* 6(1): 181–192.

Voss, Barbara L., and Rebecca Allen.

2008. "Overseas Chinese Archaeology: Historical Foundations, Current Reflections, and New Directions." *Historical Archaeology* 42(3): 5–28.

Voeten, Teun.

2010. *Tunnel People.* Oakland, CA: PM Press.

Walker, N.

2003. "Late Sovereignty in the European Union." In *Sovereignty in Transition,* ed. Neil Walker, 3–32. London: Hart Publishing.

Walsh, Justin St. P., and Alice C. Gorman.

2021. "A Method for Space Archaeology Research: The International Space Station Archaeological Project." *Antiquity* 95(383): 1331–1343.

Wang, Cangbai.

2016. "Introduction: The 'Material Turn' in Migration Studies." *Modern Languages Open.* http://doi.org/10.3828/mlo.v0i0.88

Ward, Peter M.

2014. "The Reproduction of Informality in Low-Income Self-Help Housing Communities." In *The Informal City: Beyond Taco Trucks and Day Labor,* eds. Vinit Mukhija and Anastasia Loukaitou-Sideris, 59–77. Cambridge, MA: MIT Press.

Watkins, Liz.

2014. "The Materiality of Film." In *The Oxford Handbook of the Archaeology of the Contemporary World,* eds. Paul Graves-Brown, Rodney Harrison, and Angela Piccini, 578–594. Oxford: Oxford University Press.

Watrall, Ethan.

2002. "Digital Pharaoh: Archaeology, Public Education and Interactive Entertainment." *Public Archaeology* 2(3): 163–169.

Weberman, A. J.

1980. *My Life in Garbology.* New York: Stonehill.

Webmoor, Timothy.

2014. "Object-Oriented Metrologies of Care and the Proximate Ruin of Building 500." In *Ruin Memories: Materialities, Aesthetics and the Archaeology of the Recent Past,* eds. B. Olsen and Þ. Pétursdóttir, 462–485. Abingdon: Routledge.

Wegers, P. W.

1991. "'Who's been workin' on the railroad?': An Examination of the Construction, Distribution, and Ethnic Origins of Domed Rock Ovens on Railroad-Related Sites." *Historical Archaeology* 25(1): 37–65.

Wheeler, Joshua.

2014. "The Glitch in the Video-Game Graveyard." Harpers Magazine Online. July 23. https://harpers.org/2014/07/the-glitch-in-the-video-game-graveyard

White, Carolyn L.

2020. *The Archaeology of Burning Man: The Rise and fall of Black Rock City.* Albuquerque: University of New Mexico Press.

Whitehouse, Tanya.

2018. *How Ruins Acquire Aesthetic Value. Modern Ruins, Ruin Porn, and the Ruin Tradition.* Cham: Springer International Publishing.

Wickstead, Helen.

2014. "Between Lines: Drawing Archaeology." In *The Oxford Handbook of the Archaeology of the Contemporary World,* eds. Paul Graves-Brown, Rodney Harrison, and Angela Piccini, 549–564. Oxford: Oxford University Press.

Wilk, Richard, and Michael B. Schiffer.

1981. "The Modern Material-Culture Field School: Teaching Archaeology on the University Campus." In *Modern Material Culture: The Archaeology of Us,* eds. Richard Gould and Michael Schiffer, 15–30. New York: Academic Press.

Wilkie, Laurie.

2000. *Creating Freedom: Material Culture and African American Identity at Oakley Plantation, Louisiana, 1840–1950.* Baton Rouge: Louisiana State University Press.

2001. "Black Sharecroppers and White Frat Boys: Living Communities and the Appropriation of Their Archaeological Pasts." In *Archaeologies of the Contemporary Past*, eds. Victor Buchli and Gavin Lucas, 108–118. London: Routledge.

2010. *The Lost Boys of Zeta Psi: A Historical Archaeology of Masculinity in a University Fraternity*. Berkeley: University of California Press.

2014. *Strung Out on Archaeology: An Introduction to Archaeological Research*. Illustrator: Alexandra Wilkie Farnsworth. London: Routledge.

Witmore, Christopher L.

2007. "Symmetrical Archaeology: Excerpts of a Manifesto." *World Archaeology* 39(4): 546–562.

Witmore, Christopher L., and Curtis L. Francisco.

2021. "Through the Jackpile-Paguate Uranium Mine." In *After Discourse: Things, Affects, Ethics*, eds. B. Olsen, M. Burström, C. DeSilvey, and Þ. Péturdóttir. Abingdon, UK: Routledge.

Wright, Ron, and John Schofield.

2021. "The City as Archive: How Industry and Electronic Music Forged Sheffield's Sonic Identity." *Music and Heritage* (2021): 91–102.

Wurst, LouAnn.

2002. "For the Means of Your Subsistence . . . Look Under God to Your Own Industry and Frugality": Life and Labor in Gerrit Smith's Peterboro. *International Journal of Historical Archaeology* 6(3): 159–172.

2011. "'Human Accumulations': Class and Tourism at Niagara Falls." *International Journal of Historical Archaeology* 15(2): 254–66.

2015. "The Historical Archaeology of Capitalist Dispossession." *Capital & Class* 39(1): 33–49.

2019. "Should Archaeology Have a Future?" *Journal of Contemporary Archaeology* 6(1): 168–181.

Wurst, LouAnn, and Christine L. Ridarsky.

2014. "The Second Time as Farce: Archaeological Reflections on the New New Deal." *International Journal of Historical Archaeology* 18(2): 224–241.

Wurst, LouAnn, and Stephen A. Mrozowski.

2016. "Capitalism in Motion." *Historical Archaeology* 50(3): 81–99.

Yoder, David T.

2014. "Interpreting the 50-Year Rule: How a Simple Phrase Leads to a Complex Problem." *Advances in Archaeological Practice* 2(4): 324–337.

Zielinski, Siegfried.

1996. "Media Archaeology." *CTheory* https://journals.uvic.ca/index.php/ctheory/article/view/14321

Zimmerman, Larry.

2004. "Archaeological Evaluation of the Hillside Garden Areas at the James J. Hill House (21RA21), St. Paul, Minnesota." *The Minnesota Archaeologist* 63: 118–36.

2013. "Homelessness." In *The Oxford Handbook of the Archaeology of the Contemporary World*, eds. Paul Graves-Brown, Rodney Harrison, and Angela Piccini, 336–350. Oxford: Oxford University Press.

Zimmerman, Larry J. and Jessica Welsh.

2006. "Toward an Archaeology of Homelessness." *Anthropology News* 47(2):54.

2011. "Displaced and Barely Visible: Archaeology and the Material Culture of Homelessness." *Historical Archaeology* 45(1): 67–85.

Zimmerman, Larry J., Courtney Singleton, and Jessica Welch.

2010. "Activism and Creating a Translational Archaeology of Homelessness." *World Archaeology* 42(3): 443–454. doi:10.1080/00438243.2010.497400

Zimring, C.

2004. "Dirty Work: How Hygiene and Xenophobia Marginalized the American Waste Trades, 1870–1930." *Environmental History,* 9(1): 80–101. www.jstor.org/stable/3985946

2005. *Cash for Your Trash: Scrap Recycling in America.* New Brunswick, NJ: Rutgers University Press.

Zuboff, Shoshana.

2019. *The Age of Surveillance Capitalism: The Fight for the Future at the New Frontier of Power.* London: Profile Books.

INDEX

Page numbers in *italics* indicate illustrations.

techniques in, 40, 55; scientific excavation in, 28–29; systematic documentation of, 55; toxic household products and, 55–56; transnational stories and, 22

Garbology: alcohol consumption studies, 47–48, 56; American experience and, 47, 51; archaeology and, 22, 29, 46–47; contemporary behaviors and, 56, 65; creation of modern dumps, 48; ethnoarchaeology and, 47–48; evidence of private lives in, 53; historical archaeology and, 47; surveillance schemes and, 53; transnationalism and, 65; urbanism and, 52–54. *See also* Landfills; Trash; Waste disposal

Garstki, Kevin, 107

Gas Works Park (Seattle), 164, 185

Gender: American experience and, 14; archaeologists and, 24, 106, 209; archaeology of, 24, 154; borders and, 126; Diné practices, 156; domestic space and, 98; military aggression and, 172; petro-masculinity and, 137, 187; protest camps and, 172; things and, 87. *See also* Women

Geology of Media (Parikka), 100

Gero, Joan, 209

Gibson, William, 93–94, 112

Gilliam, Terry, 94, 163

Globalization: American experience and, 15–16, 23, 111, 137; border zones and, 8, 45, 65, 118, 125–26; consumption and, 102, 111; inequalities and, 200; labor mobility, 118, 122, 127, 170, 201; movement of capital, 6, 8, 45, 65, 118, 125–27, 170, 191, 201; movement of trash and, 52, 63–64, 101–2; nation-state sovereignty and, 125; non-places and, 8; recycling and reuse, 48; supermodernity and, 9; supply chains and, 8, 15, 45, 182; waste disposal and, 64–65

Global South: American manufacturing in, 23; export of e-waste to, 64, 101, 111; favelas in, 185, 198; global capital and, 65; refugee camps, 198; structural inequalities and, 65; waste workers in, 65

González-Ruibal, Alfredo, 120–21, 134, 191

González-Tennant, Edward, 181–82

Goodwin, Lorinda, 77, 79

Gorman, Alice, 146

Gould, Richard, 3, 16–17, 58, 71–72, 177

Graffiti, 165, 176–77, *177*, 178

Grand Forks, North Dakota, 7, *143*

Grateful Dead, 90–91

Graves-Brown, P.M., 18–19

Greenham Common Airbase, 148, 172–73

Guattari, Félix, 83

Guins, Raiford, 27, 39, 95, 98–99, 103

Haag, Richard, 164, 185

Hamilakis, Yannis, 107, 109

Hanson, Todd, 142–43

Haraway, Donna, 82

Hardesty, Donald, 190

Hardt, Michael, 118–19

Harrison, Rodney, 19, 102

Hartog, François, 5

Herz, M., 129

Hickenlooper, John, 173

Hickory Creek, North Texas, 59–60

Hicks, Dan, 108, 129, 133

Hill House. *See* James J. Hill House

Historical archaeology: archaeogaming and, 106; campus fieldwork in, 150–51; capitalism and, 80; consumer culture and, 75–76; development of, 9, 19–20, 71; extractive industries and, 189–90; garbology and, 47; homelessness and, 121, 133; material culture and, 18, 75, 199; negotiation of racial identities and, 76–77, 79; pre-1950s materials, 76; quantitative analysis and, 19; race and, 172; role of theory in, 19–20; ruins and abandonment in, 172; systematic approaches to, 133–34; traditional approaches to, 24; transnationalism and, 182; women's contributions to, 209–10

Hodder, Ian, 19, 72–73, 96

Holmgren, John, 12, 108

Homelessness: Albany Bulb area, 130–31; archaeology of, 18, 121, 130–36, 165; community-building, 129, 131–33, 136, 165; creation of sense of place, 129, 131–32; displacement and, 23; expulsion assemblages, 119; invisibility and, 121, 131–32, 134–35; landfill scavenging, 133–35; loss of citizenship, 117; marginalization of, 117, 121; material culture and, 132–35; policymaking

William R. Caraher teaches in the Department of History and American Indian Studies at the University of North Dakota. He has conducted field work in Greece, Cyprus, and the United States.

The American Experience in Archaeological Perspective

Michael S. Nassaney, Founding Editor

Krysta Ryzewski, Coeditor

The American Experience in Archaeological Perspective series was established by the University Press of Florida and founding editor Michael S. Nassaney in 2004. This prestigious historical archaeology series focuses attention on a range of significant themes in the development of the modern world from an Americanist perspective. Each volume explores an event, process, setting, institution, or geographic region that played a formative role in the making of the United States of America as a political, social, and cultural entity. These comprehensive overviews underscore the theoretical, methodological, and substantive contributions that archaeology has made to the study of American history and culture. Rather than subscribing to American exceptionalism, the authors aim to illuminate the distinctive character of the American experience in time and space. While these studies focus on historical archaeology in the United States, they are also broadly applicable to historical and anthropological inquiries in other parts of the world. To date the series has produced more than two dozen titles. Prospective authors are encouraged to contact the Series Editors to learn more.

The Archaeology of Collective Action, by Dean J. Saitta (2007)

The Archaeology of Institutional Confinement, by Eleanor Conlin Casella (2007)

The Archaeology of Race and Racialization in Historic America, by Charles E. Orser Jr. (2007)

The Archaeology of North American Farmsteads, by Mark D. Groover (2008)

The Archaeology of Alcohol and Drinking, by Frederick H. Smith (2008)

The Archaeology of American Labor and Working-Class Life, by Paul A. Shackel (2009; first paperback edition, 2011)

The Archaeology of Clothing and Bodily Adornment in Colonial America, by Diana DiPaolo Loren (2010; first paperback edition, 2011)

The Archaeology of American Capitalism, by Christopher N. Matthews (2010; first paperback edition, 2012)

The Archaeology of Forts and Battlefields, by David R. Starbuck (2011; first paperback edition, 2012)

The Archaeology of Consumer Culture, by Paul R. Mullins (2011; first paperback edition, 2012)

The Archaeology of Antislavery Resistance, by Terrance M. Weik (2012; first paperback edition, 2013)

The Archaeology of Citizenship, by Stacey Lynn Camp (2013; first paperback edition, 2019)

The Archaeology of American Cities, by Nan A. Rothschild and Diana diZerega Wall (2014; first paperback edition, 2015)

The Archaeology of American Cemeteries and Gravemarkers, by Sherene Baugher and Richard F. Veit (2014; first paperback edition, 2015)

The Archaeology of Smoking and Tobacco, by Georgia L. Fox (2015; first paperback edition, 2016)

The Archaeology of Gender in Historic America, by Deborah L. Rotman (2015; first paperback edition, 2018)

The Archaeology of the North American Fur Trade, by Michael S. Nassaney (2015; first paperback edition, 2017)

The Archaeology of the Cold War, by Todd A. Hanson (2016; first paperback edition, 2019)

The Archaeology of American Mining, by Paul J. White (2017; first paperback edition, 2020)

The Archaeology of Utopian and Intentional Communities, by Stacy C. Kozakavich (2017; first paperback edition, 2023)

The Archaeology of American Childhood and Adolescence, by Jane Eva Baxter (2019)

The Archaeology of Northern Slavery and Freedom, by James A. Delle (2019)

The Archaeology of Prostitution and Clandestine Pursuits, by Rebecca Yamin and Donna J. Seifert

(2019; first paperback edition, 2023)

The Archaeology of Southeastern Native American Landscapes of the Colonial Era, by Charles R. Cobb (2019)

The Archaeology of the Logging Industry, by John G. Franzen (2020)

The Archaeology of Craft and Industry, by Christopher C. Fennell (2021)

The Archaeology of the Homed and the Unhomed, by Daniel O. Sayers (2023)

The Archaeology of Contemporary America, by William R. Caraher (2024)